PERSON-CE

Secc

Person-centred therapy, rooted in the experience and ideas of the eminent psychotherapist Carl Rogers, is widely practised in the UK and
throughout the world. It has applications in health and social care,
the voluntary sector and is relevant to work with people who are
severely mentally and emotionally distressed. As well as being a valuable sourcebook and offering a comprehensive overview, this edition
includes updated references and a new section on recent developments
and advances.

The book begins with a consideration of the principles and philosophy underpinning person-centred therapy before moving to a comprehensive discussion of the classical theory upon which practice is
based. Further areas of discussion include:

- The model of the person, including the origins of mental and
  emotional distress;
- The process of constructive change;
- A review of revisions of and additions to person-centred theory;
- Child development, styles of processing and configurations of self;
- The quality of presence and working at relational depth.

Criticisms of the approach are addressed and rebutted and the application of theory to practice is discussed. The new final section is
concerned with advances and developments in theory and practice
including:

- Counselling for Depression;
- The social dimension to person-centred therapy;
- Person-centred practice with people experiencing severe and
  enduring distress and at the 'difficult edge';
- A review of research.

Throughout the book, attention is drawn to the wider person-centred
literature to which it is a valuable key.

Person-Centred Therapy will be of particular use to students, scholars and practitioners of person-centred therapy as well as to anyone who wants to know more about one of the major psychotherapeutic modalities.

Paul Wilkins is a person-centred academic, practitioner and supervisor. After managing local authority mental health resources, he worked as a senior lecturer at Manchester Metropolitan University until 2009.

'As a succinct overview of person-centred theory and practice, this book is a valuable handbook for students as they move through their training and into the early stages of practice. It offers an up-to-date guide to the key concepts, discussions and controversies in contemporary person-centred counselling. The development of theoretical ideas is presented as a natural process, inspired by research and practice. The inclusion of child development and the impact of social and environmental forces on psychological distress offer welcome additions to mainstream person-centred thinking.'

– Connie Johnson, Senior Teaching Fellow,
University of Edinburgh; Counsellor and
supervisor in private practice

'This is an extraordinarily important book. Paul Wilkins did a great job in combining scholarly profound descriptions of the person-centred essentials with a clear and easy-to-read language. It serves the academic as well as the practitioner as both introduction and reference book to a wide range of topics from the philosophical underpinnings via an overview of criticisms and thoughtful rebuttals to the social dimensions and (as a new section to the second edition) recent developments . I like particularly that Wilkins thoroughly follows Rogers' original intentions in describing the core values of a truly *client*-centred approach to psychotherapy and at the same time does justice to the different branches and developments that originated the classical endeavour.'

– Peter F. Schmid, Sigmund Freud University, Vienna

100 Key Points and Techniques
Series Editor: Windy Dryden

Also in this series:

EXISTENTIAL THERAPY: 100 KEY POINTS AND
TECHNIQUES
Susan Iacovou and Karen Weixel-Dixon

PERSON-CENTRED THERAPY: 100 KEY POINTS, 2ND
EDITION
Paul Wilkins

PERSON-CENTRED THERAPY

100 KEY POINTS

Second Edition

Paul Wilkins

Routledge
Taylor & Francis Group
LONDON AND NEW YORK

First edition published 2010
Second edition 2016
by Routledge
2 Park Square, Milton Park, Abingdon, Oxon, OX14 4RN

and by Routledge
711 Third Avenue, New York, NY 10017

Routledge is an imprint of the Taylor & Francis Group, an informa business

British Library Cataloguing in Publication Data
A catalogue record for this book is available from the British Library

Library of Congress Cataloguing in Publication Data
Wilkins, Paul, 1946–
    Person-centred therapy : 100 key points and techniques /
    Paul Wilkins. – Second edition.
        pages   cm
    Includes bibliographical references.
    1. Client–centered psychotherapy.   I. Title.
    RC481.W538   2016
    616.89′14–dc23   2015020598

ISBN: 978-0-415-74370-9 (hbk)
ISBN: 978-0-415-74371-6 (pbk)
ISBN: 978-1-315-76519-8 (ebk)

Typeset in Aldus LT Std
by Out of House Publishing

This book is dedicated to my grandchildren:
Eleanor, Tom, Lucy and Michael

CONTENTS

Section 2
CLASSICAL PERSON-CENTRED THEORY 25

Section 3
REVISIONS, RECONSIDERATIONS
AND ADVANCES IN PERSON-CENTRED
THEORY   **69**

Section 6
PERSON-CENTRED THEORY AND PRACTICE WHEN WORKING WITH REACTIONS TO LIFE EVENTS

243

Section 7
NEWER DEVELOPMENTS, ADVANCES AND UNDERSTANDINGS: EXPANDING PERSON-CENTRED THERAPY FOR THE TWENTY-FIRST CENTURY

255

PREFACE

Since Rogers and his colleagues began to develop what was then called 'client-centred therapy' (previously 'non-directive therapy') in the 1940s and 1950s, a family of related approaches has been established around the original conceptions. Major branches of this family include focusing, experiential and process-experiential therapies. These are touched on in this book, especially in relation to theory. However, the main focus is on what in the UK is normally called 'person-centred therapy', that is an approach to therapy that has the non-directive attitude at the centre of theory and practice and which is widely taught and practised. This is closely related to client-centred therapy as it was first described but includes some newer ideas and practices. These include advances in understandings of person-centred psychopathology, reconsiderations of the necessary and sufficient conditions for constructive personality change, developments in working with people who are contact-impaired and ways in which qualitative improvements may be made to the therapist/client relationship. In taking this focus I am deliberately largely excluding a part of the person-centred family of approaches to therapy – that is those that have *experiencing* at the core of the therapeutic process. These include focusing-oriented approaches derived from the work of Gendlin (1978, 1996) and more recently addressed by, for example, Purton (2004) and process-experiential approaches, the roots of which are in the work of Rice (1974) and of which recent proponents include Greenberg and Elliott (see, for example, Elliott *et al.* 2004b), Rennie (1998) and Worsley (2002)). These approaches are particularly strong throughout continental Europe (see, for example, references to Lietaer in this book) and the journal *Person-Centered and*

Experiential Psychotherapies is a good source for original work about them (and indeed papers covering the complete spectrum of person-centred approaches). The reason for referring minimally to focusing, process-experiential and related approaches is simply that they are rich enough and different enough to deserve a book of their own. To attempt to include a consideration of them here would do neither branch of the person-centred family justice.

So, the 100 key points elaborated in this book cover 'classical' person-centred theory, recent developments in person-centred theory, criticisms of person-centred therapy (and rebuttals of these), the principles of person-centred practice, some indicative examples of how and why person-centred therapy may be done with specific client groups (in terms of their reactions to life events) and, finally, a brief review of the research evidence for the efficacy of person-centred therapy. Of course, although it was clear to me what the majority of points should be; for example, that they should include a rigorous exploration of person-centred theory and cover the major practical implementations of these as well as at least sampling mainstream theoretical and practical advances, picking only 100 key points wasn't easy. I hope my eventual choice satisfies my readers.

The book offers comprehensive coverage of person-centred therapy as it is currently conceived and practised. It will be useful not only to people training as person-centred therapists but also practitioners of the approach and anybody else who wants an easily accessible sourcebook covering the major aspects of the approach.

PREFACE TO THE SECOND EDITION

The first edition of this book was well received and is well thought of so revising it to produce a second edition, because to include new material means to lose some of the existing content, has been a challenge. However, person-centred therapy remains energetic and productive. The journal *Person-Centered and Experiential Therapies* continues to thrive and tracks new developments, new supportive evidence and much more; PCCS Books continually increases its output of person-centred titles as do other publishers. There are more national and international conferences and gatherings concerning the person-centred approach than ever before. All these and other sources contribute to the ever-increasing relevance of person-centred therapy and the person-centred approach. My task has been to respond to and reflect this dynamism and relevance while preserving all that was valuable in the first edition. So, here you will find that (because it has been valued as a resource from which to find out even more) references have been updated to include work published since the publication of the first edition (this applies to Sections 1, 2, 3 and 4 in particular) and that Section 6 (Working with reactions to life events) has been condensed which allows for the inclusion of a totally new Section 7 addressing newer developments, advances and understandings. These include the advent of the first non-CBT form of therapy in the UK to be offered as part of the IAPT (improving access to psychological therapies) programme, that person-centred therapy has a social dimension and that person-centred therapy is being effectively applied with people who experience enduring and severe mental distress. It is also here where you will find reference to the most recent research relevant to person-centred therapy.

PREFACE TO THE SECOND EDITION

Section 1

THE UNDERLYING EPISTEMOLOGY, PHILOSOPHY AND PRINCIPLES OF PERSON-CENTRED THERAPY

THE PERSON-CENTRED APPROACH IS A SYSTEM OF IDEAS AND ATTITUDES IN WHICH PERSON-CENTRED THERAPY IS ROOTED

Although it is sometimes used somewhat imprecisely to refer to a way of doing therapy, the person-centred approach is a global term for the application of the principles derived from the work and ideas of Carl Rogers, his colleagues and successors to many fields of human endeavour. It is one of the most striking things about the method of psychotherapy originating with Carl Rogers – and which has variously been referred to as 'non-directive therapy', 'client-centred therapy' and 'person-centred therapy' – that it, or rather the ideas underpinning it, gave rise to something described as an 'approach'. This is the *person-centred approach* of which Wood (1996: 163) pointed out:

> [It] is not a psychology, a school, a movement or many other things frequently imagined. It is merely what its name suggests, an *approach*. It is a psychological posture, a way of being, from which one confronts a situation.

This 'way of being' (p. 169) has the following elements:

- a belief in a formative directional tendency;
- a will to help;
- an intention to be effective in one's objectives;
- a compassion for the individual and respect for his or her autonomy and dignity;

- a flexibility in thought and action;
- an openness to new discoveries;
- 'an ability to intensely concentrate and clearly grasp the linear, piece by piece appearance of reality as well as perceiving it holistically or all-at-once': that is to say a capacity for both analysis and synthesis or the perception of gestalts;
- a tolerance for uncertainty or ambiguity.

The 'person-centred approach' is not only a way of doing counselling and psychotherapy (between which person-centred therapists do not make a distinction – Point 52) but a way of being in relationship, a relationship which can be with another individual, a group, a nation or even the planet (see Wilkins 2003: 3–5). Although an in-depth consideration of them is outside the scope of this book it is nevertheless pertinent that person-centred theory and practice extends into many other areas of human endeavour. These include education, interpersonal relationships, political, cultural and social change and approaches to research. That the person-centred approach is (for example) concerned with social justice and social change tends to impact on person-centred therapy. Also, the important elements of the approach are the drive for 'growth', that is the formative and actualising tendencies (Point 9) and the consideration of people as inherently trustworthy, capable of autonomy and to be deeply respected which has implications for the exercise of power (Point 6). This too goes to the heart of the practice of person-centred therapy. Thus knowledge of the approach as a whole informs person-centred practice. Sanders (in Thorne with Sanders 2013: 99–128) considers the overall influence of Rogers in terms of the wider field to which the person-centred approach has been applied or in which it has influence.

The first section of this book outlines some of the fundamental aspects of the person-centred approach especially as they relate to the theory and practice of person-centred therapy.

PERSON-CENTRED THERAPY HAS BEEN FROM THE OUTSET AND REMAINS A RADICAL CHALLENGE TO THE PREVAILING MEDICAL MODEL AND THE NOTION OF THERAPIST AS 'EXPERT'

Person-centred therapy was originally developed in the 1940s by Carl Rogers and his colleagues. From the outset, Rogers' intention was to provide a radical alternative to the prevailing psychodynamic and behavioural approaches to psychotherapy and also to psychiatry and the medical model in which all these can be seen as rooted. This was initially called 'non-directive therapy' and by 1951 his preferred term was 'client-centred therapy'. In the 1960s when he began to apply the principles derived from his approach to therapy to other realms of human relationship, the term 'person-centred approach' gained currency. This in turn led to the term 'person-centred counselling/ therapy' which is currently the preferred term in the UK but which may also be taken to embrace a 'family' of related approaches based on client-centred theory (Point 3).

In the various names given to the approach to therapy described by Rogers (1942, 1951, 1959) a radical alternative to (then) current approaches is indicated. In the names alone, Rogers is indicating the centrality of the relationship to the therapeutic endeavour, the focus on the client rather than on theory or technique and the importance of the therapist tracking the experience of clients rather than imposing on them. Furthermore, in his statements of the necessary and sufficient conditions for therapeutic change (1957, 1959) (Point 13), Rogers described six elements about which he (1957: 101) claims that, if they are present, positive change *will* occur *regardless* of the orientation of the practitioner 'whether we are thinking of classical psychoanalysis, or any of its modern offshoots, or Adlerian psychotherapy, or any other'. Thus Rogers was making an integrative statement about psychotherapy, not defining client-centred therapy.

So, a way of reading the statement of the necessary and sufficient conditions is as a challenge to all the elaborate theories and practices of the myriad approaches to therapy. 'Believe what you want and, providing it doesn't conflict with the necessary and sufficient conditions, do what you want, but unless the six conditions are present, change will not occur, if they are, constructive change will occur regardless.' Not only that, Rogers (1957: 101) explicitly states that psychotherapy is *not* a special kind of relationship – the conditions can be and are met in relationships of many other sorts. Implicitly, these relationships too can be the spur to therapeutic change. Herein lies a radical challenge to psychotherapy and psychiatry. This challenge is about power and how it is exercised (Points 5 and 6).

Person-centred therapy eschews diagnosis (but not necessarily 'assessment' – see Wilkins 2005a: 128–145 and Point 32) and the medicalisation of distress. However, there is an argument made by, for example, Sanders (2005: 21) to the effect that 'counsellors have abdicated the radical position occupied by Client-Centred Therapy (CCT) in the 1950s'. As Sanders (2006a: 33–35) states and explains, 'distress is not an illness'; he (2007e) explores person-centred alternatives to the medicalisation of distress.

Rather than a 'disease' model of mental distress as may be seen as dominating psychiatry or notions of 'psychosis' and 'neurosis' as may be prevalent in other approaches to psychotherapy, in the contemporary person-centred tradition there are four positions to mental ill-health. These are those based on (Wilkins 2005b: 43):

1. (psychological) contact
2. incongruence
3. styles of processing
4. issues of power.

These conceptualisations challenge not only the medicalised element of the psychiatric and psychotherapeutic professions but also the powerful pharmaceutical industry.

THE PERSON-CENTRED APPROACH EMBRACES A FAMILY OF PERSON-CENTRED THERAPIES

The approach(es) to therapy based on person-centred principles are various. They include focusing, experiential psychotherapy, process-experiential psychotherapy and creative and expressive forms too. Even the form originating directly from Carl Rogers and which has variously been referred to as 'non-directive therapy', 'client-centred therapy' and 'person-centred therapy' has shifted and adapted along the way. So just what is it that characterises the person-centred therapies?

Sanders (2004: 155) listed the primary and secondary principles of person-centred psychotherapy; the former are 'required' for person-centred practitioners and define the broad family that is the person-centred approach, the latter 'permitted' in the sense that they bring practice closer to the classic client-centred approach as it was defined in the 1940s and 1950s. Adapted as characteristics of the approach, these are as follows.

Primary principles

- The actualising tendency has primacy. It is required to believe that the process of change and growth is motivated by the actualising tendency and an error to act otherwise.
- Constructive, growthful relationships are underpinned by the active, attentive inclusion of the 'necessary and sufficient' conditions established by Rogers (1957).
- The non-directive attitude has primacy. It is mistaken to direct the content of experience either explicitly or implicitly.

Secondary principles

- There is a right to autonomy and self-determination. It is a mistake to violate the internal locus of control of another/others.
- A 'non-expert' attitude underpins relationships with others. It is a mistake to imply expertise in the direction of content and substance of the life of another. In this sense at least 'equality' is fundamental.
- The non-directive attitude and intention have primacy in that it is a mistake to wrest control of the change process from the actualising tendency in any way whatsoever.
- The therapeutic conditions proposed by Rogers (1957) are sufficient to enable encounter. It is a mistake to include other conditions, methods or techniques.
- Holism – it is a mistake to respond to only a part of the organism.

Although Sanders presented his principles in terms of the relationship between therapist and client, if it is to be person-centred, at least the primary principles apply to any relationship between individuals, an individual and a group, society or nation, groups of all kinds and individuals and groups and ecologies of all levels.

Sanders (2007a: 107–122) revisits the 'family' of person-centred and experiential therapies, explaining how the core values are seen by different authors (pp. 108–111), and characterising different approaches to:

- person-centred/client-centred therapy emphasising the centrality of the actualising tendency, the necessary and sufficient conditions and principled non-directivity (pp. 111–114);
- experiential therapies including focusing-oriented and process-experiential psychotherapies in which experiencing is at the core and the therapist is an expert process facilitator/director (pp. 114–117);

- pre-therapy – not a therapeutic approach as such but a system of techniques to come before therapy per se with clients for whom 'contact' is problematic (pp. 117–118).

The 'tribes of the person-centred nation' are explored more fully in Sanders (2012).

THERE IS A PHILOSOPHICAL BASIS TO PERSON-CENTRED THERAPY

The person-centred approach can be considered as rooted in one or more of a number of philosophical or epistemological paradigms. It is not possible to point to one of these major paradigms and to say categorically 'the person-centred approach belongs there'. Thus, the person-centred approach is not 'humanistic' (which may be considered as of the Romantic paradigm) even though it has been assigned as such and has some characteristics in common with humanistic approaches. For example (drawing on Spinelli 1994: 256–260), that person-centred therapy is 'humanistic' implies that the following are emphasised:

- the client's current experience rather than past causes which may 'explain' that experience;
- the totality of the client rather than a particular 'problem';
- the client's personal understanding and interpretation of their experience rather than the therapist's;
- the client's freedom and ability to choose how to 'be';
- an egalitarian relationship between the client and the therapist;
- the therapeutic relationship as intrinsically healing and/or growth-inspiring;
- integration of self-concept and the 'self' per se;
- the client's inherent actualising tendency and innately positive nature;
- the client's core, unitary self as a source for individual development.

However, it seems that the principles of client-centred therapy were established *before* those of humanistic psychology (see Merry 1998: 96–103) and possibly contributed to the development of that line of thought rather than being derived from it. Also, person-centred theory is an organismic theory, not a self theory (see Tudor and Merry 2002: 92). That is, it is concerned with the sum total of the biochemical, physiological, perceptual, cognitive, emotional and interpersonal behavioural subsystems constituting the person rather than a psychological construct, the self, which may be considered to be a particular and peculiar, 'culturally embedded ethnocentric concept' (see Sanders 2006b: 31) unique to Western thought.

In my view, the person-centred approach draws more on phenomenology than any other branch of philosophy. This is clearly indicated by the first two of Rogers' (1951: 483–484) propositions:

1. Every individual exists in a continually changing world of experience of which he is the center.
2. The organism reacts to the field as it is experienced and perceived. The perceptual field is, for the individual, 'reality'.

Cooper and Bohart (2013: 102–117) explore the experiential and phenomenological foundations of person-centred therapy including:

- Rogers' emphasis on experiencing as the essence of human being;
- the phenomenological foundations of this experiential perspective;
- the nature of experiencing.

Does it matter that it appears difficult or even impossible to pigeon-hole the person-centred approach in terms of a particular philosophy or meta-paradigm? Well, no. This is both because it sits well with the 'anti-establishment' origins of the approach and the notion that it is a revolutionary paradigm and because throughout the history of the approach, theory has been derived from and modified in the light of practice. The person-centred approach is not theory-driven but neither is it atheoretical. Thinking clearly about the approach, being fully conversant with its theory and, for example, tracing the conceptual and linguistic development of person-centred thought as it relates to the Western intellectual are all very important but ultimately the value of theory lies more in its construction than in its propagation. Theory informs practice but does not dictate it and is, or should be, out of immediate awareness in the moment of encounter.

5

THE PRINCIPLE OF NON-DIRECTIVITY UNDERPINS PERSON-CENTRED THERAPY

In many ways, that the therapist has a non-directive attitude is *the* fundamental and original precept of person-centred therapy; however, it is and has been controversial more or less from Rogers' early statements of the principle in, for example, the classic *Counseling and Psychotherapy* (1942). Most of this controversy centres on just what is meant by 'non-directivity'. That the non-directive therapist is a 'non-expert' (clients are the experts on themselves) has been confused with a lack of expertise. Clearly, person-centred therapists are required to have expertise in practices rooted in a particular theory and specifically to those derived from the statement of the necessary and sufficient conditions (Rogers 1957: 96, 1959: 213) and a way of being in relationship. Also, being non-directive has sometimes been operationalised as a set of passive behaviours where the therapist does little but mechanistically 'reflect' what has been heard. Empathic responding, which is at the heart of classical client-centred therapy and therefore of a non-directive approach, requires much more of the therapist than these simple behaviours (Point 20).

Rogers (in Kirschenbaum and Henderson 1990a: 86–87) wrote:

> Nondirective counselling is based on the assumption that the client has the right to select his own life goals, even though these may be at variance with the goals his counsellor might choose for him. There is also the belief that if the individual has a modicum

of insight into himself and his problems, he will be likely to make this choice wisely.

This is a statement of the right of the client to autonomy and of a belief in the constructive nature of human beings. It is not about passivity on the part of the therapist nor does it imply particular techniques. What is intended by 'non-directivity' is an attitude not a set of behaviours (see Brodley 2005: 1–4). That is, the therapist has no desire and makes no attempt to direct the course or content of the therapy or to decide goals or a desirable outcome.

Cain (2002: 366–368) challenges this conceptualisation of non-directivity as 'inflexible' and limiting of clients and (p. 369) argues that 'nondirectiveness is neither a defining nor essential component of person-centeredness'. However, others (for example Brodley 2005: 1–4; Levitt 2005: 5–16) take a different view. Grant (2002: 371–372) addresses this and comes up with two understandings of non-directiveness: *instrumental non-directiveness* and *principled non-directiveness*. The former (p. 371) 'is seen as essentially a means of facilitating growth', while the latter (p. 371) 'is essentially an expression of respect'. In Grant's (2002: 373–377) conceptualisation, instrumental non-directivity characterises 'person-centred' therapies (see Sanders' 2004: 155 primary principles), while principled non-directiveness is (Grant 2002: 371) 'essential to client-centered therapy'.

Grant (2002: 374–375) is very clear that principled non-directiveness does not involve self-abnegation or passivity on the part of the therapist.

Drawing on the work of Grant, Sanders (2006b: 82) characterises a contemporary understanding of non-directivity in the (slightly adapted) following way:

- Whilst it is not formalised in Rogers' theory it is none the less implicit in his work.
- It is an attitude, not a set of behaviours or techniques. In experienced therapists it is an aspect of character.

- It finds expression through the therapeutic conditions and is inseparable from them – all therapist responses should be 'tempered' by non-directivity.

While for some, the ethical imperative on which principled non-directivity is founded is enough to justify it, Sanders (2006b: 84–85) points out that there are arguments for the therapeutic benefits of non-directivity.

It is relevant to note that, even though he was aware of the arguments with respect to non-directivity occurring in his lifetime and in the face of Cain's (2002: 366) observation that the word 'non-directive' did not appear in the title of any of Rogers' published works after 1947, it seems that Rogers held to the principle in his later years. In Evans (1975: 26), Rogers stated:

> I still feel that the person who should guide the client's life is the client. My whole philosophy and whole approach is to strengthen him in that way of being, that he's in charge of his own life and nothing I say is intended to take that capacity or opportunity away from him.

Thus, the non-directive attitude is and was always about power in the therapeutic relationship and a belief that to exert power over another (even with good intentions) is actually counter-therapeutic.

The centrality of non-directivity to person-centred therapy is revisited in Grant (2005) who has sections on:

- historical and theoretical perspectives on non-directivity;
- the non-directive attitude in individual psychotherapy;
- ethics and applications beyond individual psychotherapy.

Although Freire (2012: 171) records that her suggestion of a special issue of *Person-Centered and Experiential Therapies* on non-directivity met with a mixed reaction, as guest editor, she solicited enough papers for *two* editions of that journal (2012, volume 11, parts 3 and 4). These include Sommerbeck

(2012: 173–189) considering non-directivity in directive settings, Bozarth (2012: 262–276) reprising 'the unprecedented premise' of non-directivity in the theory of Rogers and Moon and Rice (2012: 289–303) who write of the ethical imperatives of the non-directive attitude.

'POWER' AND HOW IT IS
EXERCISED ARE CENTRAL TO
PERSON-CENTRED THERAPY

In the study of human relationships, power and influence are problematic. How they are understood has to do with theoretical and philosophical stance as well as practical experience (see Proctor *et al.* 2006 for thoughts about power written from a person-centred perspective). There is no way any of us can divorce ourselves from the power (or lack of it) bestowed on us by our gender, class, ability, wealth, ethnicity, education, professional role and so on. All these factors affect the practice of person-centred therapy and must be acknowledged and addressed. However, at the risk of appearing naively to set them aside, there is something worth saying about fundamental person-centred attitudes and 'power' in the therapeutic relationship.

As indicated in Point 5, power in the therapeutic relationship has long been a contentious and difficult issue for person-centred therapists. The whole approach is predicated on the assumption that it is counter-therapeutic for the therapist to present as an 'expert' at least in the sense of knowing what is best for the client. This is about who has power in the relationship and the nature of that power. Quite what this means in practice may be understood differently depending on the branch of the person-centred family to which the practitioner adheres and on personal interpretation. At least for those practising in (or close to) the 'classic' client-centred tradition, this is also a matter of ethics. For example, Shlien (2003: 218) describes the client-centred method as the only 'decent' one and I (Wilkins 2006: 12) have described choosing to practise in a person-centred way as 'to make an ethical choice, to take a moral position'. This is about an aspect of power – however, power takes many shapes, some benign, some less so.

I (Wilkins 2003: 92) have argued that to be effective as a person-centred therapist it is essential to be fully present as a powerful person in the therapeutic relationship without denying or subjugating that personal power. This brings an obligation to be acutely aware of that power and to seek to exercise it in a constructive, influential way but to consciously avoid directing and dominating the other person. This is in accord with Natiello (2001: 11) who states 'I believe that a therapist needs to bring a strong sense of self and of *personal power* [original emphasis] to the facilitative relationship.' Elsewhere, Natiello (1987: 210) defines personal power as:

> the ability to act effectively under one's own volition rather than under external control. It is a state wherein the individual is aware of and can act upon his or her own feelings, needs, and values rather than looking to others for direction.

Arguably, personal power is innate – human beings are born with the facility to self-direct. Circumstances (for example conditions of worth – Point 12) can cause people to lose touch with their personal power but, given the right conditions, it can be discovered or reclaimed. However, the notion of empowering another is nonsense because it would involve the exercise of power, the 'doing' of something to another and is therefore a contradiction. Rogers (1977: 289) wrote 'it is not that this approach gives power to the person; it never takes it away'. Similarly, Grant (2002: 374) points out that 'the liberation that can come from client-centered therapy is accomplished by respecting clients as autonomous beings, not by making them autonomous beings'. A task of person-centred therapists is then to avoid *disempowering* their clients, hence the importance of the non-directive attitude.

Proctor (2002: 84–103) deals at length with the issue of power in person-centred therapy. She:

- agrees (p. 87) that the non-directive attitude leads to 'a radical disruption of the dynamics of power in therapy';
- indicates (pp. 89–90) that the therapist exercising personal power (in the form of empathic understanding) can be liberating for the client;
- discusses (p. 90) the demystification of therapy explicit in the person-centred approach as contributing to a lack of disempowerment of the client;
- states (p. 92) the importance of the therapist's intent to follow but not interpret the client's experience and to be prepared to 'self disclose' as contributing to an egalitarian relationship.

She (pp. 94–95) also warns of the danger of ignoring the power implicit in the therapist's role, stating:

> There are different powers attached to [the role of client and the role of therapist], and this inequality is established in the institution of therapy. It seems that person-centred theory may be emphasising the agency of individuals at the expense of missing the effect of structures of power on individuals. The potential implications for person-centred therapists of ignoring structural power are that they could miss opportunities to help clients from their own position, and they could underestimate or misunderstand the effects on clients' lives of any structures of power.

Proctor (p. 103) reaches the conclusion that 'person-centred therapy certainly challenges the fundamental inequality in the roles of therapist and client' and that 'there is radical potential for PCT to challenge and question the orthodox model of mental illness'. While she agrees that the facilitative conditions described by Rogers tend to increase a sense of personal power, she warns that it is dangerous to focus on equality from this perspective as it may result in ignoring other aspects of power. She is particularly concerned with issues of structural power and especially that attaching to the role of therapist.

Power in therapy is also the focus of some of the chapters in Proctor *et al.* (2006) and consideration in many of them (see, for example, Proctor 2006: 66–79).

THE ISSUE OF THE COMPATIBILITY OF USING TECHNIQUES IN A PERSON-CENTRED FRAMEWORK IS UNRESOLVED AND CONTENTIOUS

Because it is seen as to conflict with the principle of non-directivity (Point 5) and involve the exertion of power by the therapist (Point 6), the use of techniques within person-centred therapy is, to say the least, contentious. Certainly, there are those who argue that the use of any technique is incompatible with person-centred therapy (see, for example, Fairhurst 1993: 25–30). This is because, from a classical client-centred point of view, the therapist's sole role is to attend to the client's experience and process. To do anything else may be counter-therapeutic. However, many others who adopt the label 'person-centred' deviate from the classical view. For example, experiential and focusing therapists have no problems with the notion of directing clients' attention towards aspects of their experience and process while others proactively introduce activities drawing on a range of creative and expressive techniques. For example, Natalie Rogers (2007: 316–320) describes 'person-centred expressive arts therapy', Silverstone (1994: 18–23) discusses person-centred art therapy and in Wilkins (1994: 14–18) I make a case for person-centred psychodrama.

Bozarth (1996: 363) takes a 'yes but' position with respect to the use of techniques. He is of the opinion that while theory militates against the use of techniques it may be possible to do this in a person-centred way. His hesitation with respect to techniques rests on the fact that they may distract the therapist from the world of the client. In other words the therapeutic endeavour moves from being client-centred to being technique-centred. Brodley and Brody (1996: 369) come to a similar conclusion but (p. 373) qualify this stating that techniques are not compatible with 'true client-centered psychotherapy' if 'they are the result of the therapist's having a diagnostic mindset'. Rogers (1957: 103) sees 'no essential value' to the use of 'such techniques as interpretation of personality dynamics, free association, analysis of dreams, analysis of the transference, hypnosis, interpretation of life style, suggestion, and the like'.

What Rogers is sceptical about are techniques of interpretation, those which involve therapists intervening from their own frames of reference. This seems also to lie at the heart of the reservations of Fairhurst, Bozarth, and Brodley and Brody and the like. It is clear that anything centring on therapists and their frames of reference is something other than person-centred therapy. However, the 'techniques' of (for example) person-centred expressive therapists, person-centred art therapists and perhaps even person-centred psychodramatists can be viewed as those of communication and/or exploration, not interpretation. For example, Natalie Rogers (Rogers 2013: 239) argues that expressive arts enhances the therapeutic relationship in many ways because it enables a variety of internal processes. There is an argument to be made that the implicit direction of the classic client-centred therapist 'talk to me' is in reality no different from the 'direction' of the person-centred expressive therapist 'dance with me' or 'draw with me'. People communicate and express themselves via many media and to restrict them to one channel may be mistaken. Perhaps what matters is that the therapist's attention is focused on the client's experience which is responded to empathically and acceptingly regardless of the medium employed.

Section 2

CLASSICAL PERSON-CENTRED THEORY

PERSON-CENTRED PRACTICE, HOWEVER IT IS NOW CARRIED OUT, IS FOUNDED ON THEORY BASED ON EMPIRICAL RESEARCH AND OBSERVATION AS DESCRIBED BY ROGERS AND HIS COLLEAGUES IN THE 1940S AND 1950S

An early and proud boast of the founders of person-centred therapy is that its theory was firmly rooted in the empirical observation of practice. Rogers and his students saw themselves as scientists seeking to establish a basis for their beliefs and practices by actively engaging in research. Kirschenbaum (2007: 197–210) told of Rogers' early experiences of psychotherapy research and (p. 198) noted that 'when Rogers first entertained the idea of undertaking research in psychotherapy there were no precedents for him to follow'.

Rogers was not alone in this early, innovative research work. Barrett-Lennard (1998: 11–12) recorded that in the 1940s each graduate student working with Rogers typically contributed 'a discovery in method, technique or theoretical formulation in the previously uncharted field of empirical research on psychotherapy'. McLeod (2002: 88) wrote:

> Rogers was the leader of a systematic programme of research into the processes and outcomes of client-centered therapy. The client-centered research group comprised the largest centre for research in psychotherapy then in existence.

27

The first intent of Rogers was to seek to understand the process of therapy and what led to constructive change. Rogers (1967: 244) framed the theory of client-centred therapy 'not as dogma or as truth but as a statement of hypotheses, as a tool for advancing our knowledge'. The concepts underpinning person-centred therapy were being constantly revised in the light of clinical experience and research. This led Rogers to hypothesise (1957: 96) an *integrative* statement of the necessary and sufficient conditions of any successful therapeutic relationship regardless of the orientation of the therapist (see Bozarth 1996: 25–26; Wilkins 1999: 57–58) not merely a formula for person-centred practice.

The most accessible accounts of research are in Rogers (1951). These include studies of therapist techniques and attitudes (pp. 30–31, pp. 51–52), statements as to the nature of self and self-concept (pp. 136–137), process and outcomes in play therapy (pp. 267–275) and the training of therapists (pp. 444–462) as well as studies of the process of therapy and client 'change'. There is also a review (pp. 56–64) of the evidence for the basic hypothesis (p. 56) 'concerning the capacity of the individual for self-initiated, constructive handling of the issues involved in life situations' and an account of 'The Early Period of Research' in Rogers (1967: 247–266). It was from this early research that the theoretical propositions underpinning the person-centred approach first came to be stated. Throughout the 1940s, as Rogers (1951: 15) states, most of the theoretical constructs proposed by those researching client-centred therapy had centred on the nature of the self. For example, Rogers (1951) culminates in (pp. 481–524) the statement of 'a theory of personality' derived from clinical experience and the research studies illuminating the nature of self and the process of therapy. This statement is as nineteen propositions (Point 10). However, there was also important research into the non-directive approach.

The next landmark texts are Rogers' 1957 paper and his 1959 chapter. In Rogers (1959) there is a comprehensive statement of a theory of therapy and personality change, a theory of personality (including child development) and a theory of interpersonal relationships. Rogers (1957) is presented in terms of a statement of a hypothesis and its implications although throughout the paper references are made to the empirical observations underpinning the hypothesis. Rogers (1959) comprises a fuller statement of the hypothesis and hypothesises many other elements of person-centred theory. Following each statement, Rogers makes first a commentary on it and then offers an account of the evidence from research that supports the hypothesis. In the final section of this chapter (pp. 244–251), Rogers reviews 'the theoretical system in the context of research' considering, amongst other things, what has been investigated and how.

THE ACTUALISING TENDENCY IS THE CRUCIAL CONCEPT AT THE HEART OF APPROACHES TO PERSON-CENTRED THERAPY

In the theory and practice of person-centred therapy, it is held that an innate tendency within the client constitutes the sole agent for growth, 'constructive personality change' (Rogers 1957: 96), achievement of potential and so on. This agent is called the actualising tendency. Of this tendency, Rogers (1951: 487) wrote that the human species 'has one basic tendency and striving – to actualize, maintain, and enhance the experiencing organism'. However, it is clear from Rogers' later writing (see, for example, Kirschenbaum and Henderson 1990a: 380) and (for example) the commentary of Barrett-Lennard (1998: 75) that the actualising tendency is not seen as a uniquely human characteristic but that it 'is present generally in complex life forms'.

As the first of his 'primary principles of person-centred therapies', Sanders (2004: 155) indicates the primacy of the actualising tendency. He goes on to state 'it is a therapeutic mistake to believe, or act on the belief, that the therapeutic change process is *not* [original emphasis] motivated by the client's actualising tendency'. Thus the actualising tendency is fundamental to and defining of the person-centred approach.

The actualising tendency is a biological force common to all living things. It directs all organisms towards survival, maintenance and growth where growth is understood as increasing complexity and the fulfilment of potential. Bohart (2013: 86) describes the actualising tendency as *generative*.

In person-centred theory, the actualising tendency is the sole motivation for development and behaviour in human beings and beings of other kinds. In terms of 'classical' person-centred therapy, the actualising tendency in human beings propels the organism – that is the sum total of the biochemical, physiological, perceptual, cognitive and interpersonal behavioural subsystems constituting the person – in the direction of increasing independence *and* towards developing relationships. While this may at first appear to be a contradiction, in reality it is only as a person moves towards being psychologically free that there can be a corresponding movement towards open and honest encounter. Moreover, there is an increasing propensity for unfettered relating, that is, towards relationships that are mutual and equal and in which 'manipulation' plays no part. This is also because human beings are of an inherently social nature and thus, under optimal conditions, the actualising tendency drives towards constructive social behaviour. However, as Rogers (1959: 196–197) makes clear, as an individual develops a self structure so the general tendency to actualise 'expresses itself also in the actualization of that portion of the experience of the organism which is symbolized in the self'. This is self-actualising tendency. When there is a significant difference between self and organismic experience the self-actualising tendency may conflict with the actualising tendency and a state of incongruence arises (see Point 11). Rogers expands on his understanding of the actualising tendency in Rogers (1977: 237–251) (Chapter 11 of *On Personal Power*, 'A political base: the actualizing tendency') and, with respect to 'motives' and consciousness, in Rogers (1963: 1–24, 2008: 17–32).

The actualising tendency can be viewed as a springing from the *formative tendency* that is a directional tendency towards increasing order, complexity and interrelatedness found throughout the natural world and which is postulated to be (literally) universal. Rogers (1980: 134) stated that, for him, the formative tendency 'is a philosophical base for the person-centered approach'. Implicit in the notion of the formative tendency is the interconnectedness of all things and thus this must also be true of the actualising tendency.

Levitt (2008) includes reprinted chapters by Rogers, Bozarth and Merry dealing with the historical context of the actualising tendency and a section on contemporary explorations of human potential in person-centred theory in which there are considerations of the actualising tendency and formative tendency.

THE 'NINETEEN PROPOSITIONS' DETAILED IN ROGERS (1951) AND ROGERS (1959) PROVIDE AN ELEGANT STATEMENT OF A THEORY OF PERSONALITY CONSISTENT WITH PERSON-CENTRED CONCEPTS OF CHANGE

In Rogers (1951: 483–522) nineteen propositions amounting to a person-centred theory of personality and behaviour are set forth. Sanders (2006b: 17), in 'deliberately colloquial' language, describes these theoretical statements as being 'about human psychological development, the nature of human mental life, the structure of personality, how this structure can be prone to weaknesses, the nature of psychological distress, and how distress can be put right'.

As well as the original statement of these propositions by Rogers, there are neat summaries of them in Merry (2002: 34–37), including (p. 34) 'some explanations in different and perhaps more familiar terms', and Tudor and Merry (2002: 98–99).

The nineteen propositions demonstrate the person-centred view of the person as continually in process – that is personality is fluid, not fixed. Explicit in this theory is that harmful and/or inhibiting early experiences give rise to 'conditions of worth' (see Point 12) and that these give rise to emotional or psychological distress. However, people have the potential to become free of conditioning and to move towards being 'fully functioning'.

In Rogers (1959: 221–223) the person-centred theory of personality is refined and restated. The following aspects of personality are considered:

- postulated characteristics of the human infant;
- the development of the self;
- the need for positive regard;
- the development of the need for self-regard;
- the development of conditions of worth;
- the development of incongruence between self and experience;
- the development of discrepancies in behaviour;
- the experience of threat and the process of defence;
- the process of breakdown and disorganisation;
- the process of re-integration;
- specification of functional relationships in the theory of personality.

Rogers (pp. 232–233) goes on to consider the research evidence for his theory of personality.

Drawing together threads from Rogers' theoretical statements, Sanders (2006b: 21–24) characterises person-centred personality theory as:

- A phenomenological theory: it emphasises the subjective, experiential world of the individual.
- A perceptual theory: because an individual's reality is based on the perception of the world, then a change in perception leads to a change in experience and behaviour.
- A humanistic theory: it is rooted in (p. 23) 'a naturalistic philosophy that rejects all supernaturalism and relies primarily on reason and science, democracy and human compassion'.
- A holistic theory: the organism is central – human beings are (more than?) the sum total of their parts.
- A fulfilment of potential, growth-oriented theory: the person-centred metaphor for recovery is not 'cure' or 'mending' or 'reprogramming' but of growth or development to a new way of being.
- A process theory: neither personality nor self are fixed 'things', rather, being human is a process, not a state.

ALTHOUGH PERSON-CENTRED THEORY IS AN ORGANISMIC THEORY, NOT A SELF THEORY, THE NOTION OF 'SELF' REMAINS IMPORTANT

Although person-centred theory centres on the concept of the 'organism', that is the whole person comprising a number of subsystems including biochemical, physiological, perceptual, emotional, behavioural and relational systems, rather than the 'self' (see Barrett-Lennard 1998: 74–76; Rogers 1951: 484–488, 1959: 221; Tudor and Merry 2002: 91–93), and Tudor and Merry (2002: 92) state that person-centred theory may justifiably be considered as an organismic psychology rather than a self psychology, the notion of the self has importance and currency.

While person-centred theorists have offered and continue to offer re-conceptualisations of the self (for example, in terms of quantum physics) and challenges to the concept as 'culture-bound' (see Wilkins 2003: 30–34) and it is acknowledged that 'self' is a process, fluid rather than fixed, in classic client-centred theory the term is used in two principal ways. First, there is the emerging or developing self. This Rogers (1959: 200) defined thus:

> The organized, consistent conceptual gestalt composed of conceptions of the characteristics of the 'I' or 'me' and the perceptions of the characteristics of the 'I' or 'me' to others and to various aspects of life, together with the values attached to these perceptions. It is a gestalt which is available to awareness though not necessarily in

35

awareness. It is a fluid and changing gestalt, a process, but at any given moment it is a specific entity.

In a way, this 'self', the experiencing self, is what is differentiated from the organism (as a total openness to experiencing as may be the lot of an infant) through interaction with the environment and, especially, significant others. Tudor and Merry (2002: 126) add '[t]he self is thus the inner, experiencing person with reflective consciousness'. This conceptualisation of the self may be equated with the individual.

Second, there is the self-concept which, in the simplest terms, is the view one has of one's self. The move towards a state of full functioning depends on the degree of congruence between the organism and the self-concept. The person for whom there is a notable disparity will tend to anxiety, at least a degree of emotional distress and a rigidity of personality while the person for whom there is greater accord will be propelled by the actualising tendency in the direction of becoming a fully functioning person. Related to the self-concept is the 'ideal self' (Rogers 1959: 200) which is the self-concept the person would most like to possess. In terms of therapy, clients probably have the aim of becoming as close as possible to their ideal selves but theory suggests that it is greater congruence between self and organism that will correlate most strongly with the relief of distress.

Bohart (2013: 88) refers to 'the self one is' as 'to be in process, to be in touch with all aspects of oneself and to have a trusting relationship towards oneself'. This is to approach the 'fully functioning person' and may be considered as a drawing together of the experiencing self and the ideal self.

Rogers (1959: 223–224) explains how the self develops. He (p. 223) tells how, as a function of the actualising tendency, part of the experience of an individual becomes differentiated and symbolised in an awareness of being and functioning. This awareness he called 'self-experience'. It is through interaction with the environment, particularly significant others, that this representation in awareness develops into the self-concept. As this awareness emerges, the individual develops a need for positive regard. Rogers (1959: 223) states that this need 'is universal in human beings, and in the individual, is pervasive and persistent'. So powerful is this need for positive regard that it can overwhelm the organismic valuing process or the actualising tendency and thus deflect the individual from becoming a fully functioning person. As the individual continues to develop, a need for self-regard arises. Tudor and Merry (2002: 130) equate self-regard with self-esteem which (p. 129) they define as 'the value an individual has of her/himself which, in turn, relies on a self-concept to which to attach the value or esteem'.

Technically, self-regard is positive regard experienced by the individual independently of positive regard transactions (whether satisfying or frustrating) with social others. Rogers (1959: 224) writes that a need for self-regard 'develops as a learned need developing out of the association of self-experiences with the satisfaction or frustration of the need for positive self regard' and 'the individual thus comes to experience positive regard or loss of positive regard independently of transactions with any social other [and] in a sense becomes his own significant social other'. In other words, the attitude of the individuals towards themselves is no longer directly dependent on others. However, when a self experience is sought or avoided only because it enhances or detracts from self-regard the person is said to have acquired a 'condition of worth' (Point 12).

12

THE ROOT OF PSYCHOLOGICAL AND EMOTIONAL DISTRESS LIES IN THE ACQUISITION OF CONDITIONS OF WORTH

Individuals have a need for positive regard (Point 19) – in particular from 'significant others', that is important people in the immediate environment such as parents and other principal carers. As the self develops, there is also a need for positive self-regard which Merry (2002: 25) indicates as being necessary to 'develop a sense of trust in the accuracy and reliability of our own inner experiencing'. That is to say that positive self-regard allows individuals to trust their own perceptions and evaluations of the world as they experience it. In terms of person-centred theory, this position is having an 'internal locus of evaluation'. However, the need for positive regard from others, especially those to whom the individual looks for care, protection and nurture, is so strong that this internal evaluation of experience can be easily overwhelmed if love and acceptance is withheld or threatened to be withheld – that is if they become 'conditional'. So, in order to gain and maintain the positive regard of others, the individual disregards or inhibits the expression of aspects of inner experiencing that conflicts (or seems to conflict) with the needs and opinions of others because to do otherwise would risk the withdrawal of love and acceptance. When this happens, individuals rely on the evaluations of others for their feelings of acceptance and self-regard. They develop an 'external locus of evaluation', distrusting inner experiencing even to the point of abandoning it altogether. In this way, individuals learn that they are only acceptable, loveable and prized, that is 'worthy', as long as they conform to the demands, expectations and positive evaluations of others. In this way 'conditions of worth' are acquired. In order to maintain a feeling of being valued and accepted, individuals seek or avoid experiences according to how well they fit with their conditions of worth. Experiences that match these conditions of worth (and therefore the self-concept) are perceived accurately and accepted; ones that do not are perceived as threatening and are distorted or denied ('distortion' and 'denial' are the two 'defence mechanisms' described in classic person-centred theory – see Rogers 1959: 227). This leads to 'incongruence' (Point 16) between the self and experience and in behaviour. (Note: there are other propositions as to causes of incongruence, see Point 35.) It is the process of defence that leads to some expressions of emotional or psychological distress. Rogers (1959: 228) lists these as including:

> not only the behaviors customarily regarded as neurotic – rationalization, compensation, fantasy, projection, compulsions, phobias and the like – but also some of the behaviors customarily regarded as psychotic, notably paranoid behaviors and perhaps catatonic states.

However, sometimes the process of defence is unable to operate successfully. This can lead to a state of disorganisation (see Rogers 1959: 229). It is postulated that this may lead to acute psychotic breakdown. Thus incongruence arising from conditions of worth can be seen as the root of emotional and psychological distress. The client's incongruence, leading to feelings of vulnerability or anxiety, is the second of Rogers' (1959: 213) 'necessary and sufficient conditions' for constructive personality change (Point 13).

While it is theoretically possible that if a person experienced only unconditional positive regard that therefore no conditions of worth would arise and there would be no conflict between positive regard from others and positive self-regard, it is supposed that this never occurs in reality.

13

THE PROPOSAL OF SIX NECESSARY AND SUFFICIENT CONDITIONS FOR THERAPEUTIC CHANGE IS AN INTEGRATIVE STATEMENT DESCRIBING THE ELEMENTS OF ANY SUCCESSFUL THERAPEUTIC RELATIONSHIP. IT IS UNTRUE THAT THE PRACTICE OF PERSON-CENTRED THERAPY INVOLVES BUT THREE 'CORE CONDITIONS'

One of the most widespread misassumptions about person-centred theory is that there are three 'core conditions' (usually named as 'empathy', 'congruence' and 'acceptance' or 'unconditional positive regard'), the practice of which defines person-centred therapy. This is not so. The famous hypothesis of the necessary and sufficient conditions for therapeutic change (Rogers 1957: 95–103, 1959: 213) comprises six statements. From Rogers (1957: 96) these conditions are:

1. Two persons are in psychological contact.
2. The first, whom we shall term the client, is in a state of incongruence, being vulnerable or anxious.
3. The second person, whom we shall term the therapist, is congruent or integrated in the relationship.

4. The therapist experiences unconditional positive regard for the client.
5. The therapist experiences an empathic understanding of the client's internal frame of reference and endeavours to communicate this experience to the client.
6. The communication to the client of the therapist's empathic understanding and unconditional positive regard is to a minimal degree achieved.

Rogers states that, if these conditions are present, positive change will occur regardless of the orientation of the practitioner. Thus he is making an integrative statement. From a person-centred perspective, this explains why in comparative studies of the efficacy of different approaches to therapy such as Stiles *et al.* (2006) there is no significant difference between them. The assumption must be that when the hypothesis of the necessary and sufficient conditions is met and other elements of the particular therapeutic style of the practitioner do not significantly conflict with them, the effects of therapy will be broadly the same. What is important to note is that the hypothesis depends on all six conditions not merely the so-called core conditions. Exclude any and the proposition falls. Rogers (1957: 100) states this quite unambiguously: 'if one or more of [the six conditions] is not present, constructive personality change will not occur'. Although in Rogers (1959: 213) these conditions are stated slightly differently, with respect to the basic hypothesis, this is not of much significance (see Wilkins 2003: 64–65) and the same arguments apply. However, as well as including a(n integrative) statement of the necessary and sufficient conditions for successful therapy the 1959 paper comprises a statement of person-centred theory.

The assumption that there are 'core' conditions has led people to act, write and think as if it is only these which matter or at least that they are in some way more important than the other three. Actually, no ranking of the conditions is stated or implied in the original hypothesis or elsewhere in Rogers' writings. However, Rogers (1957: 100) does offer a further hypothesis to the effect that 'If all six conditions are present, then the greater the degree to which Conditions 2 to 6 exist, the more marked will be the constructive personality change in the client.' This still means that it is only collectively and in combination that the conditions are necessary and sufficient (see also Tudor 2000: 33–37). This is of great importance when any evaluation of person-centred therapy is attempted because, as is often the case, to concentrate only on the therapist conditions of empathic understanding, congruence and unconditional positive regard severally or together is to fail to put the hypothesis to the test.

14

BECAUSE THERE IS NO STATED OR IMPLIED RANKING OF THE SIX NECESSARY AND SUFFICIENT CONDITIONS AND THEY ARE ONLY EFFECTIVE IN COMBINATION, IT MAY BE A MISTAKE TO FAVOUR ONE ABOVE THE OTHER

As stated in Point 13, the hypothesis of the necessary and sufficient conditions rests on the presence of all of them. Even so, it is not uncommon to read that 'congruence takes precedence' (for example, Rogers interviewed by Hobbs 1989: 21) or that unconditional positive regard (UPR) is the curative condition (for example, Bozarth 1998: 83) or descriptions as to how empathy cures (for example, Warner 1996: 127–143) or that it is the communication or perception of empathy and/or UPR that makes for constructive personality change (for example, Wilkins 2000: 33–34). However, in some ways such statements are unhelpful or even misleading – certainly they seem open to misinterpretation. It is clear from Rogers' original formulation that no one condition is more important than the other. So how and why have people come to make statements that appear to contradict this?

When being interviewed by Hobbs (1989: 19–27), Rogers did indeed indicate that congruence takes precedence; however, this was a qualified statement. What he (p. 21) actually said was 'Empathy is extremely important in making contact with another person but if you have other feelings then congruence takes precedence over anything else.' Two things immediately strike me about this. First, it is only if the therapist has feelings other than an empathic sensing of the experience of the other that congruence takes precedence. The inference from this is that sometimes, if the therapist cannot maintain contact with the experiential world of the client because of some feeling, thought or sensation that is clearly in their own frame of reference then some action is called for. Haugh (2001: 7) offers some criteria for making a judgement about this. Perhaps what is happening in such circumstances is that the therapist is countering or avoiding incongruence by saying or doing something from their own frame of reference so that they are able to be empathic and accepting. Second, there has been some confusion between 'precedence' and importance. What (necessarily) comes first is not necessarily more important than what follows. Congruence comes before the other therapist conditions only because without it the others cannot be trusted – or are difficult or impossible to hold. So, it is not that congruence is more important than the other conditions but that therapists must be congruent in the relationship before and if their empathy and unconditional positive regard is to be perceived by clients as trustworthy.

With respect to the stated or implied greater importance of the other conditions, the state of affairs is more complex. Sometimes the apparent favouring of one condition over another is analogous to the situation with respect to congruence. For example, when Rogers (1959: 208) writes that UPR 'seems effective in bringing about change' or Bozarth (1998: 83) states that it is 'the curative factor in client-centred therapy' they are not ranking it above the other conditions. What is happening here and with respect to similar statements about empathy and the communication or perception of the therapist conditions is more likely to be attempts to understand and explain the process of therapeutic change. This is precisely what Rogers was doing when he set out the six conditions. However, from both practical experience and theoretical consideration I have come to believe that it is a mistake to think of the therapist conditions as unitary fragments, independent of each other. As Bozarth (1998: 80) states, the three therapist conditions are functionally one condition. Freire (2001: 152) echoes this, arguing that 'empathic experience and unconditional positive regard are ultimately the sole and same experience'. Mearns and Thorne (2007: 149) put it slightly differently, expressing the opinion that, in combination, the therapist conditions become 'something much larger than the parts'. Following from this it can be postulated that there is but one therapist super-condition of which congruence, UPR and empathy are but facets. This is why the issue of the importance of the conditions with respect to one another is a spurious consideration. It is also why attempts to research any single condition, while it may have value, can say nothing about the hypothesis of the necessary and sufficient conditions (see Wilkins 2003: 66–67).

15

THE NEED FOR (PSYCHOLOGICAL) CONTACT IS AN OFTEN UNCONSIDERED PREREQUISITE FOR PERSON-CENTRED THERAPY. TO BE IN CONTACT IS TO BE IN RELATIONSHIP

As Sanders (2006b: 33) states, the first of Rogers' necessary and sufficient conditions, the requirement that 'contact' (Rogers 1959: 213) or 'psychological contact' (Rogers 1957: 96) exists between client and therapist, is consistently overlooked in most books about therapy and often in the training even of person-centred therapists. This seems to be an important oversight because what is being expressed is that successful therapy depends upon there being a relationship between the client and the therapist. Rogers (1959: 207) makes this clear in his definitions of terms:

> *Contact.* Two persons are in psychological contact, or have the minimum essential of a relationship, when each makes a perceived or subceived difference in the experiential field of another.

Another way of understanding this is that for therapy to be successful each person involved must, to some small degree and on some level, be aware of the presence of the other (even if not consciously) and that this awareness constitutes a relationship. Rogers (1957: 96) writes:

> The first condition specifies that a minimal relationship, a psychological contact, must exist. I am hypothesizing that significant positive personality change does not occur except in a relationship.

Because human beings are innately relational, we have a strong need for psychological contact. Warner (2002: 92) points out that 'even moderate increases in psychological contact are of great personal and psychological value to clients'. Contact with another person, a sense of being with rather than apart, however fleeting, can lessen anxiety and existential loneliness.

In their exploration of the concept of contact, Wyatt and Sanders (2002: 8) point out that, from their reading of Rogers, 'the minimal connection between two persons – before it can be said that they are "in relationship" – is that both have a *desire and intention* [original emphasis] to be in contact with each other'. This implies that mindfulness is a necessary element of relationship, i.e. each person must make a perceptible impact on the awareness of the other. This seems to contradict the idea that a subceived impact is sufficient to constitute contact – if to be in contact is to be in relationship. Wyatt and Sanders present a view of contact as a necessary precursor to relationship and therefore to any prospect of successful therapy. This is indeed the normal situation. However, because contact can also be subceived, it is possible to build on and strengthen it. This is, for example, what lies behind pre-therapy (see Prouty 2002a, 2002b) where the therapist works in a systematic way to discover and strengthen subceived contact between the therapist and clients of impaired functioning due to (for example) psychosis, more extreme learning disability, dementia or brain damage (through organic disease or injury). Indeed, Prouty (2002a: 55) describes pre-therapy as a theory of psychological contact although his meaning is slightly different because he includes contact with the self.

Without the requirement for contact being met, the other conditions would have no meaning and no effect. In putting the relationship at the heart of the therapeutic endeavour, Rogers was making a radical statement. Because to this day in the practice of person-centred therapy the relationship is valued above all else and the radical challenge remains. Increasingly, evidence from outcome research indicates that, in counselling and psychotherapy as a whole, apart from 'client variables' – that is, what the client brings to the interaction – it is the relationship between client and therapist which correlates most strongly with successful outcome (see, for example, Krupnick *et al.* 1996). This places contact at the very centre of understanding what happens in psychotherapy. From a person-centred perspective, this awareness has led to a reconsideration of the nature of contact. For example, whereas the classic client-centred position is that contact exists or it does not (what Sanders 2006b: 36 describes as 'a binary, all-or-nothing, on-off event') others argue that there are levels of contact and/or that there are types of contact different in nature and degree. So, Cameron (2003a: 87) considers that contact may be of various depths, writing '[t]he depth of contact is what makes the difference between a rather mechanical and lifeless therapeutic relationship and one that shimmers with energy and involvement'. In two chapters, she (2003a, 2003b) names and describes four levels of psychological contact:

- *basic contact* is 'meeting', mutual encounter of perhaps the most rudimentary kind in which each person perceives the other and is affected by them;
- *cognitive contact* is about sharing meaning and involves mental processes and at least a degree of mutual understanding;
- *emotional contact* is 'being closer', an openness to one's own feelings and a willingness to receive and respond to the feelings of the other;
- *subtle contact* or intimacy which has an equivalence with 'presence' (Rogers 1980: 129), tenderness (Thorne 1991: 73–81) or even 'working at relational depth' (Mearns 1996).

These could just as well be thought of as characterising different qualities of relating.

Wyatt (2013: 150–164) reprises psychological contact considering, amongst other things, 'the evolving nature of psychological contact' (pp. 152–155) and 'psychological contact in person-centred relationships' (pp. 158–160).

16

THAT THE CLIENT IS INCONGRUENT AND AT LEAST TO SOME DEGREE AWARE OF THAT INCONGRUENCE (AS VULNERABILITY OR ANXIETY) IS A NECESSARY CONDITION FOR THERAPY

The second of Rogers' (1957) necessary and sufficient conditions for successful therapy demands that the client is (p. 96) 'in a state of incongruence, being vulnerable or anxious'. In technical terms, incongruence is a discrepancy between the self as perceived and the actual experience of the organism. Rogers (1959: 203) indicates that such a discrepancy results in a state of tension and internal confusion because in some respects behaviour is regulated by the actualising tendency and in others by the self-actualising tendency. This gives rise to 'discordant or incomprehensible behaviors'. Incongruent individuals feel at least a degree of confusion because there is conflict between their feelings and behaviour and what they consciously 'want'. According to Tudor and Merry (2002: 72), incongruence can be considered to manifest as one of three process elements: 'a general and generalised vulnerability, a dimly perceived tension or anxiety, and a sharp awareness of incongruence'.

  When individuals are unaware of their incongruence they are potentially vulnerable because a new experience which demonstrates the discrepancy between self and organism is threatening and the self-concept cannot assimilate it and thus it becomes disorganised. When individuals are aware of an uneasiness or tension of unknown cause they may be

considered as anxious. What is happening in such circumstances is that the incongruence between the self-concept and
the organism is approaching awareness (i.e. it is subceived).
The resulting anxiety results from a fear that the discrepancy
may enter awareness and so force a change in the self-concept.
This is one of the many reasons why therapy is a scary business. A 'sharp awareness of incongruence' is exactly what it
says. Whatever its precise nature, incongruence may be considered as arising from the acquisition of conditions of worth and
a lack of unconditional positive regard (Point 12).

Rogers' second condition states unambiguously that the client's incongruence is a necessary condition for constructive
personality change to occur but he also qualifies this with the
requirement that the incongruence manifests as vulnerability
or anxiety. Sanders (2006b: 43) interprets this as 'the client
needs help, and knows it'. This raises the question as to whether
it is possible to be incongruent without being vulnerable or
anxious or, to use Sanders' form, if it is possible 'that the client needs help but doesn't know it'. If so, condition two would
not be met and so some individuals at some stage of their process could be considered as unsuitable for therapy. Wilkins and
Bozarth (2001: ix–x) consider this at greater length. However,
Barrett-Lennard (1998: 79) states 'some degree of vulnerability and anxiety seems bound to apply to anyone voluntarily
in therapy and, perhaps, in most people'. While Wilkins and
Bozarth agree with this, they (2001: x) also ask 'Does condition two imply that therapy will only be successful if, in some
way and on some level, the person in the client role is suffi-
ciently aware of and troubled by incongruence to persist in the
[therapeutic] endeavour?' They go on to say 'almost certainly'.
In the context of assessment, Wilkins (2005a: 141) puts this
in the form of a question: '[i]s my potential client in need of
and [original emphasis] able to make use of therapy?' Rogers'
(1967: 132: 155) consideration of the seven stages of process is
helpful in answering this question (Points 17 and 32).

17

ROGERS' SEVEN STAGES OF PROCESS PROVIDES A MODEL FOR THERAPEUTIC CHANGE AND GUIDANCE FOR THE THERAPIST IN THE ENCOUNTER

In person-centred terms, a person's process is their way of experiencing and encountering the world, their way of making sense of all the stimuli and information to which they are exposed. Process is cognitive, behavioural, emotional and (arguably at least) spiritual. It is both in and out of awareness and it may be reflexive or spontaneous.

Rogers (1967: 132–155) proposes a continuum of personality change as seven stages of process. These are also described and illustrated in an accessible way by Merry (2002: 58–63). Briefly, at the relevant stage the client:

1. is very defensive, and extremely resistant to change;
2. becomes slightly less rigid, and will talk about external events or other people;
3. talks about her/himself, but as an object, avoiding discussion of present events;
4. begins to talk about deep feelings and develops a relationship with the therapist;
5. can express present emotions, and begins to rely more on their own decision-making abilities and increasingly accepts more responsibility for their actions;
6. shows rapid growth toward congruence and begins to develop unconditional positive regard for others;

7. is a fully functioning, self-actualised individual who is empathic and shows unconditional positive regard for others. This individual can relate their previous therapy to present day real-life situations.

The stages of process indicate something about the individual's likely way of being and so what is appropriate from the therapist. Although Merry (2002: 59) points out that there 'is a great deal of variation and individual differences in clients' processes' and Rogers (1967: 139) states that 'a person is never wholly at one or another stage of process', knowing something about a client's stage in the process continuum can inform the therapist and help in making appropriate ethical and professional decisions. For example, whether therapy is likely to be effective and should therefore be offered at all, whether pre-therapy may be a more appropriate strategy (Point 34) or whether the client is close enough to being fully functioning not to need therapeutic interventions at all.

Briefly, because they have a limited awareness of their incongruence (Point 16), people in the first two stages of processing are unlikely to willingly contract for therapy or, if they do, are likely not to stay the course. Individuals in stage three, the point at which Rogers (1967: 136) believed many people who seek 'psychological help' are at or around, are likely to commit to a therapy contract. According to Merry (2002: 60), clients in stage three of process 'need to be fully accepted as they present themselves before moving deeper into stage four'. Much of counselling and psychotherapy occurs with clients who are in stages four and five and Rogers (1967: 150) describes stage six as highly crucial. It is at this stage that irreversible constructive personality change is most likely to occur. Arguably, by stage seven, clients no longer need the companionship of a therapist on their journey towards being fully functioning. Of stage seven, Rogers (1967: 151) writes 'this stage occurs as much outside the therapeutic relationship as in it, and is often reported rather than experienced in the therapeutic hour'.

In the seven stages of process, there is not only a guide to when and for whom therapy is appropriate but an indication that different 'ways of being' by the therapist in the encounter suit different stages. Implicit in the scheme is that, for example, there are qualitative differences of intent required of the therapist dealing with a client in stage three than one at stage six (although at all stages the emphasis is on the non-directive attitude and the provision of the therapist conditions). It is therefore important that person-centred therapists have some understanding of these stages.

In the first stage of process, the individual is fixed and remote from organismic experiencing. Rogers (1967: 133) understands this remoteness from experiencing in terms of blockages of both interpersonal and intrapersonal communication and points out that individuals at this stage of processing do not experience themselves as having problems or, if they do, these problems are perceived as being entirely external. At the second stage of process, individuals can experience themselves as fully received and begin to express themselves with respect to topics not directly connected with their selves. However, amongst other things, problems are still perceived as external, there is no sense of personal responsibility with respect to problems and feelings are not recognised or owned. Rogers (1967: 132) states that a person in stage one of process is unlikely to enter therapy voluntarily and that while some people in stage two do present voluntarily, working with them is successful only to a very modest degree. In other words, it is only clients in stage three process or later stages who are likely to meet Sanders' criteria. This has implications for contracting with clients.

18

FOR THERAPY TO BE EFFECTIVE, THE THERAPIST MUST BE CONGRUENT IN THE RELATIONSHIP. THIS IS A REQUIREMENT TO 'BE' AND NOT NECESSARILY TO 'DO'

There is a great deal of misunderstanding about the third of Rogers' necessary and sufficient conditions that the therapist be congruent in the relationship. This seems to be because there is a tendency to think about and to attempt to operationalise 'congruence' as action but congruence does not involve the counsellor in *doing* anything. It is a way of being in which outward behaviour is an accurate reflection of inner state, that is there is a matching of awareness and experience. Cornelius-White (2013: 195), drawing on the words of Rogers (1957: 97) in which Rogers refers to freely being the feelings that emerge and (1959: 214) where he writes of accurately being himself in the relationship as support, adds 'the therapist's expression or communication' as an element of congruence. However, another way of understanding both these statements is that the emphasis is on 'being'.

Brodley (2001: 56–57) concludes from the original formulations of congruence by Rogers that it is defined in terms of distinction between self and experience, not in terms of the therapist's behaviour. She (p. 57) also points out that, according to the statement of the necessary and sufficient conditions, there is no requirement that the client perceive the congruence of the therapist. So, although it is a necessary condition for therapy it is not necessary that it is communicated.

However, it seems to me (see Wilkins 1997a: 38) incongruence does jar and is more likely to be directly perceived or at least subceived in such a way as to disrupt the therapeutic endeavour. Cornelius-White (2007: 174) is of the opinion that congruence (and therefore incongruence) is perceived largely through unconscious body language.

Strictly speaking, the therapist's congruence is not about an interpersonal interaction but an intrapersonal state. Whereas empathy and unconditional positive regard are, congruence is not the product of the therapeutic relationship although it may be affected by it. It is possible to be congruent alone. Congruent therapists are not necessarily *doing, saying* or *expressing* anything; they are *being* totally themselves and are fully present and aware of the flow of their experiencing.

According to Haugh (1998: 45), the requirement for congruence on the part of therapists is not so that clients experience them as real and genuine but to facilitate their ability to be empathic and to hold unconditional positive regard for their client. In terms of the client experience, it is a sensing of the therapist's congruence (whether in awareness or subceived) that gives credence to and confirms these attitudes. A congruent therapist is a trustworthy therapist.

Although it is often confused with honesty, directness and self-disclosure, being congruent is not about communicating the feelings and experiences of the therapist to the client. However, Rogers did make repeated references to the importance of the therapist's willingness to express feelings and attitudes. This has led to what some (for example Bozarth 1998: 74–78 and Haugh 1998: 46) consider the erroneous conclusion that there are therapist behaviours which would convey the therapist's congruence. However, there is agreement that at least sometimes (even if rarely) one or more things may be necessary to maintain congruence (Points 70, 71 and 72).

Haugh (2001: 7) draws together statements about congruence from Rogers' work and presents an overview of the characteristics of the practice of a congruent therapist. She offers four suggestions as to the timing of congruent responses:

1. when the therapist's feelings are interrupting the core conditions;
2. when these feelings are persistent;
3. when to not do so would result in the therapist not being 'real' in the relationship;
4. when it is appropriate – appropriateness is to be assessed on the preceding points.

Generally speaking, at least in terms of classic client-centred therapy, therapist responses are confined to attempts to communicate an understanding of the client's experience. But, as Haugh indicates, there may be times when, because congruence takes precedence (because an incongruent therapist is unlikely to be or to be perceived to be empathic and accepting), it is incumbent upon therapists to respond from their own frame of reference. Nevertheless, 'being congruent' is not a licence to confront, contradict or express an opinion about the client nor is it about offering an emotional reaction to the client or the client's material. Furthermore, self-disclosure has nothing to do with being congruent. Although there appears to be some place for the former in person-centred therapy, Barrett-Lennard (1998: 264–267) reporting a study conducted in 1962 shows that the hypothesis that the therapist's 'willingness to be known' would relate to positive outcome in person-centred therapy was unproven.

19

UNCONDITIONAL POSITIVE REGARD, THE LINCHPIN ON WHICH PERSON-CENTRED THERAPY TURNS PRESENTS A REAL CHALLENGE TO THE THERAPIST. HOWEVER, WITHOUT THIS QUALITY OF ACCEPTANCE THERE IS A STRONG POSSIBILITY THAT THERAPY WILL BE UNSUCCESSFUL

The unconditional positive regard (UPR) of the therapist for the client is a necessary condition for constructive change. Some writers (for example Bozarth 1998: 88; Wilkins 2000: 33–34) indicate that it is the active facilitator of constructive change and Freire (2001: 152) describes it as 'the revolutionary feature of the person-centered approach'. However, UPR presents real personal, ethical and professional challenges to therapists. This is partly because, however accepting of others we believe ourselves to be, it is likely that at least to some extent we carry prejudice and fear. Masson (1992: 234) in his critique of person-centred therapy asks: 'Faced with a brutal rapist who murders children, why should any therapist have unconditional regard for him?' Of course there is no reason at all why any therapist *should* but without being able to offer UPR the therapeutic endeavour will be pointless. The hypothesis of the necessary and sufficient conditions asserts that *if* a person, regardless how 'bad', consistently experiences the six conditions and perceives the empathic understanding and unconditional positive regard of another then change *will* occur. However, it may very well be that this is a big 'if'. In such cases, it is important to realise that this does not prove that the hypothesis is correct or that some people are beyond redemption but rather that the limitation is in the therapist. Luckily, although human beings share a tendency to be unaccepting of some things, these are not necessarily the same things. Thus a client to whom, for whatever reason, one therapist finds it difficult to offer UPR may find the qualities of acceptance, warmth and prizing easily extended by another. Also, it seems that by addressing our own fears and unresolved issues so increasing our unconditional positive self-regard we can increase our ability to offer UPR to others (see Wilkins 2003: 73–74). Herein lies some of the personal, ethical and professional challenges referred to above. For example, these challenges lead to an ethical requirement to reach some assessment as to the likelihood of the therapist being able to offer enough UPR to facilitate change and a professional responsibility to 'refer on' or decline the contract if not and a personal and professional responsibility for the therapist to continually address anything that limits the ability to practise.

The requirement to offer UPR is a challenge in another way. Within this condition and the hypothesis of the necessary and sufficient conditions as a whole there is what appears to be one of the 'necessary paradoxes' of person-centred therapy. The hypothesis is about change; therapists tend to have an aim to facilitate change in their clients and yet the fourth condition requires that the therapist accepts the client as the client is. There can be no requirement or even anticipation on the part of the therapist that the client will change because this would be unaccepting. Freire (2001: 145) presents the 'paradox of unconditional positive regard' as 'that a person must accept herself in order to change'. The client's acceptance is contingent on the acceptance of the therapist. She (p. 152) goes onto summarise features of person-centred therapy that relate to UPR. These (slightly adapted) are:

1. Therapists do not try to change clients. The unconditional acceptance of the client's experience is the therapist's sole aim.
2. The greater the extent to which the therapist can trust the actualising tendency of the client, the greater will be the extent to which the therapist can experience UPR for the client.
3. Therapists experience UPR for clients to the extent that they have unconditional positive self-regard.

These features require that person-centred therapists 'let go' of any desire or demand that their clients change and that they continually address their unconditional positive self-regard.

20

'THE IDEAL PERSON-CENTRED THERAPIST IS FIRST OF ALL EMPATHIC.' 'BEING EMPATHIC IS A COMPLEX, DEMANDING, STRONG YET SUBTLE AND GENTLE WAY OF BEING'

The above heading is constructed from words used by Rogers (1975: 4–6) in his updating of his views on empathy. They reflect the widespread person-centred belief that empathy is an essential attribute of a successful therapist. In Rogers (1957: 101), being empathic is defined as 'to sense the client's private world as if it were your own, but without ever losing the "as if" quality'. Being empathic is to perceive the internal frame of reference of the other with accuracy while at the same time not becoming absorbed in or overwhelmed by it. Sanders (2006b: 66) makes a useful distinction between perceiving the world of another person and experiencing it. He writes 'I cannot *feel* someone else's hurt, fears and joys. I can, though, see their thoughts and feelings accurately and *understand* them [original emphases].' It is this sensing and the communication of it to the client that constitutes the empathic process in therapy. To passively sense and understand is not enough, however accurate the understanding. In his later paper, Rogers (1975: 4) offers a richer definition:

> The way of being with another person which is termed empathic has several facets. It means entering the private perceptual world of the other and becoming thoroughly at home in it. It involves

being sensitive, moment to moment, to the changing felt meanings which flow in this other person, to the fear, rage or tenderness or confusion or whatever he/she is experiencing. It means temporarily living his/her life, moving about in it without making judgements, sensing meanings of which she is scarcely aware, but not trying to uncover feelings of which the person is totally unaware, since this would be too threatening. It includes communicating your sense of his/her world as you look with fresh and unfrightened eyes at elements of which the individual is fearful.

This is asking a lot and Rogers goes on to point out how complex and demanding the task of being empathic is, referring to it (p. 4) as a 'strong yet subtle and gentle way of being'. It is these things but, because it involves real contact with the experience of another, it can also be richly rewarding.

An important element in Rogers' statement is the notion that being empathic involves the communication to the client of the therapist's sense of their experience (Point 21). Unless the client perceives the therapist's deep understanding of their experience it is unlikely to be helpful, however accurate and complete it may be.

Rogers (1975: 5–6) published a review of empathy research, the findings of which may be summarised thus:

The ideal therapist is first of all empathic.

- Empathy is correlated with self-exploration and process movement.
- Empathy early in the relationship predicts later success.
- The client comes to perceive more empathy in successful cases.
- Understanding is provided by the therapists, not drawn from them.
- The more experienced the therapists, the more likely they are to be empathic.
- Empathy is a special quality in a relationship and therapists offer definitely more of it than even helpful friends.
- The better integrated the therapists are within themselves the higher degree of empathy they exhibit.

- Experienced therapists often fall far short of being empathic.
- Clients are much better judges of the degree of empathy than are therapists.
- Brilliance and diagnostic perceptiveness are unrelated to empathy.
- An empathic way of being can be learned from empathic persons.

By and large, after over thirty years, these statements remain broadly true but needless to say thinking and researching empathy has continued (Freire 2013: 175–176 presents a brief summary of research findings on empathy). Sanders (2006b: 69–73) offers an accessible overview of the work of those who have built on the classical client-centred view of empathy.

21

THE EFFECTIVENESS OF A THERAPIST'S UNCONDITIONAL POSITIVE REGARD AND EMPATHIC UNDERSTANDING DEPENDS ON THE EXTENT TO WHICH THEY ARE PERCEIVED BY THE CLIENT

Together with the 'contact' prescribed in condition one (and probably more than it), the elements of condition six, the communication to and/or perception by the client of the therapist's UPR and empathic understanding is relatively little understood or discussed and yet Rogers is very clear that unless this happens to at least a minimal degree change will not occur. In Rogers (1957: 96) the sixth condition is articulated in terms of the communication to the client of the therapist's empathic understanding and UPR while in Rogers (1959: 213) the emphasis is on the client's perception of these from the therapist. These two different formulations are not in conflict but together aid a complete understanding of the desired process. In effect, what this condition states is that change depends on the client being and feeling understood and accepted, however dimly. Not only must the therapist have an understanding of the client's experience and have unconditional positive regard for that client, the client must be aware of and receive these at least to some extent. If the latter does not occur then condition six has not been met regardless of how empathic and accepting therapists believe themselves to have been. This places the client at the centre of the therapeutic endeavour but it also lays a responsibility on the therapist. In some way, therapists must communicate (or make available) to the client their understanding of the client's experience and UPR for the client. To be effective, this cannot be a mechanistic or uniform process. It need not be verbal but it must involve high-quality attention to the client's process and a perceivable intention to understand the client's experience and both of these must be presented in a climate of warmth, regard and genuineness. 'Communication' as a therapist behaviour is explored in Points 82 and 83. However, there is more to the sixth condition than a requirement for particular behaviours from the therapist.

It is in the sixth condition that the 'super-condition' postulated in Point 25 may be seen to operate. Essentially, the client experience is of being received 'warts and all' and yet not found wanting, being seen with faults and fears but not judged and all this within the framework of the therapist's genuineness. This can be a singularly powerful experience for both parties and it can result in a 'moment of change'. Various attempts to explore this 'high level' experience have been made and terms such as 'presence', 'tenderness' and 'relational depth' have been applied to it. These are returned to in Points 25 and 38.

IN PERSON-CENTRED THEORY, THERE IS NO ACCEPTANCE OF THE UNCONSCIOUS AS A REPOSITORY OF REPRESSED FUNCTIONS AND PRIMITIVE DRIVES OR DESIRES AND THEREFORE 'TRANSFERENCE' IS OF LITTLE OR NO RELEVANCE

While the possibility of an 'unconscious' faculty to the human mind is not denied in person-centred theory, classically, whether or not it exists is seen as largely irrelevant to the process of therapy. This is because person-centred therapy is phenomenological, concerned only with the client's current experiencing. Anything of which a client is unconscious or unaware is by definition unknown and therefore unknowable to the therapist. Any view as to the 'unconscious' processes of the client or interpretation of them could only come from the frame of reference of the therapist. This is at odds with person-centred practice. Also, the notion of a particular structure to the mind (for example, id, ego, superconscious) does not find wide acceptance amongst person-centred theorists. When it is discussed at all, writers are likely to take the view that there is a constant flow between the 'conscious' and the 'unconscious' and to suggest a process model for the human mind (see, for example, Coulson 1995; Ellingham 1997; and Wilkins 1997a). In reality, it is only with respect to 'transference' that the unconscious causes much of a stir in person-centred theory.

It is largely true that person-centred theorists tend not to pay much attention to transference. There are two basic positions with respect to it. Either transference may (sometimes) be a part of the interaction between client and therapist but that to 'work' with it would be counter-therapeutic or it is an artefact of the psychoanalytic mindset which has no reality. Rogers' own position seems to have been close to the former. He (see Kirschenbaum and Henderson 1990a: 129–130) thought that if and when transference feelings occurred, the normal process of person-centred therapy would move through them and that there was absolutely no need for the therapist to permit the dependence that is seen as legitimate, even encouraged and supported, in other approaches to therapy. That is to say, the therapist should continue to be present as an empathic, accepting and congruent person and not be changed in response to the transferential process of the client.

Some other person-centred theorists are not as inclined to accept the psychodynamic notion of transference as Rogers may have been. Most notably Shlien (1984: 153–181) offered a 'countertheory of transference' which he hoped would be instrumental in developing a person-centred model of the unconscious. Shlien (p. 151) was of the view that 'transference is a fiction, invented and maintained by the therapist to protect himself from the consequences of his own behaviour'. This paper was responded to by Lietaer (1993: 35–37) who took the view that not only does transference exist but that it is relevant to practice. The situation with respect to countertransference is similar except that in Wilkins (1997a: 38) many of the processes described as countertransference may, in terms of person- centred theory, be described as empathy.

One way in which supposedly unconscious material may become relevant in the course of person-centred therapy has been suggested by Mearns and Thorne (2000: 175–176). They propose a reconfiguration of the classic view of the concept of self such that it includes subceived material; that is material which is in some way impacting on the person even though it is not in awareness (and so is not accepted by the person as part of the self-concept). Rogers (1959: 200), in his definition of subception, writes 'it appears that the organism can discriminate a stimulus and its meaning for the organism without utilizing the higher nerve centres involved in awareness'. Mearns and Thorne (p. 175) use the term 'edge of awareness material' and define self as 'self-concept + edge of awareness material'. This formulation is, as they point out themselves (p. 176), a departure from the phenomenological position at the core of person-centred theory (self = self-concept amongst other things). They also write of the potential danger that 'this widening conception of Self could lose its discipline in holding to the edge of awareness and wander into the unconscious'.

Section 3

REVISIONS, RECONSIDERATIONS AND ADVANCES IN PERSON-CENTRED THEORY

PERSON-CENTRED THERAPY IS NOT BASED ON AN OSSIFIED, MID-TWENTIETH-CENTURY THEORY BUT ALIVE, DYNAMIC AND BEING ACTIVELY RESEARCHED AND DEVELOPED

While there is a view that much of what needs to be known about the practice of classic client-centred therapy was stated more or less completely in the works of Rogers and his colleagues published in the 1950s, this is probably held by a minority of people describing themselves as person-centred. For the most part, there is an acceptance that Rogers did not provide all the answers and a certainty that he did not address all the issues raised in and by the practice of counselling and psychotherapy in the modern world. More or less from the days of the Chicago Center, person-centred theory has been thought about and reflected on and modified in response. For example, Eugene Gendlin, one of Rogers' leading colleagues and whose background was in philosophy, became more and more interested in how clients were facilitated to express, symbolise and articulate experience. From this interest flowed the development of focusing and thence (with other influences) experiential psychotherapy which many see as the second major branch to the person-centred family of therapies. Others also took the basic ideas of client-centred therapy in different directions. Notable amongst them was Laura Rice who incorporated some ideas from cognitive therapy traditions in her work. This led to an increased interest in the micro-processes of psychotherapy and ultimately to a way of doing and understanding psychotherapy which is sometimes called process-experiential therapy and the notion that those therapists in the broader person-centred tradition are process experts. This process of review, revision and expansion continues with, for example, the move into 'Emotional-Focused Therapy' as a derivative of the process-experiential strand (see Elliott *et al.* 2004b).

After a period of doldrums through, in particular, the 1970s and the 1980s, there have been many efforts to understand and explain the processes of person-centred therapy, to explore its effectiveness and to fill some of the gaps in knowledge through active, empirical research. Some of this research has addressed the efficacy of the classical non-directive approach (see, for example the work of Brodley, Bozarth, Freire and Sommerbeck) but a great deal of it has been directed towards expanding person-centred theory and/or understanding person-centred practice in wider and different contexts. These include clarification of child development, reconsideration of incongruence, examinations of the client/therapist relationship and ideas about psychopathology.

Although there has been a great deal of research by experiential and process-experiential therapists (see the journal *Person-Centered and Experiential Psychotherapies* for contributions to these fields of endeavour as well as to person-centred therapy per se) and this has cast light on the effectiveness of person-centred therapy as a whole, this is outside the remit of this book and the rest of this section addresses revisions, reconsiderations, expansions and additions to mainstream person-centred therapy only. However, increasingly, research efforts do not neatly separate classical client-centred therapy, person-centred therapy and (for example) emotion-focused therapy but explore two or more approaches from the person-centred nation together. A good example of this is the work done at the University of Strathclyde by Robert Elliott and his colleagues and students.

Research into, reconceptualisations and reconsiderations of person-centred therapy are in many ways one of the foci of Points 86–100 but are also found throughout this book.

24

FROM THE OUTSET, AN UNDERSTANDING OF CHILD DEVELOPMENT AND PSYCHOTHERAPY WITH CHILDREN AND YOUNG PEOPLE HAS BEEN FUNDAMENTAL TO THE PERSON-CENTRED APPROACH

It is frequently assumed that person-centred theory has no position with respect to child development. This is an error. It is often forgotten that Rogers' first major publication (Rogers 1939) was *The Clinical Treatment of the Problem Child*. Also, early luminaries of the approach Clark Moustakas and Virginia Satir were child psychotherapists. It is reasonable to assume that the development of person-centred theory was informed by practice with children and done in the light of contemporary knowledge of child development and child psychopathology. Rogers (1959: 221–223) considers aspects of personality relevant to child development and (p. 222) postulated that:

The individual, during the period of infancy, has at least these attributes:

1. He perceives his *experience* as a reality. His *experience* is his reality.
    a   As a consequence he has greater potential *awareness* of what reality is for him than does anyone else, since no one else can completely assume his *internal frame of reference*.

2. He has an inherent tendency toward *actualizing* his organism.
3. He interacts with his reality in terms of his basic *actualizing* tendency. Thus his behavior is the goal-directed attempt of the organism to satisfy the experienced needs for *actualization* in the reality as *perceived*.
4. In this interaction he *behaves* as an organized whole, as a gestalt.
5. He engages in an *organismic valuing process*, valuing *experience* with reference to the *actualizing tendency* as a criterion. Experiences which are *perceived* as maintaining or enhancing the organism are valued positively. Those which are perceived as negating such maintenance or enhancement are valued negatively.
6. He behaves with adience toward positively valued *experiences* and with avoidance toward those negatively valued.

All this amounts to a comprehensive theory of the development of the human organism from which ways of understanding child development and psychotherapeutic practice with children may be easily derived. For example, from Rogers' statement of the necessary and sufficient conditions, Biermann-Ratjen (1996: 13) derives the necessary conditions for development in early childhood. These are:

1. That the baby is in *contact* with a significant other.
2. That the baby is preoccupied with *evaluating experience* which might possibly arouse *anxiety*.
3. That the *significant other person* is *congruent in the relationship* to the baby, does not experience anything inconsistent with her self-concept while in contact with the baby when it is preoccupied with evaluating his experience.
4. That the significant other is *experiencing unconditional positive regard* toward the baby's processes of evaluating his experience.
5. That the significant other is *experiencing an empathic understanding* of the baby's experiencing within his *internal frame of reference*.

6. That the baby gradually *perceives* both the unconditional positive regard of the significant other person for him and the empathic understanding so that in the baby's *awareness* there is gradually a *belief or prognosis* that the unconditional positive regarding and empathically understanding object would when reacting to other experiences of the baby also exhibit positive regard and empathic understanding.

Cooper (1999: 64) and Mearns and Thorne (2000: 106–108) link the need for positive self-regard to the development of plural 'selfs' or configurations of self (Point 27). In their consideration of relational depth (Point 38), Mearns and Cooper (2005: 8) argue that infants have a basic need

> not only to bond with others, but also to interact and communicate with them … They want to be loved, but they also want to interact with that other and that love, to give as well as to receive, and to experience an immediate and engaged contact.

They (pp. 17–34) go on to explain how difficulties in adulthood may be linked to a failure to experience 'relational depth' in infancy and childhood. Biermann-Ratjen (1996: p. 14) is clear that positive regard is the precondition for self development and she links her model to psychopathology. Warner (2000: 149–150) also explores links between child development and psychopathology.

Cooper (2013a: 118–128) revisits person-centred development and personality theory and (pp. 125–128) presents critiques and developments of the original model.

Behr *et al.* (2013: 266–281) address person-centred therapy with children and young people concluding (p. 277) that person-centred therapy is 'a specific area of person-centred work, as well as a major therapeutic approach in its own right'. Hölldampf *et al.* (2010: 16–44) reviewed outcome studies of the effectiveness of person-centred therapies with children and (p. 34) report that the studies they looked at provided strong evidence for effectiveness. Lastly, Keys and Walshaw (2008) comprises fifteen chapters addressing person-centred practice with children and young people.

25

IN THE VIEW OF SOME, THERE ARE TIMES WHEN THE INTEGRATION OF THE NECESSARY AND SUFFICIENT CONDITIONS LEADS TO ANOTHER, 'TRANSFORMATIONAL' QUALITY KNOWN AS 'PRESENCE'

Over the years, there have been indications from some person-centred writers that there are times in the therapy session when there is a kind of peak experience, transforming both client and therapist. In his later years, Rogers (in Kirschenbaum and Henderson 1990a: 137) described this quality and named it 'presence'. He wrote:

> When I am at my best, as a group facilitator or a therapist, I dis-cover another characteristic. I find that when I am closest to my inner, intuitive self, when I am somehow in touch with the unknown in me, when perhaps I am in a slightly altered state of consciousness in the relationship, then whatever I do seems to be full of healing. Then simply my presence is releasing and helpful.

Rogers indicates that presence is a medium for personal growth and that it is a self-transcending aspect of therapy. Thorne (1991: 73–81) tells of something very similar and uses the expression 'the quality of tenderness' to describe the active principle of transformation. Both Rogers and Thorne indicate that there is a transcendental, spiritual or mystical dimension to this quality. While no way denying this, Schmid (1998a: 82) identifies presence with encounter

(Point 31). He (2002: 182–203) expands on this with respect to the requirement for contact/psychological contact and (pp. 198–199) states that presence 'is the proper term for the "core conditions" in their interconnectedness as *the* [original emphasis] way of being and acting of the therapist'. Schmid's view can be seen as emphasising 'presence' as the (inevitable?) outcome of high-quality attention in the therapeutic endeavour.

That is, presence is a result of a peaking of the therapist conditions (or perhaps the super-condition alluded to in Point 14). Also, because Schmid sees person-centred therapy in terms of dialogue, that is encounter, presence must flow from that and not from the therapist per se.

Although it has been described as 'the fourth condition' (more properly the fourth therapist-provided condition), there seems to be consensus that it is the product of the therapist-provided conditions as they are ideally, not something 'extra' and distinct from them. For example, Barrett-Lennard (2007: 130) states that presence 'implies "being all there", absorbed in the immediate relation with one's whole, deeply attentive and connecting self' and Wyatt (2007: 150), while acknowledging the 'extra-dimensional' quality of presence and that it can be described (amongst other things) as electric, intense and/or transformative, also notes that 'at these times all of Rogers' conditions are simultaneously present'. None of this takes away from the transformative, transpersonal effect of the experience of presence. However, Mearns (1994: 7–8) points out that although presence can be described in terms of mystical language, it is equally possible to refer to it in terms of classical person-centred theory. He says that presence arises from the combination of two circumstances. The first of these is a blending of high degrees of congruence, unconditional positive regard and empathic understanding and the second (p. 8) is:

> that the counsellor is able to be truly *still* [original emphasis] within herself, allowing her person to resonate with the client's experiencing. In a sense, the counsellor has allowed her person to

step right into the client's experiencing without needing to do anything to establish her separateness.

His understanding of presence has been instrumental in leading Mearns to develop the idea of working at relational depth (Point 38).

However presence arises, it is the ultimate manifestation of the person-centred therapist's intention to *be* with the client rather than to *do* something to them, for them or even with them. In my experience, for all that it arises from them, it transcends the therapist-provided conditions and it is transformative. I also see it as being co-created and co-experienced, not something engendered by the therapist alone. However, this does not mean that the experience of 'presence' cannot be prepared for or encouraged. Geller and Greenberg (2002: 75–77), while stating that the experience of presence cannot be assured in a session, indicate that the capacity for it can be enhanced through preparation (Point 84).

Geller (2013: 209–222) explores 'therapeutic presence' defining and describing it, explaining it in terms of the necessary and sufficient conditions and presenting research on it in terms of process and outcome. She (p. 220) states that research has suggested that presence is essential to effective therapy. While I don't disagree with this, it seems to me that 'presence', 'relational depth' (see Point 38) and the hypothesised super-condition of which congruence, unconditional positive regard and empathic understanding are all facets may very well be different ways of understanding the same phenomenon.

26

FOR SOME, IN CLASSIC PERSON-CENTRED THEORY THE NOTION OF THE 'INDIVIDUAL/ SELF' AS A DISCRETE ENTITY IS OVER-EMPHASISED, INCOMPLETE AND/OR CULTURE BOUND

Even though it is in many ways defined as fluid and changing and the concept of the organism is more important (Point 11), even within the person-centred tradition the concept of 'self' is criticised, questioned and/or found wanting. For example, Holdstock (1993: 229–252) indicates that it may be necessary to revise the person-centred concept of the self in order to take account of how the self is perceived in other cultures and paradigms. Of the concept of self in other cultures, Holdstock (p. 230) writes:

> the extended concept of the self may even include the deceased as well as the larger universe of animals, plants and inanimate objects. Power and control are not considered to rest predominantly with the individual but within the field of forces within which the individual exists.

Subsequently, others echoed this challenge. Briefly, what is questioned is 'self' as a unitary, demarcated entity in some way separate from the world. What is proposed is a 'relational' self intertwined not only with other people but the environment. For example, Mearns and Cooper (2005: 5) argue that people are 'fundamentally and inextricably linked with others' and Cooper (2007: 85–86) draws attention to and discusses the view that (p. 85) 'human beings [are] fundamentally woven into their social, political and historical context rather than separable from it'. Bohart (2013: 87) argues that there is no conflict and that 'to perceive Rogers' concept of self as culture-specific is to misunderstand it'. This is because 'there is no reason why Rogers' view of the self, as a conceptual map, could not include a map of the self as connected and sociocentric'.

It is this awareness of and emphasis on the relational aspects of being in the world over the 'individualistic' view of people imputed to Rogers' original theory of personality and development that leads Mearns and Thorne (2000: 182–183) to propose a process of 'social mediation'. Social mediation is proposed as a counter-balance or (Mearns and Thorne 2007: 24) 'a restraining force' to the actualising tendency. The idea springs from the recognition that people are in relationship and that a free, unmediated, unmoderated expression of the actualising tendency may be detrimental to the person. This restraining force works in such a way as to ensure that the person not only moves towards being fully functioning but does so in such a way as to preserve, maintain (and possibly even enhance) the social contexts in which they exist. This is then the basis for further growth. Mearns and Thorne (2007: 24) encapsulate their development of theory thus 'the person *takes other people in their life into account* [original emphasis] in the course of their own maintenance and development'.

Cooper (2007: 86–88) also considers 'self-pluralistic perspectives' as a divergence from Rogers' original conceptualisations of personality and human development. He points out that person-centred theorists and those of related 'tribes' persuaded by these ideas 'have argued that a focus on the individual not only overlooks the multiplicity of which the individual is a part, but also the *multiplicity by which the individual is constituted* [original emphasis]'. That is to say, people are composed of a number of facets, each of which manifests differently in the world. These facets are named differently in different therapeutic modalities, for example, psychosynthesists talk in terms of 'subpersonalities', psychodramatists in terms of 'roles' but a term popularised in person-centred circles by Dave Mearns is 'configurations of self' (Point 27). There is nothing intrinsically unhealthy about 'self as a multiple entity' but emotional distress may arise when configurations are in conflict or relate to each other in abusive ways.

THE PERSON MAY CONSTITUTE A MULTIPLICITY OF 'SELVES' RATHER THAN A UNITARY SELF

Recently, a number of person-centred scholars (for example Cooper 1999; Keil 1996; Mearns 2002; Mearns and Thorne 2000: 174–189; and Warner 2005) have explored what they believe to be the limitations of the classical model of self as unitary and proposed revisions to this. Not all these authors are of exactly the same view but for each of them the notion of 'self-plurality' has important ramifications for practice and requires adaptations to theory. However, it is of particular importance to note that advocates of the 'multiple self' model all see this as healthy and normal, not pathological. Cooper (2007: 86–88) presents a helpful discussion of these views and the differences and similarities between them. By way of example, one way in which the idea of a plural self has reached particular prominence is through the work of Mearns (1999, 2002) and Mearns and Thorne (2000, 2007).

The notion of self as a constellation of self-concepts is what Mearns (1999: 126) calls 'configurations of self' and defines as 'a number of elements which form a coherent pattern generally reflective of a dimension of existence within the Self'. Configurations of self are explained more fully in Mearns and Thorne (2000: 101–119). Mearns and Thorne (2007: 33) represent the notion of configurations in the context of 'self-dialogues'. They refer to 'self-pluralist theory' 'where the person appears to symbolise their self as comprising different *parts, voices, subpersonalities, sub-selves* [original emphasis]' or, in their terms, configurations. They (pp. 34–38) contextualise their ideas in relation to self-pluralist theory and offer four theoretical propositions concerning configurations. These are:

1. Configurations may be established around introjections about self.
2. Configurations may also be established around dissonant self-experience.
3. Formative configurations assimilate other consistent elements.
4. Configurations interrelate and reconfigure.

What this means is that quasi-independent elements of the self-concept can arise in one of two ways (although Mearns and Thorne 2000: 117 state 'there may be other pathways'). These are through the incorporation of an evaluation taken from others which may be positive or negative or through the encapsulation of an experience which is at odds with other aspects of the self-concept. Once established, a configuration can expand and grow by incorporating similar elements. Moreover, configurations are dynamic. They can and do change and change in relation to one another too. Throughout their description and analysis of configurations of self, Mearns and Thorne emphasise their protective nature. In other words, configurations of self are helpful ways of interfacing with the world having different functions and abilities. In more extreme cases, particular configurations may even be about survival. Warner's (2005: 94) concept of dissociated process involving the existence of 'parts' with 'a variety of opposing strategies for responding to emotional pain' offers an illustration of this.

However they arise and for whatever reason, normally, it is not that individuals comprise a multiplicity of selves that is deleterious or in any way indicative of a need for therapy but psychological distress may arise when the relationship between configurations is conflictual or disharmonious.

28

EMPATHY IS SEEN AS MULTIFACETED AND COMPLEX BUT IT IS IMPORTANT TO REMEMBER THAT EMPATHIC UNDERSTANDING IS WHAT IS ESSENTIAL TO EFFECTIVE THERAPY

Almost from the outset of person-centred therapy there have been efforts to deconstruct and understand the empathic process. Recently, these have included 'reconsiderations' by Barrett-Lennard (1997), Bozarth (1997) and Shlien (1997), an analysis as to how empathy 'cures' (Warner 1996: 127–143), a description of 'five kinds of empathy' (Neville 1996: 439–453), an edited volume concerned with the history, theory and practice of empathy (Haugh and Merry 2001) and a recapitulation and updating of the classic client-centred view (Freire 2007). The intention behind each of these works and others addressing empathy is to explore and explain the concept, to make what it is and/or how it operates clearer.

There have also been attempts to deal with misconceptions about empathy. For example, in his iconoclastic manner, Shlien (1997: 67) writes that in his opinion 'empathy has been over-rated, underexamined and carelessly though enthusiastically conceived' and (p. 79) that empathy 'is not much of a theory, explains hardly anything, tells us nothing of the mechanisms'. Shlien is not attacking one of the bedrock six conditions but his chapter is an attempt to re-establish that condition five requires that the therapist experiences *empathic understanding* of the client's internal frame of reference. This, he (p. 73) considers to be different from empathy as such. Rather it is a particular kind of understanding 'distinct from the types of understanding that come from external frames, such as diagnostic, or judgemental, or suspicious interrogation'. It is empathic understanding that (p. 67) 'promotes healing from within'. Empathy, he argues throughout, is nothing special, animals of all kinds can do it, whereas empathic understanding and the communication of it requires effort to acquire and attention of the highest order. This is an important correction. In person-centred therapy, it is not enough to 'feel' the client's pain, emotional distress or joy whatever form that feeling takes. It is on the therapist's understanding of the client's process and the perception of that understanding by the client that the effectiveness of therapy depends. In other words, although empathy may be a visceral, somatic or emotional experience, at least a degree of cognitive processing is required to turn it into empathic understanding. Shlien (1997: 67) values sympathy because it is a type of commitment and writes '[e]mpathy alone, without sympathy, and even more, without understanding, may be harmful'. Another way of understanding this may be that it is only when the experience of another is understood rather than simply echoed or resonated with can it be accepted.

While it is clear that empathic understanding (and its perception by the other – see Point 21) rather than empathy per se is what is effective in person-centred therapy, there are arguments as to what is to be understood and responded to. For example, Grant (2010: 220–235) states that there can be two targets of empathic understanding – experiences and communications. He is of the opinion that only intended communications are proper targets for classical client-centred therapy and that to respond to experience is to be directive.

29

ALTHOUGH THE BASIC HYPOTHESIS DOES NOT CALL FOR IT, THE COMMUNICATION TO AND/OR PERCEPTION OF THE THERAPIST'S CONGRUENCE BY THE CLIENT HAS RECENTLY RECEIVED ATTENTION

Wyatt (2001a) edited a volume concerning congruence and in her introduction to it she (p. vii) reports that from the 1950s when Rogers first used the term, it received little further attention until the late 1980s. One of the ways in which it has been thought and written about since then is in terms of how it may be communicated. This is partly the focus of Cornelius-White's (2013: 199–204) consideration of congruent communication and expanded ideas of congruence. While the classical client-centred position is that congruence is rarely, if ever, directly communicated in words but rather, as Cornelius-White (2007: 174) explains, via body language which is the product of internal congruence, some writers have become concerned with the appropriateness and nature of 'congruent responses' and (Wyatt 2001b: 79–95) 'the multifaceted nature of congruence'.

Although it is 'being' which is important about congruence, some person-centred theorists have explored how it operates and its facets. For example, Lietaer (1993: 18) is of the opinion that 'genuineness' has two facets, an inner one he calls 'congruence' which is about 'being' and the availability of experience to awareness (and thus close to the original formulation of Rogers) and an outer facet he names 'transparency' which 'refers to the explicit communication by the therapist of his

conscious perceptions, attitudes and feelings'. Making it clear
that the separation is in some ways artificial, Lietaer goes on
to explore the differences between these aspects and in Lietaer
(2001a: 36–54) revisits his ideas. In discussing transparency, he
(pp. 42–47) emphasises the importance of the 'personal presence' of the therapist and explains the place of 'self-disclosure'
in the therapeutic encounter. By the former he means that the
therapist 'shines through' as a real, recognisable and present
person. The second element of transparency, self-disclosure, he
sees as contributing to person-centred therapy moving away
from the classical tradition to a more interactional form of
therapy of which a dialogue between therapist and client is a
legitimate part. While such a dialogic form to person-centred
therapy may contribute to (for example) 'working at relational
depth' (Point 38), self-disclosure is something for the therapist to approach with caution and perhaps to do rarely if at all.
Lietaer (p. 47) himself qualifies his ideas stating that it is enor-
mously important that 'self-disclosing responses [are] embedded in a fundamental attitude of openness: openness towards
oneself (congruence) and openness towards the experiencing
self of the client (unconditional positive regard)'.

Tudor and Worrall (1994: 198) identify four components of
congruence. These they call:

- self-awareness
- self-awareness in action
- communication
- appropriateness.

The first two elements share much with congruence as
described by Lietaer but they argue that congruent communication involves more than transparency. In their view,
'apparency' 'which has a more active, relational, transitive
quality' is an important aspect of congruence. Being apparent
is to do with the *appropriate* communication of the therapist's experience. Therapists need to (p. 199) 'think clearly' in
order to discriminate between appropriate and inappropriate
congruent responses. For them (p. 201), it is more relevant to

focus on 'communicating our experiencing than on disclosing our experience'. Congruent responses should normally focus on the communication of the here-and-now experience of the therapist rather than the sharing of some aspect of personal history. While this can be related to the position of (for example) Mearns and Thorne (2007: 139–142) who (p. 142) suggest that appropriate congruent responses are those 'that are *relevant* to [the] client and that are relatively *persistent* or *striking* [original emphases]', the subdivision of congruence is seen as unnecessary and unhelpful by some (see Point 18).

30

ALTHOUGH IT REMAINS UNDER-RESEARCHED, UNCONDITIONAL POSITIVE REGARD HAS BEEN RECONSIDERED AND RE-EVALUATED

In Wilkins (2003: 75), I report on the relative lack of research into the nature and function of unconditional positive regard (UPR). Watson and Sheckley (2001: 185) also comment on the paucity of research into UPR attributing it to 'a number of factors, including the difficulty of defining the construct, poor research tools, and an increased interest in the working alliance'. However, there are a number of 're-conceptualisations' and reconsiderations of the notion. These include explorations from a classic client-centred position and from the point of view of experiential psychotherapy and even philosophical and religious expositions (see, for example, Bozarth and Wilkins 2001).

From a client-centred perspective Bozarth (1998: 83–88) reprises UPR and (p. 83, p. 88) describes it as 'the core curative condition in Rogers' theory' and Freire (2001: 145) reaches the conclusion that not only is UPR 'the primary therapeutic healing agent' but that it is 'the distinctive feature of client-centered therapy'. From a similar viewpoint, I (Wilkins 2000: 23–36) 'reconsider' UPR and also reach the conclusion (pp. 33–34) that, in terms of theory and my experience as therapist and client, the communication of UPR is the active facilitator of constructive change. Behind this view lies the recognition that as the client perceives the unconditional positive regard of a congruent therapist experiencing empathic understanding, the client's *positive self-regard* increases. UPR is the factor that frees the client from conditions of worth (see Point 17). Writing from his position as a leading exponent of experiential psychotherapy, Lietaer (1984: 41–58) discusses UPR as (p. 41) a 'controversial basic attitude in client-centered therapy' and sees it as potentially in conflict with congruence. He also (p. 41) considers that 'while unconditionality is not impossible, it is improbable'. Revisiting UPR, Lietaer (2001b: 88) describes it as 'a multi-dimensional concept' and (pp. 93–98) considers what limits UPR or renders it a difficult attitude to hold towards another. The dimensions of UPR Lietaer (2001b: 88–89) recognises are:

- *positive regard* which is the affective attitude of the therapist toward the client;
- *non-directivity* as the attitude of non-manipulation of the client;
- *unconditionality* or constancy in accepting the client.

In accord with other experiential therapists (for example Hendricks 2001: 126–144; Iberg 2001: 109–125), Lietaer understands UPR in terms of therapist behaviour as much as a basic therapeutic attitude. While accepting that there is 'general compatibility' between the classical and experiential positions with regard to respecting the client's self-direction, Bozarth (2007: 185) considers that the two approaches involve substantially different views of UPR and that this has implications for practice.

Bozarth (2013: 182–184, 189) returns to the divergence of views about UPR between classical client-centred therapists and those who lean more towards an experiential modality and (p. 188) offers some 'critical reflections for the future'. He emphasises that 'one consideration for the future might lie in the definition of positive regard as making a difference in the experiential field of the therapist that is stimulated by the client's self-expression'.

31

PERSON-CENTRED THERAPY IS ROOTED IN A PHILOSOPHICAL AND ETHICAL TRADITION: THE WORK OF PETER SCHMID

Peter Schmid has been described as 'the philosopher of the person-centred approach'. While he is not alone in seeking to understand the philosophical traditions behind person-centred therapy and the implications these have for practice, it is true that his work on the anthropological and epistemological foundations of it have made a significant impact. Of particular concern to Schmid, drawing on the work of the philosophers Emmanuel Levinas, Martin Buber and many others, are the concept of human beings as essentially relational, the process of encounter and the dialogical nature of person-centred therapy.

In one of his first works published in English, Schmid (1998b: 38–52) explains the importance of the concept of the *person* and (p. 39) why the paradigm shift from an objective view of human beings (*what* is a human being?) he sees as underpinning much of psychology and psychotherapy to a subjective view (*who* are you?), which characterises the person-centred approach, is truly radical. Treating someone as an object leads in the direction of diagnosis, treatment and cure; attempting to discover who someone is involves the process of encounter. It is clear that for Schmid 'encounter' is different from 'relationship'. In my view and in my interpretation of Schmid, it is in encounter that each of us may discover and change ourselves through interaction and dialogue with the Other (see below).

An exploration of Western philosophical thought and rea-
soned argument lead Schmid (1998b: 45) to declare 'the two
most important principles of the person-centred image of the
human being'. These are that 'we live through *experience*,
and we live in *relationships* [original emphases]'. In Schmid
(1998a: 74–90) dealing with 'the art of encounter' and stressing
the relational nature of the person, he (p. 81) writes that, from
a person-centred perspective, 'each encounter involves *meeting reality* and *being touched* by the essence of the *opposite*
[original emphases]'. What Schmid is drawing attention to is
encounter as a process of engagement involving acknowledgement, the meaning of which (to do the sort of thing Schmid
himself does so well) implies not only recognition of the Other
(p. 81) but also responding to and greeting the Other (dialogue).
In this way, the Other cannot be seen as an anonymous stran-
ger but becomes a(nother) person; someone real with whom
there is at once communion and from whom there is separation.
This consideration leads Schmid (p. 82) to link encounter with
Rogers' notion of 'presence' (Kirschenbaum and Henderson
1990a: 137) and 'tenderness' (Thorne 1991: 73–81) (Point 25)
and it clearly relates to the concept of 'relational depth' (Point
38). Schmid (1998a: 82) writes:

> In the encounter philosophical perspective, presence is the authen-
> tic attitude *to be* [original emphasis], to fully live in the pres-
> ence: unconditionally accepting the Other, empathically becoming
> involved in his or her presence, without any prior intention, that is
> with openness and a wonder towards experience.

Revisiting his characterisation of the person-centred approach,
Schmid (2003: 110) lists three distinguishing qualities:

1. Client and therapist spring from a fundamental 'We'.
2. The client comes first.
3. The therapist is present.

Schmid (p. 110) considers that 'we exist only as part of a "We"',
and that (p. 111):

> This We includes our history and our culture. It is not an undifferentiated mass, nor is it an accumulation of 'Mes'; it includes commonality *and* [original emphasis] difference, valuing both equally. Only common esteem for diversity constitutes and accepts a We.

Schmid (2003: 111, 2007: 38–39) is clear that essential to the understanding and acceptance of 'We' is the recognition and acceptance of another person as 'Other'. That is 'that the Other really "stands counter", because he or she is essentially different from me'. Schmid (2007: 39) writes that to stand counter 'means to give room to each other and to express respect'. It is only the recognition of standing counter to others that allows encounter. Of encounter, Schmid (2002: 201) writes:

> To encounter a human being means to give them space and freedom to develop themselves according to their own possibilities, to become, and to be fully the person he or she is able to become. On the one hand this is opposed to any use as a means to a particular end or any 'intention' and on the other hand it is also opposed to interaction based on role or function.

So, from a person-centred perspective there is no valuing of sameness or difference but respectful acceptance of the Other in his or her own terms. Moreover, the We implies a connectedness, an interrelatedness that, in my view (Wilkins 2006: 12) 'goes far beyond the self, even beyond the organism'. All this links to the importance of the non-directive attitude (see Point 4) and, for example, leads Schmid (2007: 42–43) and Wilkins (2006: 12–13) to see person-centred therapy as centring on ethics.

Schmid (2013) continues his scholarly effort to examine and explain the ethical and philosophical antecedents of person-centred therapy and (2014) how his thinking leads him to propose a 'person-centred sociotherapy' (see Point 92).

32

ALTHOUGH DIAGNOSIS HAS NO PLACE IN PERSON-CENTRED PRACTICE, ASSESSMENT MAY BE AN ETHICAL OBLIGATION

'Assessment' has long been contentious in the context of person-centred therapy. This is largely because assessment is equated or conflated with diagnosis and the latter is believed to be an inappropriate adoption from the medical model implying that there is an underlying problem (disease) which, if it can be identified, can be 'treated' and a cure effected. This is completely at odds with classic client-centred therapy because it puts the problem before the person. Sanders (2013: 18) re-emphasises the inappropriateness of diagnosis in person-centred therapy noting that 'classical client-centred therapy makes no distinction between medical diagnoses, therapist interpretations or expert interventions ... all are injurious to the client's recovery'.

Although Rogers (1951: 221–223) does refer to 'the client-centered rationale for diagnosis', this clearly puts the client and the client's experience at the heart of the process. Furthermore, Rogers (pp. 223–225) immediately follows his rationale with 'certain objections to psychological diagnosis'. As Mearns (2004: 88–101) explains (p. 88), 'problem-centered is not person-centered' and (p. 90) although two clients may have the same or similar 'problem' their needs from therapy and the therapist may be different. Another objection to diagnosis is exemplified by Sanders (see, for example, 2006a: 32–39, 2007b: 112–128) who argues that the concept of mental illness is inappropriate and oppressive. Sanders (2007b: 119) considers 'distress' more relevant than 'disease' and sees distress as arising from psychological and social causes rather than biological causes. He (pp. 120–122) goes on to present arguments with respect to psychodiagnosis, stating (p. 122) that resistance to it 'can be justified in terms of philosophy, theory and effectiveness'.

The above views reflect some of those published in a symposium on psychodiagnosis published in 1989. These are explored in Wilkins (2005a: 135–138) and (p. 138) summarised as representing three main views:

1. Psychodiagnosis is irrelevant to person-centred therapy and may actually be harmful.
2. Although there are problems with psychodiagnosis, assessment and diagnosis are realities in the world of psychotherapy and it may be that person-centred therapists must take this into account.
3. If assessment focuses on the client and the client's self-knowledge then not only is it compatible with person-centred theory but it is also an advantage in the practice of person-centred therapy.

The first two positions may be represented as 'purist' and 'pragmatic' respectively and they are concerned with diagnosis. The third is different: it is concerned with assessment. In crude and simple terms, diagnosis is a process of 'labelling' a person as having a particular (kind of) problem while assessment is a (mutual) process by which a decision is made as to the likelihood that therapist and client can and will build an effective therapeutic relationship. Assessment may take place over time. Assessment is not inimical to person-centred theory and practice. Indeed the necessary and sufficient conditions and the seven stages of process can be seen as contributing to a person-centred scheme for assessment (see Wilkins 2005a: 141–143). Such a scheme sets aside the notion of the therapist as expert, able to reach a definitive conclusion as to the nature of the client's difficulties and rather concentrates on the likelihood of establishing a relationship in which the necessary and sufficient conditions will be met. It also highlights the potential limitations of the therapist. Person-centred therapists are ethically obliged to ask themselves if a potential client stands in need of therapy and if they can offer an effective relationship to that client. The criteria in Wilkins (2005a: 141–142) provide a system for making such a judgement (see also Point 59).

Lastly, Gillon (2013: 418) is of the opinion that both assessment and case formulation can be compatible with person-centred therapy and Moerman (2012: 214–223) presents research demonstrating how person-counsellors 'assess' when working with suicidal clients.

33

PERSON-CENTRED THEORY INCLUDES WAYS OF UNDERSTANDING PSYCHOPATHOLOGY. THESE DIFFER FROM THE PREDOMINANT 'MEDICAL MODEL'

For the most part, in the West the treatment of people experiencing mental and/or emotional distress has been dominated by practitioners who adhere to the medical model whether they are medically trained or not. That is to say that a way of thinking about and responding to physical ailments has been applied wholesale to disorders of thought and feeling. However, the applicability of a model which goes something like *(symptoms) – diagnosis – treatment – cure – (lack of symptoms)* has, at least from a person-centred point of view, not been proved. A second influence on understanding psychopathology has been psychoanalysis. It is from this source that some of the familiar terms associated with psychological distress arise – for example, 'borderline' and 'narcissism'. Historically, both these ways of thinking about people have been opposed by person-centred practitioners although more recently there has been some move towards developing a common or inclusive language especially by person-centred practitioners who work in medical settings. This rejection by person-centred practitioners has been criticised largely on the basis that person-centred theory lacks a model of child development and a model of psychological distress. This is easy to refute (see Wilkins 2003: 99–107, 2005b: 43–50, Point 24).

From the outset there has been a model of child development as part of person-centred theory (see Rogers 1959: 222) and a linking of this to the development of distress (Rogers 1959: 224–230). This has subsequently been refined and developed by (for example) Biermann-Ratjen (1996: 13–14). There are in fact four major contemporary positions with respect to mental ill-health within the person-centred tradition. These are those based on:

1. (psychological) contact (see Point 34)
2. incongruence (see Point 35)
3. styles of processing (see Point 36)
4. issues of power (see Point 37).

While they share a great deal, each of these approaches to understanding emotional and mental distress has been developed primarily from a particular theoretical proposition or philosophical attitude.

1. Understanding or working with mental distress in the context of 'contact' derives from the first of the necessary and sufficient conditions requiring that client and therapist are in (psychological) contact. The underpinning question is what to do if this is not so and there is an assumption that the absence of contact is in itself distressing.
2. The notion that it is incongruence which gives rise to mental and emotional distress is a straightforward reading of the second of Rogers' six conditions. It is incongruence expressed as anxiety or vulnerability that leads a client to therapy. This incongruence can be anywhere on a spectrum from mild unease to acute or chronic suffering of the most disturbing kind.
3. Models in which 'difficult' process is the basis for distress derive from Rogers' (1967: 27) description of life as 'a flowing, changing process in which nothing is fixed' and the recognition that sometimes this process may be interrupted, distorted, stagnant or in some other way deviate from the ideal.

4. That psychological distress relates to issues of power rather than to intrinsic, intrapersonal and interpersonal dynamics is based on the assumption that its causes are social and/or environmental. Perhaps this draws on person-centred philosophy as much or more than its theory of personality. It relates to the non-directive principle and the attitude to the exercise of power (Points 5 and 6). The foundation of this understanding of distress is that 'madness' is socially defined and that social and political circumstances at the very least contribute to mental ill-health and are possibly causal.

34

PRE-THERAPY AND CONTACT WORK CONSTITUTE AN IMPORTANT, PERSON-CENTRED WAY OF WORKING WITH 'CONTACT IMPAIRMENT' AND EXTREME MENTAL AND EMOTIONAL DISTRESS

With respect to psychological contact and mental distress and person-centred therapy, the work of Garry Prouty is of pre-eminence (Points 15 and 68). Proutyg asked the fundamental question 'What happens if the first of the necessary and sufficient conditions is not met?' This led to the development of a person-centred system of thought and practice embracing clients with (for example) profound learning difficulties or schizophrenia. This became known as pre-therapy (see Prouty 2002a and 2002b) which (2002b: 55) is described as 'a theory of psychological contact ... rooted in Rogers' conception of psychological contact as the first condition of a therapeutic relationship'. According to Krietemeyer and Prouty (2003: 152) pre-therapy theory 'was developed in the context of treating mentally retarded or psychotic populations'. This is because, in Prouty's experience, such people are 'contact-impaired' and have difficulty forming interpersonal connections. Pre-therapy theory led to the development of a set of practices by which psychological contact could be established (see case studies presented by Krietemeyer and Prouty 2003: 154–160 and Van Werde 1994: 125–128) and for which Dekeyser *et al.* (2014: 206–222) and Prouty (2001: 595–596) summarise the research evidence.

Pre-therapy work with clients of different types is exemplified by Sommerbeck's (2011: 235–241) introduction to pre-therapy with people diagnosed with psychoses, her (2014a: 67–73) work with people at the difficult edge (see Points 96 and 97) and Carrick and McKenzie's (2011) work with people on the autism spectrum.

Pre-therapy is a deeply respectful way of working with people *before* psychological therapy as it is usually understood can take place. So, in its original form and intent at least, it is not a complete therapy but a preparation for therapy. The primary aim of pre-therapy is to restore the (psychological) contact which, because it is a prerequisite for forming a reciprocal relationship, was named by Rogers as the first essential for constructive personality change. Pre-therapy is underpinned by contact theory of which the elements are as follows.

1. **Contact functions** – the client's process. An assumption is that people who are not contact impaired have the ability for:
   • 'reality contact' or an awareness of people, things, places and events they encounter;
   • 'affective contact' or awareness of their feelings and emotions;
   • 'communicative contact' or the ability to symbolise and represent their experience of their environment to themselves and others through the medium of language.
2. **Contact reflections** – the therapist's responses. Essentially, these are what the therapist or contact worker does to (re-) establish contact with the client. Contact reflections are of five types. These are (after Sanders 2007d: 31 and Van Werde and Prouty 2007: 240):
   • *Situational reflections* to reflect aspects of the shared environment (people, places, happenings and things) in order to facilitate reality contact. For example, 'You are sitting on the floor. The floor is red.'
   • *Facial reflections* which describe in words or mimic the facial expressions of the client. This facilitates affective contact. For example, 'You have tears in your eyes.'

- *Body reflections* which reflect verbally or by imitation the body language, movement and postures of the client which may help to establish reality contact or affective contact. For example, holding an arm erect when the client does.
- *Word-for-word reflections* which involve repeating back what the client says word for word, however bizarre or irrational. This develops communicative contact.
- *Re-iterative reflections* which entails repeating any previous reflections to which there was a response – in other words, if it works, do it again.

3. **Contact behaviours** – the client's behaviours as they give an indication of the extent to which clients can express themselves or make contact with another. One respect in which these are important is as a measure of change following pre-therapy.

Contact theory is expanded on in Sanders (2007d: 24–31) and Van Werde and Prouty (2007: 238–243).

Sanders (2007c: 18) states that pre-therapy methods 'may be used to help restore, strengthen or sustain contact' with people:

- in a state of severe psychotic withdrawal, catatonia or regression;
- suffering from dissociative states;
- with learning disabilities which impair communication and contact, from mild to severe and enduring;
- suffering from dementia;
- suffering from terminal or degenerative illness which impairs communication or contact, including those, for example, whose palliative care causes drowsiness due to pain-killing drugs (see Van Werde 2014);
- with temporary contact impairment due to an organic condition;
- suffering from a brain injury or damage.

The practice of pre-therapy is dealt with in Point 68.

35

CLIENT INCONGRUENCE, WHICH CAN BE UNDERSTOOD AS CAUSED IN VARIOUS WAYS, IS A SOURCE OF MENTAL AND EMOTIONAL DISTRESS

An important person-centred approach to understanding psychopathology hinges on the second of the necessary and sufficient conditions – that is that incongruence is central to mental/emotional distress. In his exploration of the links between incongruence and mental health, Tengland (2001: 169) sees incongruence as contributing to ill-health 'since it often reduces the person's ability to reach vital goals'. This is because when we experience something that conflicts with how we see ourselves and we cannot make the outer reality fit with our self image we tend to feel tense, anxious, confused or frightened. To phrase it more formally, when a person has a poor self-concept which is out of touch with the organism, disturbance results and in extreme cases this manifests as distress or even 'madness'. This can be framed in terms of conditions of worth (Point 12) which is the classic client-centred view. However, within the broader person-centred family, some theorists have argued that incongruence can arise from causes other than conditions of worth (for example, genetic or other biological causes, life events such as abuse early in life or post-traumatic stress disorder) and there have been attempts to develop models of distress based on understanding incongruence per se.

For Speierer (1996: 300) client-centred therapy *is* the treatment of incongruence. His contention is that incongruence is the root of emotional distress and that (p. 229) it has three main causes. These are:

- the acquisition of conditions of worth and/or conflict between societal and organismic values;
- bio-neuropsychological limitations – either genetic or as a result of injury or trauma;
- life-changing events of such intensity as to cause (for example) intrusive flashbacks.

Speierer's theory constitutes a divergence from classic client-centred therapy because he suggests that different 'disorders' arise from different types of incongruence and so (p. 307) different therapeutic strategies can be offered according to the nature of the disorder and the needs of the client. This Speierer calls the 'differential incongruence model' (see Speierer 1996, 1998). However, this can be seen as in direct conflict with the classical client-centred perception of psychodiagnosis as potentially harmful to clients and definitely of unproven benefit (Point 32).

Biermann-Ratjen (1998) also writes about incongruence and psychopathology. She devotes sections to 'post-traumatic distress disorder', 'psychogenic illness' and 'neurosis' as manifestations of incongruence. She relates incongruence to (child) development, indicating that it is the stage at which development is interrupted that determines the nature of distress.

Warner (2007a: 154–167) reviews person-centred theory and practice with respect to client incongruence and psychopathology exploring reformulations of the concept of incongruence, person-centred models of psychopathology and research into client incongruence. She (p. 164) reaches the conclusion that person-centred therapists are particularly well placed to work with clients diagnosed with severe disorders and that the 'person-centred approach in work with clients of all levels of severity of symptoms' should be proactively promoted.

While seeing it as a major contributor to depression, Sanders and Hill (2014: 104–107) broaden the notion of incongruence as underpinning mental and emotional distress (and therefore depression) to 'self-discrepancy'. This, they (p. 105) say, 'brings together a more broadly-based palette of self discrepancies which are considered to be precursors for experiences which might be diagnosed as depression'.

36

THE CLIENT'S STYLE OF PROCESSING MAY RESULT IN MENTAL AND EMOTIONAL DISTRESS

Emotional and mental distress may be understood in terms of styles of processing. That is, in some individuals and for a variety of reasons, rather than the fluid form described as desirable, process is 'difficult' for the client, the therapist or both. For example, Warner (2001: 182–183) describes three kinds of 'difficult' process. She later (see Warner 2007b: 143–144) added a fourth, metaphact process. These are also considered in Warner (2014).

- *Fragile process*. Individuals with a fragile style of processing tend to experience core issues at very low or very high levels of intensity and have difficulty holding onto their own experience. They are often diagnosed as borderline or narcissistic. Because of the fragile connection with their own experience, they often have difficulty accepting the point of view of another person without feeling overwhelmed or that their experience has been annihilated. Warner (2007a: 160) indicates that fragile processing is likely to have arisen from a lack of empathic care-giving at crucial stages in early childhood or 'around newer edges of their experience that have not previously been received by themselves or others'.
- *Dissociated process*. Clients experiencing a dissociated process go through periods when they quite convincingly experience themselves as having 'selves' that are not

integrated with each other. That is as having multiple selves, one or more of whom may or may not be aware of the existence of some or all of the others for some or all of the time.

- Sometimes they experience a fragmentation or disunity of self that can be (literally) maddening to them and appear 'crazy' to others. People with dissociated process may appear to function well enough for years without being aware of their various 'parts' by keeping busy but leading restricted lives. However, it is likely that past experiences will return disturbingly and disruptingly at times of crisis. This type of processing has been identified with 'multiple personality disorder' and 'dissociative identity disorder' and almost always results from severe early childhood trauma.

- *Psychotic process.* Clients experiencing a psychotic form of processing have impaired contact with themselves, others and the world. They have difficulty in formulating and/or communicating their experience in a way which makes cohesive sense and have equal difficulty making sense of their environment. People with a psychotic form of processing may hear voices and/or experience hallucinations or delusions which are alienating. The label 'schizophrenic' is one of many which may be attached to people experiencing psychotic processing.

- *Metaphact process.* In this style of processing ordinary facts and metaphors are joined into a single hybrid form when the person is trying to make sense of something new or emotionally complex. This can sound very strange and irrational but Warner (2007b: 144) says metaphact processing 'is a lot like deaf sign language' in that it can seem crazy to someone to whom it is unfamiliar but is really an eloquent form of communication. Warner (2014: 133–135) includes more of her understanding of this style of processing and she makes reference to some relevant research.

In her various papers, Warner describes the possible origins of these styles of processing and effective ways of working with each group of clients in a person-centred way.

37

THE CAUSES OF MENTAL AND EMOTIONAL DISTRESS ARE ENVIRONMENTAL, SOCIAL AND TO DO WITH POWER AND POWERLESSNESS. THE MEDICALISATION OF DISTRESS IS AN ERROR

Amongst person-centred thinkers, there is a widespread and increasing view that the causes of emotional and mental distress are not intrinsic, interpersonal and a response to relationships with significant others but that their origin is social and/or environmental. Also, there is an assumption that 'madness' is socially defined and that social and political circumstances at the very least contribute to mental distress and are possibly (or even likely to be) causal. There is also a belief that the imbalance and abuse of power relate to mental ill-health and that it is only if power in all its aspects is openly addressed that therapy can be successful. For example, Proctor (2002: 3) is clear that 'there is much evidence to associate the likelihood of suffering from psychological distress with the individual's position in society with respect to structural power'. She (pp. 3–4) shows how women are more likely than men to be diagnosed with a range of disorders and that working class people are as a whole over-represented in the mental health services. Similarly, Sanders (2006a: 33) states that there is growing evidence that psychological distress has social, not biological, causes. He goes as far as to say that there is no such thing as mental illness and (pp. 33–35) makes a strong, evidenced argument against what he calls 'biological psychiatry', that is psychiatry based on a diagnosis-treatment-cure model for specific 'disorders' such as schizophrenia and depression.

What is being argued by Proctor, Sanders and many others is that medicalised psychiatric systems are essentially systems of control and power. It follows that if distress flows from an experience of inequality and power and an encounter with psychiatric services is disempowering, then (biological) psychiatry may be making people worse rather than better. Not only that, but the whole idea of treating specific 'illnesses' with medicine or by other physical means is based on a false premise (i.e. the biological/medical model of distress) for which, according to Sanders (2006a: 32), there is 'hardly a jot of evidence'. This is not a new position nor is it confined to person-centred therapy. Essentially, the antipsychiatry movement of the mid-twentieth century and currently critical and positive psychologies make the same arguments. For example, Read *et al.* (2004: 3) (a clinical psychologist, a psychiatrist and professor of psychiatry and a professor of experimental clinical psychology respectively) consider that the notion that mental illness is an illness in the same way as a physical disease is not supported by research. They also say that adherence to the medical model leads to ignoring or even actively discouraging any discussion or exploration of what is going on in the lives, surroundings and societies of people experiencing distress. Of course, in many ways it is insufficient to criticise one model of distress and helping without proposing another and that is just what person-centred therapists are seeking to do.

For example, one way of correcting the potentially oppressive power imbalance in therapy is its demystification. A way in which this may be done is through the therapist's willingness to be known. Also, a person-centred model to address power issues could involve working at 'relational depth' (Point 38) but it would also have to take account of inequalities of structural power both within and without the therapy relationship.

Sanders and Tudor (2001: 148) see person-centred therapy as offering a radical view of psychology and psychotherapy and a critical contribution to contemporary concerns about the mental health system. Throughout their chapter, with respect to working with mental and emotional distress, they are very clear that to consider individuals separately from the social and political milieus in which they live is mistaken. In a later work, Sanders (2007e: 188–191) advocates and describes a person-centred social model of distress. This he (p. 190) writes is 'multidisciplinary as it embraces the material, social, psychological, biological and spiritual aspects of being human'.

38

FOR SOME, AN EXTENSION TO PERSON-CENTRED WORKING IS EMBRACED IN THE CONCEPT OF 'RELATIONAL DEPTH'

'Relational depth' is a term coined by Mearns (1996) and it is considered at length in Mearns and Cooper (2005). What is being talked about is a degree of psychological contact between client and therapist which is qualitatively different from the ordinary. It is about high-quality encounter of the kind described by Rogers (1986: 137) as involving 'presence' and by Thorne (1991: 73–81) as to do with 'tenderness' (Point 25) but which Mearns (1994: 7–8) sees as something more prosaic but no less profound. In a nutshell, the deep personal self-knowledge of the therapist and a willingness to engage with the client wholly and without artifice (and a similar willingness on the part of the client to be 'real') brings about a level of contact which is transformative. Relational depth has at least some equivalence with intimacy (in the sense of mutual engagement and openness). Mearns and Cooper (2005: xii) offer the following 'working definition' of relational depth: 'A state of profound contact and engagement between two people, in which each person is fully real with the Other, and able to understand and value the Other's experiences at a high level.'

And (p. 36) they characterise the therapist's experience of meeting at relational depth thus:

A feeling of profound contact and engagement with a client, in which one simultaneously experiences high and consistent levels of empathy and acceptance towards that Other, and relates to them

in a highly transparent way. In this relationship, the client is experienced as acknowledging one's empathy, acceptance and congruence – either implicitly or explicitly – and is experienced as fully
congruent in that moment.

In other words, relational depth is conditions three, four, five
and six at high level and in concert with the addition of some
client qualities and what might be thought of as elements of
mutuality. In this notion of relational depth, 'depth' refers to
closeness to personal reality and 'truth', a fullness of subjective
lived experience, not to contact with some hidden inner core.
Also, what is 'deep' is not superior to, merely different from,
other ways of being in relationship.

In practice, the conceptions behind working at relational
depth are different from classic client-centred therapy in at
least as much as the emphasis is no longer on a non-directive
attitude nor on facilitating emotional change but on the dialogue between client and therapist. It is 'relationship-centred
therapy' rather than client-centred therapy because the
agency of change (while still primarily the actualising tendency) is the co-created space between and within the dyad
of therapist and client. Arguably, this is nothing new but
this stance has previously been implicit rather than explicitly stated and explored in terms of theory and practice.
Besides Mearns and Cooper, other prominent exponents of
a dialogical approach to client-centred therapy include Peter
Schmid (Point 31) and Barrett-Lennard (2005). A justification
for focusing on and emphasising the relationship in therapy
is that research evidence points to the fact that, besides whatever clients bring and/or do themselves, most of the variance
in the outcome of therapy can be attributed to the quality of
the relationship per se. An explanation for this may be that
much emotional and mental distress is caused by the *absence*
of or *difficulty in achieving and maintaining* close personal
contact – that is an existential loneliness – and that relational
depth achieved in therapy (or anywhere else for that matter)
begins to change this. It is postulated that the way this healing happens is that the sense of connectedness resulting from

contact at relational depth allows the client to move beyond the feeling of being totally alone to a feeling of being recognised, received, perceived and understood by at least one other. This is transformative; a relief in itself but also giving rise to the hope that such deep human contact is possible outside the therapy hour and with others. Not only that, but contact at relational depth, because it is redolent with acceptance and empathic understanding, allows the client to move towards fundamental issues to do with their very existence and which may have previously been denied to awareness.

Knox *et al.* (2013) comprises an edited book addressing many aspects of relational depth and there are research papers focusing on it, for example Knox and Cooper (2011: 61–81) and Wiggins *et al.* (2012: 139–158).

CRITICISMS OF PERSON-CENTRED THERAPY – AND REBUTTALS

39

THE THEORY AND PRACTICE OF PERSON-CENTRED THERAPY HAS BEEN SUBJECT TO A GREAT DEAL OF CRITICISM. THIS CRITICISM IS OFTEN BASED IN MISUNDERSTANDING

Criticism of person-centred therapy usually comes from an ignorance of theory and the way it is implemented. For example, there appears to be a belief that being 'person-centred' involves little more than being 'nice' to people, lending a sympathetic ear but to little effect. It is quite common to hear therapists of other orientations say that while attentive, accepting listening might be helpful in the initial stages of a therapeutic relationship (if indeed it is helpful at all) the serious work happens when expert knowledge and technique are brought into play. In other words while there is (sometimes grudging) acceptance that the six conditions are necessary they are not deemed to be sufficient.

More charitably, there is a view that while person-centred therapy 'works' for the worried well or to help people in acute (but relatively trivial) distress anyone who is more seriously disturbed, 'mentally ill' or who has deep-rooted problems needs the stronger medicine of another approach. Given the research evidence for the efficacy of person-centred therapy and the respect accorded to Rogers, why this view is held is difficult to understand. One view is that there is something about person-centred therapy which is intrinsically threatening to therapists of other orientations and that this leads to wilful ignorance or contemptuous dismissal (see, for example, Mearns and Thorne 2000: ix–x).

It may also be that person-centred theorists, researchers and practitioners bear a responsibility for failing to promote the approach by being too insular and precious, preaching principally to the converted. Certainly, it appears that the person-centred resistance to conventional hierarchical organisations has done the approach no favours. For example, the experience of the (few) person-centred therapists who attended the first World Congress for Psychotherapy in Vienna in 1996 was that person-centred therapy was easily dismissed by therapists of other orientations because it was not represented by a properly constituted international professional body. Modalities practised by far fewer people and often on the fringes of approaches to psychotherapy were accorded more respect because they were represented in that way. Partly in reaction to this, the World Association for Person-Centered and Experiential Psychotherapies was formed.

For some, the view of person-centred therapy as relatively trivial leads the belief that something must be added to it for it to be effective. However, there is no need for this. There is ample evidence for the efficacy of person-centred therapy (see Point 99 and throughout this book) and most of the common criticisms are easily rebutted. The preceding sections, and works under the imprimatur of leading publishers including the publications of PCCS Books and *Person-Centered and Experiential Therapies*, the leading international journal for the approach, will help you formulate your own rebuttals. To help you along, this section comprises some of the most common criticisms made of person-centred therapy and how they can be answered.

40

IT IS UNTRUE THAT PERSON-CENTRED THEORY HOLDS THAT THERE IS AN IDEAL END POINT TO HUMAN DEVELOPMENT AND THIS HAS IMPLICATIONS FOR THERAPY

Person-centred therapy has often been criticised for implicitly incorporating the notion of human beings as in some way inherently 'good' and that, given the right conditions, they will develop constructively to achieve some ideal state. Central to this criticism is the actualising tendency (Point 9). It is assumed that this leads to an ideal end point to growth which may be a state of 'self-actualisation' or a fully functioning person and which is the pinnacle of the individual achievement of potential. However, in terms of person-centred theory, when it is used at all, the term self-actualisation refers to a concept different from that of Maslow in that it is not a peak state resulting from the satisfaction of a hierarchy of needs.

In person-centred terms, self-actualisation is a process, not a state. Moreover, it applies only to that part of the person delineated as the 'self' which is a subsystem of the whole person (or the organism). This subsystem is also called the self-concept which is, as the term suggests, the way people see and/or construct themselves. There is also the concept of 'self-structure' which Tolan and Wilkins (2012: 5–6) indicate is the self-concept (the view a person has of themselves) plus the values and beliefs that person has about the world in general but this too is mutable. Self-actualisation is not a goal of either therapy or normal, healthy living and it does not necessarily result in optimal functioning because it is about maintaining the self-concept. Furthermore, the process of self-actualisation may conflict with the actualising tendency. For example, the need of the self for positive regard or affirmation from others may be more compelling than experiences which are of positive value in actualising the organism (see Rogers 1959: 224). That is to say it is possible, because of conditions of worth, for a person to respond to and internalise the values of others as part of the self-concept thus setting up an uncomfortable tension between the constructive directionality of the actualising tendency and needs imposed by the social environment. Bohart (2013: 87–88) broadly agrees with the above argument and rebuts criticisms under the following headings:

- Is the concept of self-actualisation a Western, culturally specific notion?
- Is self-actualisation always positive?

Arguments as to the nature of the 'fully functioning person' are essentially similar, for while this too may be taken as indicating that there is some ideal human state, it does not. In defining the 'good life' (that is being fully functioning) Rogers (1967: 186) wrote 'it is not, in my estimation, a state of virtue, or contentment, or nirvana, or happiness'. Like self-actualisation, the fully functioning person refers to a directional development, not a state of being. Being fully functioning is characterised by an openness to experience, increasingly existential living (that is living in the present with awareness of each moment) and an increasing trust in the organism. This is exemplified in Rogers' Process Scale (a tool for psychotherapy research) of which Rogers (1961: 33) says:

> [It] commences at one end with a rigid, static, undifferentiated, unfeeling, impersonal type of psychological functioning. It evolves through various stages to, at the other end, a level of functioning marked by changingness, fluidity, richly differentiated reactions, by immediate experiencing of personal feelings, which are felt as deeply owned and accepted.

The emphasis is clearly on a process of 'becoming'. Bohart (2013: 93) usefully explains the relationship of actualisation to the fully functioning person. He states 'fully functioning persons are persons who are operating in such a way ... that allows the actualizing process to operate most effectively'.

So, person-centred theory neither states nor implies that there is an ideal state which is to be the objective of therapy and/or personal growth. Moreover, as Merry (2000: 348) points out, because 'the theory of actualization is a natural science theory, not a moral theory', no values are implied.

41

IT IS UNTRUE THAT THE MODEL OF THE PERSON ADVANCED IN PERSON-CENTRED THEORY IS INADEQUATE TO EXPLAIN PSYCHOPATHOLOGY AND LEADS TO AN UNPROFESSIONAL DISREGARD FOR ASSESSMENT

The person-centred approach has been criticised as lacking a theory of personality and, in particular, of child development and thus as having an inadequate view of how mental and emotional distress may arise. This is often more focused and the criticism becomes one of the absence of an explanation for 'psychoses' and 'neuroses' as they are defined and understood in the medical model and, to some extent, in psychoanalysis. It is claimed that from this lack of clarity about the origins of distress there arises a disregard for assessment and this amounts to professional irresponsibility. Leaving aside the evident logical flaw of criticising one theory because it does not give rise to the same conclusions as another, is this charge true and does it matter one way or the other?

First, there is in fact a well-developed person-centred model of the person (see Rogers 1951: 483–522, 1959: 221–223 and Point 8). On the face of it, there is little about the human organism that this statement of theory does not explain. It considers both 'healthy' and 'dysfunctional' development and shows how therapeutic change can occur. Additionally, Biermann-Ratjen (1996: 13), drawing on Rogers' six conditions, offers a list of

120

the necessary conditions for self-development in early child-hood (Point 24).

Similarly, others have pursued the understanding of the causes of mental distress. This has been particularly evident in, for example, the exploration of the roots of incongruence and the links of these to mental ill-health (Point 35) and in Warner's concept of difficult process (Point 36). Furthermore, Joseph and Worsley (2005) and Worsley and Joseph (2007) provide a comprehensive account of person-centred theory and practice with respect to emotional and mental distress. As well as considerations of person-centred theory with respect to psychopathology and research, these books include (for example) explorations of person-centred practice with people experiencing:

- psychotic functioning;
- antisocial personality disorder;
- post-traumatic distress;
- maternal depression;
- the legacy of childhood abuse;
- 'special needs';
- autism and Asperger's syndrome;
- eating disorders;
- long-term depression.

Pearce and Sommerbeck (2014) also present accounts of person-centred therapy 'at the difficult edge' (that is to say with clients who may be said by others to be 'mentally ill'). This work is a focus of Point 97. Tolan and Wilkins (2012) contains other evidence for the effectiveness of person-centred therapy with people who are experiencing more severe forms of mental and emotional distress including people sexually abused as children, people experiencing post-traumatic stress disorder and those who have a different approach to reality (i.e. who are 'psychotic').

With respect to assessment, if that is (erroneously) under-stood to result in diagnosis, there may be a charge to answer.

Clearly and axiomatically there is no place for diagnosis in classic client-centred therapy (Point 32). The perceived problem of diagnosis is that it labels and fixes the client – the fear is that therapy becomes problem-driven rather than client-centred. From another perspective, diagnosis can be seen as helpful because it allows the development of a mutual understanding between a variety of healthcare professionals and because it facilitates the therapist's understanding of the client's process. Arguably, combining these two attitudes to diagnosis plays a part in person-centred practice with people experiencing mental distress. For example, Warner's concept of difficult client process allows both correspondence to psychiatric ideas and the challenging of them.

Looked at another way, assessment is an essential part of the process of person-centred therapy. Indeed, Wilkins and Gill (2003: 184) have shown that, even though they do not describe it as such, when meeting a client for the first time, person-centred therapists do indeed conduct a process that could legitimately be called 'assessment' although its aim is not diagnosis. It is an ethical and professional obligation for the person-centred therapist to ascertain the likelihood of being able to offer the potential client the therapist conditions or at the very least to make a sincere attempt to do so. To this end, Wilkins (2005a: 140–143) suggests criteria for person-centred assessment drawing on the necessary and sufficient conditions and the seven stages of process (Point 32).

42

IT IS UNTRUE THAT PERSON-CENTRED THEORY INCLUDES AN UNDULY OPTIMISTIC VIEW OF HUMAN NATURE AS FUNDAMENTALLY 'GOOD' AND THAT THIS LEADS TO A NAIVE DISREGARD FOR DESTRUCTIVE DRIVES AND AN AVOIDANCE OF CHALLENGE AND CONFRONTATION IN THE THERAPEUTIC ENDEAVOUR

There is a widely held view that person-centred theory holds that people are 'essentially good'. This presumed assumption is criticised in the light of the observed behaviour of people. For example, how can the perpetrators of the Nazi Holocaust, the Killing Fields of Cambodia, ethnic cleansing in too many conflicts to name be fundamentally good? In Kirschenbaum and Henderson (1990b: 239–255) there is a debate between Rogers and Rollo May which addresses this. While Rogers (pp. 237–238) acknowledges the vast amount of destructive, cruel and malevolent behaviour to be encountered in the world, he does not find that people are inherently evil. However, this is not the same as stating that people are innately good. As Shlien and Levant (1984: 3) note 'we are basically both good and bad'. Neither are assumed by theory but the potential to change is.

The concept of the inherent goodness of people plays no part in the classic statements of person-centred theory. Furthermore, in 'A note on the nature of man' (see Kirschenbaum and Henderson 1990a: 401–408), Rogers (p. 403) considers 'what man is *not* [original emphasis]', stating:

> I do not discover man to be well characterised in his basic nature by such terms as *fundamentally hostile, antisocial, destructive, evil.*
>
> I do not discover man to be, in his basic nature, completely without a nature, a tabula rasa on which *anything* may be written, nor malleable putty which can be shaped into any form.
>
> I do not discover man to be essentially a perfect being, sadly warped and corrupted by society. In my experience I have discovered man to have characteristics which seem inherent in his species, and the terms which have at different times seemed to me descriptive of these characteristics are such as *positive, forward-moving, constructive, realistic, trustworthy* [original emphases].

While Rogers is clearly stating that people are not intrinsically evil, he is not confirming that people are 'good'. Rogers' statement was not meant to imply moral judgement but was the result of empirical observation, not a declaration of desirable or admirable qualities. Arguments about 'inherent goodness' are spurious – it is neither stated nor implied. Primarily, Rogers is making a statement about the biological and psychological nature of people: we are constructive and tend to grow, to move towards the achievement of potential. However, person-centred theory does hold that people are of worth but even this does not imply 'goodness'. Being constructive, trustworthy and of worth does not amount to inherent and innate saintliness!

Nothing in person-centred theory leads its practitioners to conclude that feelings such as envy, murderous rage, bitterness and hatred are to be avoided. These are well within the repertoire of normal human emotions and are encountered and met in the context of therapy and in ourselves. However, that someone is feeling murderous, spiteful or sadistic does not alter that they are of worth. Sometimes such feelings are directed towards the therapist and, when that happens, they are met, acknowledged and worked with. Quite why when so many person-centred writers have referred so often to the expression of 'negative' emotions the myth persists that we deny and avoid such normal ways of being mystifies me.

In the therapist-provided conditions, person-centred therapists have a powerful tool for aiding clients to contact and express powerful, negative and shameful feelings. They are able to convey to clients something like: 'I know that you feel murderous, I can even feel it within me – this does not frighten me nor does it change my sense of you as a person of worth.' This usually happens beyond words but is all the more powerful for that. Theory and experience lead me to the knowledge that this can lead to an even deeper connection with destructive impulses, negative and shameful emotions, bitterness and the like. It is when this connection is deeply felt and openly expressed that change of some kind is likely to occur.

43

ROGERS' (1957/1959) STATEMENT OF THE NECESSARY AND SUFFICIENT CONDITIONS HAS BEEN CHALLENGED. WHILE MANY ACCEPT THE NECESSITY OF THESE, THE SUFFICIENCY IS DOUBTED

Although person-centred theory has never asserted that the so-called 'core conditions' of empathy, unconditional positive regard and congruence are necessary and sufficient conditions for constructive personality change (the hypothesis demands all six conditions, Point 13), research into and criticism of the hypothesis of the necessary and sufficient conditions usually concentrates on them.

Wilkins (2003: 67–69) reviews the research evidence for the hypothesis showing that, while there is evidence for the primacy of the relationship in the therapeutic endeavour (which is implicit in Rogers' statements), the basic hypothesis remains unproved (but in spite of efforts to do so, neither has it been disproved). This is at least partly because efforts to investigate the hypothesis as a whole are rare if indeed they exist at all. Most research concentrates on the therapist-provided conditions, usually singly, sometimes in combination. Bozarth (1998: 165–173) reviews the findings from research into therapist attitudes and argues that they demonstrate the effectiveness of Rogers' conditions.

The proposition that Rogers' conditions are both necessary and sufficient is often dismissed by therapists of other orientations and even 'modified' by some therapists who consider themselves to be in the wider person-centred family of approaches. The principal argument is that while the 'core conditions' are necessary or at least helpful in the forming of a therapeutic relationship they are not sufficient. Something else is needed. Notions of what the 'something else' is vary with the orientation of the critic but it always rests on techniques and expertise available to them but apparently eschewed by person-centred practitioners. There are even arguments that the therapist-provided conditions may be counter-therapeutic (for example, empathy may encourage a client to wallow in self-pity rather than to change). Often, while broad agreement with person-centred theory is indicated, there are suggested refinements and additions. For example, Dryden (1990: 17–18) notes that while rational-emotive behaviour therapists agree with the need for the therapist-provided conditions (acceptance and genuineness in particular) he doubts the value of 'warmth' because (p. 18) it may reinforce the client's need for love and approval and the 'low frustration tolerance that many clients have'. This reflects a real philosophical and theoretical difference between the two approaches. In terms of person-centred theory, it is unconditional positive regard (for which 'warmth' is one of Rogers' synonyms) that decreases conditions of worth (Points 12 and 19) and increases self-regard. This results in an increasing internalisation of the locus of evaluation and therefore a decreasing need for the 'approval' of others. Because such differences are rooted in different, unproved theoretical constructs (usually to do with the nature of people), arguing about them can be fruitless. However, it is acceptable to reject attacks based solely on a different belief and certainly to refuse to be diminished by them (but remember this works the other way round too).

While there is widespread agreement in the wider person-centred community that the six conditions are necessary and sufficient, this does not mean that person-centred practitioners are unthinking about them. They are constantly being 'reconsidered' (for example, congruence by Tudor and Worrall 1994, empathy by Bohart and Greenberg 1997 and unconditional positive regard by Wilkins 2000), reviewed and readdressed (for example in the series Rogers' Therapeutic Conditions edited by Gill Wyatt for PCCS Books). Currently, it seems that research into the effectiveness of psychotherapy indicates that (apart from what the client brings and does) the major 'change factor' is the relationship between therapist and client. Arguably, that is exactly the weight of the hypothesis of the necessary and sufficient conditions.

44

PERSON-CENTRED THERAPY IS SEEN AS ARISING FROM AND BOUND TO A PARTICULAR CULTURE MILIEU AND THIS LIMITS ITS RELEVANCE AND APPLICABILITY

Rogers and his early colleagues and collaborators were, for the most part, well-educated, middle-class, white American men. It is widely held that the theories and practices they developed reflect who and how they were. That is to say that person-centred therapy is essentially the product of a mid-twentieth century, white, North American, male perspective. Perhaps (for example) it is true that a cultural emphasis on rugged individualism did contribute to the development of humanistic psychology and thus person-centred thought. However, if this was the sole influence, then the actualising tendency and other theoretical precepts are artefacts of a particular time, place and culture and their relevance to any other time, place and culture is at least questionable. This in turn would mean that the applicability of person-centred therapy is limited because it fails to take note of variations in culture. Needless to say, person-centred practitioners do not accept this criticism wholesale. For some, person-centred theory, because it is organismic, natural and universal (Point 11), is independent of culture and there is appreciation from outside the approach of the anti-intellectual, non-racist, non-sexist qualities inherent in person-centred therapy. However, for other person-centred practitioners, although this is true, culture is something to be consciously taken into account in both theory and practice.

'Cultural awareness' has been an issue for person-centred practitioners from the earliest of days. Rogers (1951: 437) believed it to be important that therapists had at least some knowledge of their clients' cultural setting and that it was important to actively learn about 'cultural influences very different from those which have molded [the counsellor]'. The issue of cultural differences has featured in person-centred writing ever since. For example, Holdstock (1993) pointed out that the concept of 'self' and 'I' differed between cultures and that this had implications for the practice of person-centred therapy and there have been more recent attempts to address (for example) issues of gender and ethnicity.

One of the major concerns of person-centred practitioners with reference to difference is that of power. For example, men and women, black and white, poor and wealthy are different in their daily experience of power and oppression and this plays a part in psychological development. A major criticism is that such differences are not allowed for in person-centred theory. With respect to gender, some notable person-centred writers of critiques and theoretical modifications include Wolter-Gustafson (1999) who considers Rogers' theory of human development with reference to feminist and postmodern ideas and Natiello (1999) who shows how conditions of worth lead to gender splitting and how gender typing challenges congruence. In addition there is a major work edited by Proctor and Napier (2004) concerned with intersections between feminism and the person-centred approach. Similarly, attention has been given to issues of race and ethnicity by person-centred theorists and practitioners. Of particular note in this respect is Moodley et al. (2004: 85–174) presenting the views of a number of people on race and culture in person-centred counselling and Proctor et al. (2006: 143–231) where the contributors address socio-political issues and the therapy relationship. All the above and a number of other writers are raising awareness of the shortcomings of person-centred practice in the absence of cultural awareness. This is the major concern of Lago (2007: 251–265) who (p. 255) considers the tensions and criticisms in relation to difference and diversity within the person-centred approach and (pp. 261–262) makes recommendations 'for person-centred therapists working across difference and diversity'. Two further works by this renowned person-centred author relevant to the issue of working transculturally are Lago (2010: 73–85) which concerns developing empathic capabilities to work interculturally and inter-ethnically and Lago (2011a) which is an edited, contemporary review of research and practice across transcultural counselling and psychotherapy.

45

IN IGNORING 'TRANSFERENCE' PERSON-CENTRED THERAPY IS SEEN AS NAIVE AND SERIOUSLY LACKING

An area in which person-centred theory is seen to be lacking is with respect to 'transference' and other 'unconscious' processes (Point 22). This view is characterised by the assumption that person-centred practitioners seek to 'avoid' transference issues by being congruent and non-directive and thus ignore an important process to the detriment of their clients. In this analysis, person-centred therapists are seen as encouraging, through their actions and approach, positive transference (being supportive and 'parental' in the best sense of the word) but as denying the client expression of 'negative' transference feelings. This prevents real, in-depth therapy. The 'discouragement of negative transference' argument seems to be rooted in the assumption that the attitudes of person-centred therapists amount to a bland 'niceness'. However, in context, confrontation and challenge may be part of the process of therapy. Person-centred therapy depends (amongst other things) on the expression of real feelings *in the moment* and this can and sometimes does include anger at the therapist.

In person-centred terms, either transference may (sometimes) be part of an interaction but it would be counter-therapeutic to work with it (because to do so would avoid the 'here-and-now' interactions and attribute the dynamic almost solely to the client's process) or it is a psychoanalytic theoretical construct with no reality. While Rogers (in Kirschenbaum and Henderson 1990a: 129–130) acknowledged that in the therapeutic encounter there could arise emotions having little or nothing to do with the therapist's behaviour these were of no practical relevance.

Other person-centred theorists have expressed stronger views. Most notably, Shlien (1984: 153–181) proposed a 'counter theory of transference' which he intended to be instrumental in developing an alternative theory of the unconscious. Shlien (p. 153) was of the view that 'transference is a fiction, invented and maintained by the therapist to protect himself from the consequences of his own behaviour'. More recently, Mearns and Cooper (2005: 53) expressed the opinion that transference phenomena occur only in comparatively superficial levels of relationship and disappear altogether when working at relational depth (Point 38). They (p. 159) go further and claim that concentrating on transference phenomena actively blocks relational depth. This neatly reverses the familiar claim of psychodynamic therapists and puts working with transference in the position of being counter-therapeutic. Of course there are person-centred therapists who take different views about the existence and importance of transference phenomena. For example Lietaer (1993: 35) takes the view that while transference does exist it is how it is worked with in person-centred therapy that is different. He points out that transference phenomena dissolve of their own accord as a result of a good working relationship and that person-centred therapy does not 'provide a *priority in principle* [original emphasis] to working with a problem in the here-and-now relationship'.

It is also true that transference is a theoretical construct used by some people to describe a process they observe and to which they attribute significance. It is a concept, not a verified process and, if it occurs at all, there are different explanations for it. These include person-centred explanations. It is possible that person-centred practitioners observe the same processes as therapists of other orientations but name and understand them differently. For example, in Wilkins (1997a: 38) I point out that some of the many processes described as 'countertransference' may, in terms of person-centred theory, very well be described as empathy.

As yet, there is no more proof for one theoretical position than another. To argue against one theory as if another were proven is illogical and spurious. Additionally, it isn't that person-centred practitioners are ignorant of transference phenomena but that there is an alternative explanation for them and different ideas about the relevance of transference to practice.

46

THE NON-DIRECTIVE ATTITUDE IS A FICTION AND AN IRRESPONSIBLE DENIAL OF POWER

The principle of non-directivity is the bedrock of person-centred therapy (Point 5). This is sometimes criticised as a denial of the inevitable greater power of the therapist in the therapeutic relationship and/or as a practical impossibility. In the first place, it is argued that because therapists are invested with knowledge and expertise and the client has neither, it is the former who has control of the session. Thus there is an inevitable imbalance of power. Indeed, because the second of Rogers' conditions requires that the client is at least to some extent vulnerable and anxious and this is likely to provoke and invoke feelings of powerlessness and a sense of a lack of control, person-centred theory may even seem to confirm this inevitability. In these circumstances, whether therapists wish it or not, at least some clients are likely to follow what they perceive to be directions from them. So, the argument goes, for person-centred therapists to pretend they are non-directive is to deny reality and leads to an avoidance of the issue of the power imbalance in the therapeutic relationship. Also, it is argued that therapists have skills, knowledge and experience that they are professionally and ethically obliged to employ to the client's advantage. This is something person-centred practitioners are assumed to avoid and in so doing deprive and disadvantage their clients. All this is rooted in a misapprehension as to what in person-centred theory is meant by non-directivity.

In one of Rogers' earliest works (*Counseling and Psychotherapy*, 1942), he wrote a chapter entitled 'The directive versus the nondirective approach' (see Kirschenbaum and Henderson 1990a: 77–87). In essence, the difference between these two positions relates to who chooses the client's goals. In person-centred therapy, a non-directive stance relates first and foremost to the clients' right to choose their own life goals even if these conflict with the view of the therapist. The belief is that clients have insight into themselves and their problems and are best placed to make the right choices at the right time. This is about trusting the actualising tendency (Point 9). However, according to Kirschenbaum and Henderson (1990a: 62), Rogers did come to fear that a non-directive approach had come to emphasise particular therapist techniques at the expense of therapists' attitudes towards the client. From this it can be inferred that non-directivity is less to do with particular therapist behaviours (such as confining responses to 'reflection') and everything to do with the therapist's recognition of the client as an autonomous person with a unique personal wisdom. The clients are the experts on their own lives and ways of being in the world.

Arising from all this, there seems to be a misassumption that person-centred practitioners are relatively passive, responding only to direct input of some kind from their clients – specifically by merely reflecting the client's words. This in turn leads to the belief that anyone can practise person-centred therapy. However, it has been clear from the earliest days that person-centred practice does require and depend on considerable knowledge and expertise at least in the sense of adherence to a form of practice rooted in a belief in the actualising tendency and at which the necessary and sufficient conditions lie at the heart. With respect to expertise, the issue is about power, mystique and their misuse.

The non-directive attitude remains at the heart of classical client-centred therapy (see, for example, Levitt 2005). In this and related forms of practice, clients formulate their own goals and therapists are companions on the journey, not leaders. Person-centred therapists cannot have goals for their clients, cannot presume to know what outcomes are desirable for them. It is by tracking clients' subjective experiences (empathically, acceptingly and congruently) that person-centred therapy 'works'. What matters most is not what is said or done by the therapist but what the client experiences, i.e. it is an essential precept that the efficacy of person-centred therapy depends on clients perceiving themselves as not being directed to a particular course of action, belief or code of conduct. Within the broad spectrum of person-centred practice, there are different ways of achieving this aim.

47

THE CONCERN FOR POWER IN THE THERAPEUTIC RELATIONSHIP SHOWN BY PERSON-CENTRED THERAPISTS IS MISCONCEIVED AND MISDIRECTED

As indicated in Points 5, 6 and 37, the issue of power has long been considered as important in the practice of person-centred therapy. At the very heart of the approach lies the therapist's eschewal of the direction and domination of the client. However, this appears to conflict with what is generally agreed to be an inherent imbalance in the power dynamic in which the therapist has knowledge and expertise and the client is vulnerable and anxious. Also effective person-centred therapy depends on therapists being fully present as powerful people. However, rather than denying their power in a relationship, person-centred therapists are required to be acutely aware of it and to exercise it in a constructive, influential way. It is also hoped that as the therapeutic relationship develops, as the result of increased reciprocal trust, there is a move towards the sharing of power or, more correctly, the establishment of a co-operative and collaborative endeavour in which therapist and client are equal although they have different aims, focus on different things and function differently. That is to say, in the person-centred relationship 'equality' is not about being the same but being of the same worth.

For at least some outside the approach this belief in the desirability and achievability of equality within the therapeutic relationship solely through reliance on the necessary and sufficient conditions is a naive (and potentially dangerous) myth.

However, as already pointed out, person-centred therapy does not involve therapists relinquishing their power. To do so would be incongruent and therefore clearly counter-therapeutic. Moreover, it is a theoretical precept backed by empirical observation that when, in the absence of direction, clients are met congruently with empathic understanding and unconditional positive regard they do change and this change involves an increased sense of their own power, an internalisation of their loci of evaluation.

There is a problem here. Clearly, by offering clients the therapist conditions person-centred therapists are seeking to influence them even if not to direct them. This is about being powerful even if the direction and end point of change are not an issue for the therapist. This relates to what Proctor (2002: 87–97) calls 'role power'. However, while recognising the inherent power imbalance in the roles of therapist and client, she (p. 87) points out that, through the non-directive attitude, person-centred therapists seek to avoid client *disempowerment*. This is an important distinction. It is possible and desirable to experience personal power without exercising authoritarian power (*power over*). It is this refusal to disempower the other, to take responsibility for the course and direction of the therapeutic encounter, that allows the emergence of 'power-from-within' (see Proctor 2002: 90), however weakly experienced up to that point.

Perhaps part of the problem with respect to power is the different ways in which this can be understood. In our prevailing culture we tend to think of power in terms of authority, control and supremacy. In this understanding, power is about getting your own way almost regardless of the cost to others. There are other ways of conceiving of power. Bozarth (1998: 21) argues that, from a person-centred perspective, 'power' is closer to its Latin roots – *posse* is 'to be able'. He is of the opinion that in this reading to be powerful is to be all you are capable of being. Writers influenced to at least some extent by feminist principles have also offered elegant analyses of power and its manifestations (see, for example, Marshall 1984; Natiello 1990; Proctor

2002). Essentially, the views expressed by such authors are that not only is there authoritarian power over others, there is personal power (power from within) and collaborative power. The latter is joint enterprise, openness with respect to information, responsiveness to the needs of all, mutual respect, co-operation rather than competition and personal empowerment. It is these notions of collaborative power and power as a force moving people towards what they can be that are the heart of person-centred therapy.

48

PERSON-CENTRED THERAPY IS A PALLIATIVE FOR THE WORRIED WELL BUT LACKS THE DEPTH AND RIGOUR TO DEAL WITH PEOPLE WHO ARE 'ILL'

A popular view of person-centred therapy is that it is mild and inoffensive, great for people who want and need little more than a sympathetic ear but, in reality, anodyne and weak so of little or no use to anyone with real mental distress. People with mild neuroses and acute but everyday problems may gain something from the opportunity to just talk to someone who will listen in a non-judgemental way but person-centred therapists lack the knowledge and skills to deal with deep-rooted psychological problems. Paradoxically, another view held by (for example) Kovel (1976: 116) is that person-centred therapy is adequate when working with people who are so deeply disturbed and dysfunctional as to be 'unsuitable' for psychotherapy (ground which, via pre-therapy and contact work, person-centred therapy has proudly claimed for its own – Point 34). What both these views amount to is the assumption that person-centred therapy is a palliative but that it is ineffective with people experiencing deep-rooted emotional distress. Even though there is an increasing recognition that person-centred therapists do work with people who may be called mentally ill this is seen as a recent development and the old myths persist. In reality, at least from the days of the Wisconsin project in the 1960s which involved investigating the efficacy of person-centred therapy with people diagnosed as 'schizophrenic' (see Barrett-Lennard 1998: 267–270), there has been evidence of person-centred practice with people who may be described as 'severely disturbed'.

In part, questions about the efficacy of person-centred therapy with people experiencing extreme mental and/or emotional distress go back to the sterile argument about the difference between 'counselling' and psychotherapy (see Wilkins 2003: 100–104). For the most part, because it is the client who determines the nature, duration and 'depth' of the therapeutic relationship, person-centred therapy admits of no such difference. This does not mean that person-centred therapists do not do what others may call 'psychotherapy'. Even a fairly cursory glance at the person-centred literature will demonstrate this. There is a body of work addressing a person-centred take on psychopathology (Point 33) and person-centred therapists have published accounts of their work with people who are (amongst other things) contact impaired (Point 34), experiencing difficult process (Point 36), diagnosed as 'borderline', 'psychotic', having a 'personality disorder' and so on (see Lambers 1994: 105–120). More recently, Joseph and Worsley (2005) and Worsley and Joseph (2007) have produced two edited volumes addressing the theory and practice and research evidence for person-centred practice with people experiencing a variety of 'psychopathological' ways of being in the world and Pearce and Sommerbeck (2014) covers 'person-centred practice at the difficult edge'.

While, in the English-speaking world, evidence for the applicability of person-centred therapy to working with people experiencing extremes of emotional and mental distress does seem to have been in short supply from the 1960s until the end of the twentieth century, there is sufficient published work to demonstrate that person-centred practitioners do not confine their work to the 'worried well'. Alongside developing practice has been developing theory. It is now clear that person-centred therapy is at least as effective with 'psychopathological' states as any other approach.

49

PERSON-CENTRED PRACTICE COMPRISES SOLELY 'REFLECTION' AND THIS IS A TECHNIQUE OF LITTLE EFFECT

At least superficially, the practice of classic client-centred therapy can appear to be little more than parroting the client's words. Sometimes this is referred to as 'reflecting'. However, this is in some ways an unfortunate term. Although, when faced with a therapist who represents what they have said, this may be like having a mirror held up to them the better that they can understand what they said this is not the intention of person-centred therapists. Rogers (in Kirschenbaum and Henderson 1990a: 127–128) was clear that when he confined his responses to the frame of reference of the client he was not trying to 'reflect feelings' but ascertaining that he had heard and correctly understood the client's communication. In such 'reflective' responses therapists are asking the implicit question 'Have I understood you? Is this what you are experiencing?' Moreover, when such responses are made in an accepting way there is an implicit assertion from the frame of reference of the therapist which is something like 'I understand the feelings you are experiencing, the events you are describing and something of how it is to be you in this moment and this knowledge does not alter my perception of you as a person of worth.' Of course, person-centred therapists respond not only to expressions of feeling but to expressions of other kinds including thoughts, bodily sensations, fantasies, memories and so on.

Exactly what person-centred therapists are doing when they 'reflect' is actually quite sophisticated and far from trivial. Indeed Rogers (in Kirschenbaum and Henderson 1990a: 127) quotes Shlien as saying that, in the right hands, reflection is 'an instrument of artistic virtuosity'. Reflection is at the heart of person-centred practice because it is about being non-directive (Point 5) and communicating the therapist conditions. If, when reflecting, the therapist's intention *is* to hold a mirror up to the client so that they may see themselves (with the notion that something will happen as a result) then what is going on has moved away from attempting to understand the client's experience and to communicate this with empathy and unconditional positive regard and moved into responding from the therapist's frame of reference. In some way and on some level 'mirroring' responses are the results of the therapist taking the decision that the client should see/hear something of what the therapist believes them to have expressed. This is in effect 'doing' something to clients rather than accompanying them on their journeys and so moves away from their perceptual worlds. However, if the intention is to check therapists' perceptions of what is being experienced and to offer empathy and unconditional positive regard then this is the non-directive attitude in action.

Person-centred therapists are not confined to reflecting only the words of the client. An aim in the therapeutic encounter is to understand and respond to the whole of the client's experience. Quite a lot of what we perceive of communication is about something other than the words spoken per se. Non-verbal communication and empathic sensing may also tell something of the client's way of being in the moment. This too can be 'reflected'. Again, the aim of therapists is to check their perceptions of unvoiced feelings, scary thoughts and the like. However, it is important that such responses do relate to the client's experience and are not the result of some interpretation on the part of the therapist.

In person-centred therapy there can be no delving into the 'unconscious'. Even if the therapist perceived unconscious material unavailable to the client (which is probably impossible from a classical client-centred point of view), because it would not be recognised or owned and more importantly because it would be directive, it would be mistaken for the therapist to offer what amounts to an interpretation. However, there is a notion of the 'edge of awareness' (see Rogers 1966: 160 and Mearns and Thorne 2007: 78–82). Briefly, this concept involves the assumption that there are things (thoughts, feelings, sensations, intuitions) just below the threshold of awareness. Sometimes, these can be perceived or empathically sensed by the therapist and when they are reflected the client experience is instant recognition: 'Yes – that's it!' Responding to 'the pool of implicit meanings just at the edge of the client's awareness' (Rogers 1966: 160) is contentious and certainly requires caution. However, it is clear that working with 'edge of awareness' material by making 'reflections' *is* part of the person-centred tradition.

There is an argument from some classical client-centred therapists to the effect that it is directive to respond to anything other than the client's communications. Grant (2010: 225) refers to this as 'taking only what is given'. He writes 'One does not *give* – offer, share, intentionally communicate – feelings, perceptions, states of mind, ideas, or any other item or aspect of one's experience, *except* [original emphases] insofar as one gives them in communications'. Therefore anything not communicated is not the proper target for non-directive client-centred therapy. While broadly speaking I agree that it is the job of person-centred therapists to respond to what is willingly communicated, I also believe that such communication goes way beyond words.

50

BECAUSE OF ITS OBSESSION WITH 'NON-DIRECTIVITY' THE PRACTICE OF PERSON-CENTRED THERAPY RESULTS IN HARMFULLY SLOPPY BOUNDARIES

Person-centred therapists have been accused of an apparent professional and ethical laxness because of an assumed disregard for boundaries inherent in person-centred theory. To a large extent, this is the result of a misunderstanding of just who is person-centred and a confusion of the behaviour of individuals with what person-centred practice actually involves (see Wilkins 2003: 121–122). In reality, how person-centred practitioners operate with respect to boundaries is, for the most part, no different to therapists of other orientations. However, it is true that, from a theoretical perspective at least, because of the concern with power (Points 5, 6 and 37), the stance of person-centred therapy with respect to 'boundaries' is different from some others. This is about the non-directive attitude and the stance of person-centred therapists as 'non-expert' with respect to the client's process.

A lot of structural boundaries in therapy are a matter of convention and/or imposed by the therapist (for example, the duration and frequency of sessions, the length of contracts, where and when meetings take place). However, there is nothing in person-centred theory that delimits where, how often and under what conditions 'therapy' takes place. Given the centrality of the client's experience to person-centred therapy and the non-directive attitude of its practitioners, it would seem that person-centred theory indicates the desirability of flexibility with respect to at least some boundaries. Because of the history of the development of counselling and psychotherapy, a lot of what has come to be accepted as desirable or even mandatory about boundaries is rooted in psychodynamic theory and practice (see Wilkins 2003: 124–125). Person-centred theory is based on entirely different premises and to judge it on the basis of other models of the person and nature of therapy is mistaken and unfair. Nevertheless the person-centred therapist has rights and preferences and ethical obligations, any or all of which must be taken into account in the setting and operation of structural boundaries (see Wilkins 2003: 128). It may be that, for some therapists, working with some clients, some of the time it is appropriate to move beyond the conventions of meeting for an hour, once a week in the therapist's room but this is something to be carefully considered and preferably discussed in supervision and/or with colleagues beforehand.

Primarily, it is with respect to 'power' and client autonomy that person-centred therapy may differ most from other approaches. Because clients are deemed to be the best experts on their own lives and driven by their actualising tendencies in the direction of positive fulfilment of their potential, the person-centred therapist cannot ethically take responsibility for the client. To take such responsibility would be to impose the will of the therapist and to deny the client the right to exercise (or fail to exercise) personal power. That is, it would be directive. However well intentioned the direction, by definition, it would be counter-therapeutic and, arguably, unethical. This has implications with respect to (for example) who ends therapy, how it ends and what are the responsibilities of therapists towards former clients. Conclusions with respect to such issues may very well be different from those held in other approaches. Essentially, from a person-centred perspective, within a given ethical framework, what is important about boundaries is that they are functional, allowing a justifiable flexible response to particular clients rather than structural – that is boundaries as a set of predetermined behaviours (see Mearns and Thorne 2000: 48).

Section 5

PERSON-CENTRED PRACTICE

THE FOUNDATIONS OF PERSON-CENTRED PRACTICE

51

RESPONSIBLE PERSON-CENTRED PRACTICE REQUIRES A STRONG THEORETICAL FOUNDATION AND PARTICULAR ATTITUDES AND PERSONAL QUALITIES

Beginning and continuing person-centred practice involves more than acquiring theoretical knowledge and practical skills. In common with other approaches there are many things to consider and do before proceeding to the meat of the thera-peutic encounter.

Of course, there is a need for appropriate training and this should include the acquisition of practical skills and a thorough grounding in person-centred theory as set out by Rogers, his colleagues and successors (Sections 2 and 3, Point 53). However, there is more to being a person-centred practi-tioner than this. Person-centred practitioners tend to talk of 'being person-centred' as if it is not only a way of doing ther-apy but of being in the world. While, arguably, it is possible to be a client-centred therapist without being a 'person-centred person' (that is, carrying the values and attitudes of the person-centred approach into endeavours and encounters other than therapy and perhaps to the whole of life) person-centred practice does involve embracing a philosophy (at least in the lay sense of the word). Something of this philosophy is dis-cussed in Point 4. What flows from this philosophical stance is a deep respect for people as autonomous, intrinsically healthy beings, a commitment to the non-directive principle (Point 5) and a willingness to eschew 'power over' (Points 6 and 37).

Effective person-centred training will probably address all of these things.

Even for the experienced person-centred practitioner these attitudes remain fundamental to day-to-day practice and are at its core. Although preparation for practice is an issue in any approach to therapy, person-centred theory and practice emphasise some different things and most things differently. This subsection is about the groundwork person-centred therapists must do.

52

PERSON-CENTRED PRACTICE TAKES PLACE IN MANY CONTEXTS AND THE TERMS 'COUNSELLING' AND 'PSYCHOTHERAPY' APPLY TO SOME OF THESE BUT ARE OFTEN INTERCHANGEABLE

Person-centred principles have been and are applied to many fields of human endeavour. They are, after all, about a way of being in relationship and this has an important part in (for example) education, social, political and cultural change, work with families and children and even research but most famously it is known as a way of doing counselling and psychotherapy. However the principles are applied, the theory and practice described as relevant to therapy are likely to be of importance.

The term 'counselling' has many different meanings in different cultures. Even in the UK there is not complete agreement as to what the term means. All of this leads to different assumptions as to what a counsellor actually does. 'Counselling' may even include the giving of advice or even a disciplinary function. Neither is there agreement as to the exact meaning of the term 'psychotherapy'. With respect to person-centred therapy, the situation is different again for, in terms of theory, there is no difference between counselling and psychotherapy. That is, they are not (for example) distinguished by notions of the degree of 'depth' or duration. Person-centred practice is about therapists responding to clients and the client's subjective experience whatever it may be in the same way and with the same intent whether they are being told about acute mild anxiety or the gut-wrenching, chronic pain of horrendous early abuse. In other words, regardless of what the client brings to the therapy session, the therapist relies upon the body of theoretical knowledge set forth in the earlier part of this book and elsewhere and responds congruently with empathic understanding and unconditional positive regard. At least from a person-centred perspective, perceived differences between counselling and psychotherapy are cultural, historical and political and stem from vested interests.

Ultimately, disagreements as to the differences between counselling and psychotherapy are sterile because they rest on different definitions. That is, there is a basic assumption that 'psychotherapy and counselling are the same (or different) because I believe them to be'. This leads to fruitless, circular arguments. However, within the person-centred world the two terms are used in such a way as to imply that they are different in some ways. For example, the lead international organisation for the approach is the World Association for Person-Centered and Experiential Psychotherapy and Counseling and some training organisations allow people who complete training in person-centred counselling to go on to do a further period of training to qualify as person-centred psychotherapists. There is no agreement as to what the difference might be and, rather than use either term, many person-centred practitioners refer to what they do simply as 'therapy'. It is the practice of a person-centred way of working and in particular person-centred therapy with which this section of the book is concerned. However the practice is described, the same principles apply.

53

THE FIRST STEP TOWARDS PERSON-CENTRED PRACTICE IS A THOROUGH GROUNDING IN PERSON-CENTRED THEORY

One of the great and potentially dangerous myths about person-centred practice is that it is in some way 'theory free' and that therefore almost anyone can do it on the basis of very little knowledge. The belief is that person-centred therapy is easy to learn – it is just a matter of being friendly and understanding. Actually there is a big difference between being a person-centred therapist and acquiring a set of skills derived (often somewhat loosely) from the thought and practice of Carl Rogers. Practising in a person-centred way requires a great deal more than a passing acquaintance with the so-called core conditions. While it is true that during the therapeutic encounter the focus of the therapist must be on the client's current experience rather than theoretical interpretation this can only be done effectively and safely when the therapist has a real understanding of person-centred theory. Haugh (2012: 15–17) refers to the fourfold importance of theory and (p. 16) writes 'it is imperative that [in the therapeutic encounter] theory is "held lightly"'. She says that rather than pigeonholing a client, theory should help the therapist stay beside the client.

What is needed then is a thorough grounding in all aspects of person-centred theory, a real understanding of the practicalities of relating to clients, a deep commitment to an ethical stance which includes respect for the client as a self-determining person, attention to the self-development of the practitioner probably including extensive experience in a peer group and many hours of supervised practice. The best way of achieving this is to attend a training course acknowledged as person-centred by the person-centred community. Courses which include 'person-centred counselling' as a core model do not necessarily offer full training in person-centred therapy. Effective practice as a person-centred therapist should include not only knowledge of the necessary and sufficient conditions but also (for example) of the person-centred model of the person and the need for positive self-regard, the roots of and reasons for the non-directive attitude, an understanding of and belief in the actualising tendency and appreciation of how conditions of worth arise and how they affect development. A good place to start with all this is to read the classic works of Rogers (for example, 1951, 1957, 1959) and also the re-presentations of this basic theory by (for example) Mearns and Thorne (2000, 2007), Merry (2002) and Sanders (2006b).

54

PERSON-CENTRED PRACTITIONERS WORK WITH CLIENTS, NOT PATIENTS

Although it might seem inconsequential and common to many approaches to therapy, the fact that person-centred practitioners refer to the people they work with as clients rather than patients is significant. The term 'client' was originally used by Rogers in 1940 and he intended it to indicate a therapeutic relationship of a different kind to that common up to that time. Although it is now often taken for granted, the notion of working with 'clients' embodies much of the person-centred attitude and stance towards people. It is about seeing them as autonomous and self-determining. Additionally, whereas 'patients' are 'sick' and are dependent on medical practitioners for a cure, person-centred theory does not allow that people who seek the help of a therapist are in need of diagnosis and expert guidance. Rather there is the explicit knowledge that each of us contains within us the seeds of our own growth and healing. We may need a companion but never someone to take over and decide what is wrong and how to put it right. It is not the expertise in terms of skills, techniques and interpretations of the therapist which is helpful but the ability to embody the attitudes of congruence, empathic understanding and unconditional positive regard. In its time, this was a subversive, revolutionary move away from the prevailing medical/psychiatric model and, in many ways, it remains such.

What this attitude means for practice is highly significant. It is axiomatic that the client's process is trustworthy and that all individuals are to be respected. Conveying this from the outset and throughout the relationship is a primary responsibility of the person-centred therapist. This means thinking about how clients are met and greeted, how the terms of a contract (including fees) are presented and (if possible and relevant) negotiated, the layout of the room in which the therapeutic encounter will take place and so on. Each of these things (and others) contributes to the client's sense of being respected, valued and trusted. Although there are some obvious things (for example avoidance of furniture and the arrangement of furniture that conveys differences in status – no little chair for the client facing a big chair behind a big desk for the therapist!), it is impossible to be prescriptive about these things because no two therapists are alike and our settings and circumstances vary. What is important is that, within whatever constraints there may be, therapists find ways of warmly and congruently indicating to their clients the collaborative and non-directive nature of the therapeutic relationship.

55

AN OBJECTIVE OF PERSON-CENTRED PRACTICE IS TO OFFER A HEALING RELATIONSHIP. THIS COMPRISES SEVERAL INGREDIENTS INCLUDING THE SIX NECESSARY AND SUFFICIENT CONDITIONS

In a way, it goes without saying that person-centred therapy is a helping relationship, the objective of which is to offer the client opportunities for healing and/or growth – this is the aim of counselling and psychotherapy as a whole. However, person-centred theory has a particular take on how this can be done in practice. The necessary and sufficient conditions resulted from the empirical observation of what actually does promote 'constructive personality change'. Basically, this amounts to an understanding that it is the quality of relationship that matters, not expert knowledge and the application of technique. There is a great deal of support for the conclusion that what clients find helpful is a caring, respectful, understanding relationship in which they can examine and analyse their thoughts and feelings without hindrance or interference (see, for example, Howe 1993; Proctor 2002: 89–90). The first task of the person-centred practitioner is to offer a relationship of this quality. The foundation stone for this is the therapist's attitude and commitment to the non-directive attitude and a belief in the client's actualising tendency and (therefore) trustworthy process. From this attitude and belief stems the desire and ability to implement the six necessary and sufficient conditions (not just the so-called 'core conditions'). This is because, although the therapist-provided conditions of congruence in the relationship, empathic understanding and unconditional positive regard are vital, it is only in the context of the contact between client and therapist, the anxiety and vulnerability of the client and the client's reception and perception of the therapist's respect and understanding that they are effective. To lose sight of any one or more of the necessary and sufficient conditions is to risk losing an understanding of what is happening in the relationship as a whole and the needs and perceptions of its participants. Instead, concentrating only on the core conditions is equivalent to paying attention only to the behaviour, feelings and intentions of the therapist. The questions become 'Am I congruent/empathic/accepting' rather than 'Are my client and I in contact?', 'Does my client need therapy and is what I can provide likely to be useful (i.e. is my client not only incongruent in our relationship but vulnerable and/or anxious)?' and 'Is my client perceiving empathy and unconditional positive regard from me?' Concentration on the therapist-provided conditions changes what is going on from a relationship to something the therapist does to the client.

Another danger of relying solely on being congruent in the relationship and providing empathy and UPR is that these are transformed from relational qualities which are part of a complex collaborative and co-created relationship to therapist-provided skills – something 'done to' the client rather than a way of being in relation to the client. This is detrimental to the healing relationship because that is about not just the therapist but what both client and therapist bring to the relationship and how they collaborate to co-create it. Also, it may in any case be a mistake to think of the therapist-provided conditions as three distinct entities. Although in his classic statements of the necessary and sufficient conditions Rogers chose to identify and characterise three therapist-provided elements, it is likely that this was to allow for the description of what many believe to be in reality one thing (Point 14). Certainly, when it comes to the phenomenon of 'presence' (Point 25) and working at relational depth (Point 38), separating these conditions seems to be irrelevant and possibly to interfere with the healing relationship.

56

BECAUSE PERSON-CENTRED THERAPY RELIES ON HOW THE THERAPIST IS RATHER THAN WHAT THE THERAPIST KNOWS, THERE IS PROFESSIONAL OBLIGATION ON PERSON-CENTRED THERAPISTS TO ATTEND TO THEIR OWN GROWTH AND DEVELOPMENT

The importance of a thorough grounding in theory to the successful practice of person-centred therapy has already been indicated (Point 53) but this alone is not sufficient to ensure that therapists can offer an effective relationship. Because person-centred therapy emphasises the importance of not only the 'person' of the client but also the person of the therapist, there is a professional obligation on the latter to attend to personal growth and development. Just as an athlete keeps in and improves physical condition by exercise and training so, for the good of their clients and their own health, person-centred therapists are strongly advised to attend to their psychological and emotional well-being. However, whereas an athlete keeps in trim to avoid loss of muscle tone and strength, the objective of the person-centred therapist's attention to psychological well-being is, for example, to avoid 'burnout' (see Mearns 1994: 29–33) and a subsequent decrease in effectiveness and quite possibly illness.

Of course, this is not unique to person-centred therapy but whereas some other approaches include definite ideas as to the place of personal therapy in training and in continuing professional development (CPD) in principle person-centred approaches are not prescriptive about this. However, it is likely that programmes of person-centred training will include some form of personal development as well as professional training. This may serve as grounding for further development in the course of practice. The aim of personal development is to enable therapists to increase their ability to work effectively with clients in ways that are safe for both parties and to incrementally increase this effectiveness. It is about dealing with blind spots and limits to unconditional positive self-regard so that it is possible to encounter the pain of clients empathically and with unconditional positive regard. It is also about maintaining the energy and enthusiasm that effective person-centred therapy demands.

Working intensively with clients can be stressful and it is certainly demanding of the personal resources of the therapist. This stress can be ameliorated through supervision and the support of colleagues but effective working necessitates positive and proactive steps on the part of the person-centred therapist to engage in rest and recreation. This is because the symptoms of burnout include a decreasing ability to be congruent since there is an increasing need on the part of the practitioner to protect and preserve those parts of the self-structure that are experienced as under almost intolerable pressure. The need to be congruent in the relationship is one of the six necessary and sufficient conditions, all of which are needed for constructive personality change to occur. Without congruence on the part of the therapist then the prospect of therapeutic change is limited. Also, when under such stress, the therapist is likely to become more problem-focused than client-centred (because the former seems more tractable and/or less demanding of the personal resources of the therapist) and more rigid with respect to contracting boundaries. This involves significant loss of the ability to empathise with the client and will almost certainly be experienced as lacking unconditional positive regard. These things also amount to a significant move away from a non-directive attitude towards directivity. Again, there is a conflict with the demands of person-centred theory. There may even be a tendency to become increasingly self-deceptive with respect to the efficacy and depth of client work. Mearns (1994: 31) writes about the possibility of person-centred therapists reacting to burnout by becoming over-involved with their clients, presenting themselves as powerful or even omnipotent agents of change rather than as facilitators of the client's own change process. This is, once again, a move towards a directive, 'expert' stance involving decreased empathy (because it is about the therapist's frame of reference) and unconditional positive regard (because it involves envisaging and imposing the therapist's 'solution'). The possibility of burnout is a matter for supervision but its prevention and 'cure' is about attention to personal development.

Just as because it is based on client need and the client's personal process of change, it is impossible and undesirable to be prescriptive about ways in which the personal and professional growth of person-centred therapists should be done. Each of us has different qualitative and quantitative development needs at different times. Personal therapy of some kind is a traditional resource for therapists because it includes the maintenance of psychological, emotional and spiritual well-being, increasing understanding of human nature and personal growth. Other ways of doing this include spiritual or meditative practice, systematic reflection on personal experience (for example through dream-work or journal keeping), reading creative or imaginative literature and creative approaches to relaxation (see Wilkins 1997b: 123–142).

5.2

THE INITIAL PROCESSES
OF PERSON-CENTRED
THERAPY

57

IN PERSON-CENTRED THERAPY, GETTING STARTED WITH A NEW CLIENT IS AN INVOLVED AND INVOLVING PROCESS

Although in the eyes of some, person-centred therapists are seen as 'casual' or even cavalier in their attitudes to practice, particularly with respect to contracts and boundaries, beginning therapy with a new client in fact requires that the therapist considers a number of issues and carries out a number of processes concerned with these very things. This includes an assessment process (although many person-centred practitioners neither call it such nor think of it in that way – Point 32), 'contracting', that is agreeing with the client the terms and conditions of therapy however flexible these may be, and also considering and being explicit about the boundaries to be imposed by the therapist and/or by the institution or service under the auspices of which therapy will be offered. All of these involve a careful consideration of ethical and professional issues and they are addressed in the following Points. It is in the nature of person-centred therapy that exactly what is done and how it is done will vary for each client/therapist relationship. Person-centred therapy is about the encounter of two individuals, a meeting of persons, and so each beginning is idiosyncratic and not about working methodically through a checklist. However, there are professional and sometimes institutional obligations to be sure that the client is clear about what is likely to happen and what the limitations of the offer of therapy are.

However it is done, the process of 'initiating' therapy is not some stand-alone element, a separate thing to be done first and something different from therapy proper. A first meeting with a client may be described as an assessment meeting or a contracting session (and this may very well be a necessary aspect of it) but it is vital to realise that the therapy relationship begins at the moment of first contact (which may even be before a face-to-face meeting). Therefore, the therapist must be available to the client as a respectful, full and present person even if there are administrative tasks to perform. Whatever else happens, it is essential that the client's needs are not overridden by the therapist's need to get the paper work in order and to tick all the necessary boxes. Even in this process, person-centred therapists should pay attention to their clients and respond with unconditional positive regard and empathic understanding. First-time clients and even ones with a good understanding of the therapeutic process tend to be uneasy and anxious at the first meeting with a therapist. If the therapist is over-concerned with gathering or passing information it is likely that the client will be deterred (because some of the client's more subtle or tentative expressions of need are missed) and/or that they will miss something the therapist thinks is important. In these early stages, just as in an established therapeutic relationship, the therapist's primary responsibility is to enter the experienced world of clients in such a way as to meet them with genuineness, warmth and understanding.

58

CONTRACTING AND STRUCTURE IN PERSON-CENTRED THERAPY

As Tolan (2003: 129) notes, all relationships have rules and, of course, this includes the relationship between therapist and client in person-centred therapy. These rules include those to do with boundaries of time, space and allowable behaviour (from either party and between them), the issue of confidentiality and perhaps how and by whom payment will be made. These rules are about safeguarding the client and the therapist and perhaps about meeting the needs of the institution or organisation under the auspices of which therapy takes place. It only takes a moment to realise that at the outset, most of these rules are likely to be known by the therapist but not by the client. One of the initial tasks of therapy is to make them explicit and to agree how they will operate.

Imposing rules and conditions from the frame of reference of the therapist can seem like a contradiction of the principle of non-directivity and the autonomy of the client. However, although the terms 'person-centred' and especially 'client-centred' seem to imply an emphasis on the rights and desires of the client, this does not mean that this is to be achieved at the expense of the rights of the therapist. It is the relationship which is the agent for change and this involves two people. A healing relationship will only be created when the needs of both parties are met. One of the duties of person-centred therapists is to ensure their continued well-being so that they are able to be available as congruent, empathic and accepting people to all their clients. This means that they must structure their sessions in such a way as to preserve and protect themselves while still being fully available to their clients. This is one of the things boundaries are for. That said, there is room for flexibility in person-centred therapy and rules are not necessarily rigidly imposed once and for all. Person-centred therapy is a process of negotiation and re-negotiation. It is the co-creation of a healing relationship. However, it is the task of the therapist to lay down the ground on which this co-creation can proceed.

From the moment of first contact with a client, it is incumbent on person-centred therapists to make an explicit statement of the 'rules' which will govern the relationship. This includes obvious things like where and when meetings will occur and for how long, payment, what to do about cancellations and so on. This is what Tolan (2003: 130) calls the 'business contract' but she also draws attention to another aspect of contracting, the 'therapeutic contract'. By addressing the needs and expectations of the client and the role of the therapist, this involves the beginnings of the equalisation of power deemed desirable in person-centred therapy. In the beginning stages of therapy, the therapist has a lot more knowledge about what is likely to happen and how it may happen than does the client. Knowledge is power. One way of ameliorating this imbalance is to 'demystify' the process of therapy by explaining something of what will happen including the responsibilities of the therapist.

Because (by definition) clients are vulnerable or anxious they are unlikely to take in every aspect of what they are told about the contract they are embarking on in a 'contracting session' so it is good practice to have at least the essential points in the form of an information sheet. This sheet can be given to the client before the first meeting, during it or at the end but whenever this happens the client can be encouraged to read it and to ask questions about its contents. The person-centred therapist's job is then to respond to the things that the client asks about but not necessarily to go into detail about what is not questioned. However, these may be raised later and should, of course, be addressed then.

However it is done and whatsoever its content, the contracting session is not something which stands outside therapy proper – it does not occur *before* establishing a therapeutic relationship, it is part of the process of doing this. Therefore, even the 'business' aspects of contract setting are conducted in accord with the necessary and sufficient conditions. It is very likely that even in this process clients will be communicating something of their needs and/or ways of being – this is to be responded to appropriately.

59

ASSESSMENT IN PERSON-CENTRED PRACTICE

Alongside the contracting process, the initial stages of the person-centred therapeutic relationship will involve some sort of assessment process. The theoretical arguments for and against assessment and diagnosis in the context of person-centred therapy were made earlier (Point 32). While diagnosis is seen as unnecessary, unhelpful and even potentially harmful to the course of person-centred therapy, assessment of the client is viewed similarly. However, in practice many, if not most, person-centred practitioners do make an assessment of the likelihood that they will be able to offer a relationship including Rogers' six conditions to the particular client, at the particular time, in the particular place even if they call it something else. This is something other than diagnosis and the emphasis is on the (potential) relationship not the client. Under the right circumstances, the client will make constructive personality changes. Any limitation to this prospect is more likely to lie with the therapist and, in a way, part of person-centred assessment is the gauging of the therapist's ability by the therapist.

One way of assessing the likelihood of successful person-centred therapy is for the responsible therapist to ask a series of questions based on the necessary and sufficient conditions. Thus:

1. Are my potential client and I capable of establishing and maintaining contact?

2. Is my potential client in need of *and* able to make use of therapy? That is to say, is my potential client in a state of incongruence and vulnerable and/or anxious?
3. Can I be congruent in the relationship with my potential client?
4. Can I experience unconditional positive regard for this potential client?
5. Can I experience an empathic understanding of the potential client's internal frame of reference?
6. Will my potential client perceive at least to a minimal degree my unconditional positive regard and empathy?

If the answer to one or more of these questions is 'no' then the necessity for the six conditions has not been met and, by definition, therapeutic change will not occur. Under these circumstances it is incumbent on the person-centred practitioner to address the shortcoming, perhaps in supervision or, if the unlikelihood of offering an appropriately effective relationship persists, to decline the contract. This is assessment.

An additional aid to assessment lies in the seven stages of process (Point 17). These indicate a client's likely way of being and so what is appropriate from the therapist. Although there is a great deal of variation and individual difference in clients' processes and no one is ever wholly at one stage or another, nevertheless knowing something about the client's stage of process can help the therapist make appropriate ethical and professional decisions.

The stages of process imply that there are qualitative differences and differences of intent required of the therapist dealing with clients at different stages. For example, people in stages 1 and 2 are unlikely to willingly enter therapy or, if they do, are unlikely to stay. People in stage 3 are likely to commit to a counselling contract but perhaps without fully understanding the implications. Such clients need to be fully accepted as they are if they are to progress to subsequent stages. It is probable that empathic responses confined to the client's apparent and current experiencing are likely to be most effective. People in stages 4 and 5 constitute the bulk of clients. They have some insight and an agenda for change. Here, responding to edge of awareness material (Point 22) and working at relational depth (Point 38) become possible and 'presence' (Point 25) may spontaneously occur. Stage 6 is highly crucial. It is at this stage that irreversible constructive personality change is most likely to occur. The full repertoire of the person-centred practitioner is appropriate to this stage. By stage 7, the journey is more or less over – or at least it can now take place without the companionship of a therapist. Reaching a judgement about these things is assessment and requires appropriate action.

Together, the necessary and sufficient conditions and the seven stages of process provide an appropriate practical assessment scheme for person-centred therapy. They provide a guide to:

- deciding the likelihood of establishing a successful therapeutic endeavour;
- monitoring the process of therapy;
- the nature of appropriate therapist responses and ways of being (although this is less important).

While it is important to remember that these are guidelines and that every relationship is unique requiring unique responses, they are essential to sound person-centred practice.

60

ESTABLISHING TRUST

Person-centred therapy is predicated on trust. First there is the axiomatic basic trust in the person as of worth and propelled by the actualising tendency to achieve potential. In other words, clients are to be trusted – given the right climate, they will do what they need to do as and when they need to do it. (The prime requirement of person-centred therapists is to establish this trust in the potential of others. It is to this end (and others) that training in the approach and attention to personal growth are directed (Points 53 and 56). The belief that the necessary and sufficient conditions are precisely that is fundamental to person-centred therapy. From this follows a trust in the process of therapy. Sometimes this is expressed glibly as 'trust the process' but this shouldn't be taken to imply a laissez-faire attitude is good enough. As Tudor and Merry (2002: 145) point out, it is also necessary to 'process the trust'. Trusting the process is about full engagement with and an understanding of what is happening and about being actively facilitative. However, it is a given that, for person-centred therapy to work, person-centred therapists must trust their clients, the process and themselves. But it is also true that the client must be equally trusting of the same elements. It is unlikely that clients will have a realistic trust in the therapist and the process of therapy when they first present and certainly not in their organismic experiencing (otherwise they wouldn't need therapy). Therefore 'establishing trust' is something to be addressed in the early stages of the therapeutic relationship.

Trust is important in the therapeutic relationship because it allows greater openness and less defensiveness. Trust is the precursor to change. However, trust cannot be engendered in the client by the therapist at will. To use a cliché, trust must be earned and the way that person-centred therapists do this is to be trustworthy. Trustworthiness is a product of the therapist conditions of congruence ('I am as I appear'), unconditional positive regard ('I see and accept you as you are') and empathic understanding ('I accurately sense how it is to be you'). Given these attitudes, clients will come to realise that the therapist does not intend to manipulate them into doing something and that acceptance is not conditional. Clarity about the nature of the 'business contract' (Point 58) underpinning the therapeutic relationship is also part of the process of becoming trustworthy. Stating the boundaries of therapy and holding to them is about trust. Explaining the likely process of therapy and the role of both therapist and client (the therapeutic contract) deals with some of the uncertainty and fears the client may have. This too helps with trustworthiness. Any attempt to address the initial power imbalance between therapist and client will also help. This involves openness and honesty on the part of the therapist. However, for the client to recognise the trustworthiness of the therapist may be a slow process. After all, for many clients trust is a big issue. They may have learned that to trust others is dangerous and to have incorporated this into their self-concept. One way to facilitate the establishment of trust is to unconditionally accept the client's lack of trust.

To re-iterate, the establishment of trust is most likely to occur in response to the therapist's genuine acceptance, warmth and understanding. It is likely to be gradual and to increase as the experience of being accepted for whom and what they are becomes more apparent to the client. In response to this, the client will allow more experience into awareness and, as this too is accepted, so the trust will be yet deeper.

5.3

THE BASIC ATTITUDES UNDERPINNING PERSON-CENTRED PRACTICE

61

NON-DIRECTIVITY IN PRACTICE

Although much of what has been discussed in the previous section and much of what will come later is either implicitly or explicitly concerned with implementing a non-directive attitude in the practice of person-centred therapy, this is such an essential principle it is worth saying something specific about it. The theoretical position with respect to the non-directive attitude is examined in Point 5. What is important to remember is that being non-directive is to do with accepting clients as people of worth and the 'experts' on themselves and their ways of being in the world. However, this is not a mere philosophical stance but a practical position involving ethical implementation. It is also something about which myths and misunderstandings have arisen both outside and within the person-centred approach.

First, being 'non-directive' is not about being passive, merely parroting the client's words for fear of deflecting them from their subjective experience of the world. Being non-directive involves actively communicating an understanding of the client's lived experience. Consider the following client statement:

I really hate myself. I am thinking of ending it all. Don't you think that would be best?

The simplistic, misguided 'non-directive' response may be something like:

You hate yourself and are thinking of killing yourself and you wonder if I think that would be for the best.

However, a response more in line with the non-directive attitude would be:

> *You are really struggling at the moment and feel really bad about yourself. Things are so awful that you can see no future and are wondering if you'd be better off dead.*

Depending on what else had been expressed (tone of voice, posture, gesture, facial expression, etc.) a non-directive approach could include reference to emotions expressed other than in words:

> *You are really struggling at the moment and feel really bad about yourself. When you told me that, I could see tears in your eyes and there was a catch in your voice. Things are so awful that you can see no future and you are wondering if you'd be better off dead.*

In the latter response, nothing has been introduced from the therapist's frame of reference. Although there is what might be a reference to the client's emotional state it is either in the form of an observation (tears, a catch in the voice) or as a re-framing of the client's own words. It is possible to go further than this and to respond to the feelings expressed by the client by actually naming them but not going beyond them or to do so to a minimal extent:

> *You are really struggling at the moment and you are feeling hurt and in pain. You're so desperate and desolate that you wonder if you'd be better off dead.*

This can be an effective way of doing therapy but it still isn't quite what is meant by 'being non-directive'.

Ideally, and, to be honest, not always practically, being non-directive involves the therapist in actively experiencing and responding to the experienced world of the client. It really is the walking in someone else's shoes sometimes used as a metaphor for the person-centred counselling process. It is about being with and within the client's experience rather than observing it. This involves high-quality attention to the entire client and leaves no room for analysis, diagnosis and the like from the therapist. It is about implementing the therapist-provided conditions in their entirety and in concert.

As Brodley (2006: 46) pointed out, being non-directive in person-centred therapy is not about behaving in a set way but it is an attitude. While being non-directive does not permit all forms of behaviour (specifically those to do with imposing the therapist's frame of reference on the client) it does allow many and various responses to the client depending upon the client's expressed experience (whether or not that expression is in words).

Although I take a (slightly?) different view as to what is 'given', when it comes to being non-directive Grant's (2010: 225) dictum 'take only what is given' is a good yardstick when practising non-directively.

62

CLIENTS ARE THE EXPERTS ON THEMSELVES AND ARE ACTIVE AGENTS IN THEIR OWN GROWTH AND HEALING

Research evidence indicates that, in the process of therapeutic change, much of what happens is as a result of the client's contribution (see, for example, Bohart 2004; Bohart and Tallman 1999, 2010). This can be in the form of the client/therapist relationship and/or what are sometimes called 'extratherapeutic variables' which include such things as the client's resources. That is to say, as well as responding to the therapist's congruently expressed unconditional positive regard and empathy, clients are somehow actively contributing to their process of constructive personality change. In effect, therapy is a collaborative effort and not something the therapist does to or for the client. Indeed, it may even be that the client is doing most of the active work.

How this seems to work is that clients are good at making positive use of nearly everything that happens in a therapy session. They do this, for example, by looking beyond the superficial things that are said or done and respond to the more consistent and stable attitudes and values of the therapist and they make positive use of whatever they can. They do this in their own way, regardless of what the therapist may have intended. For example, as a counselling student, I witnessed a group therapist react very angrily and (apparently) unacceptingly towards a client. He shouted at her, called her a wimp and was generally rather aggressive and confrontational. However, in the course of the diatribe he said 'Has it ever occurred to you that just because your mother was mad it doesn't mean you are?' While I expected the client to be damaged by the process and to feel unheard, she seemed positively buoyed up and even glowed. What I suspect happened is that she didn't 'hear' all the confrontational, attacking stuff but she did hear the deeply accepting statement of her worth and sanity. She made constructive use of the bit of the interaction that served her purpose.

Also, there are times when clients will steer therapists in the direction they need to go. This is perhaps most commonly done by responding to only the part of a therapist's voicing of empathy and positive regard – perhaps even twisting it a little. In such cases it is imperative that the therapist picks up on the client's hint. This is not always as simple as it sounds and requires a super-sensitivity ('What of the things I said has my client actually responded to?') and a willingness to let go of the ideas formulated as to the client's experience regardless of how accurate these may seem to be (see Point 63).

As Sanders (2006b: 92) points out, that clients can make use of poor responses is not an excuse for poor practice. The point is that clients do not simply passively receive what the therapist puts before them but are active agents in its receipt and processing. Clients recover, grow, heal even when they don't seem to be doing what psychotherapeutic theory says they should. In every way, the client is in charge. The implication for practice is that, yes, it is necessary to be non-directive and to communicate the therapist-provided conditions but most importantly the therapist's job is to trust the client to run the change process in their own way and not to obstruct or hinder them in that. However, this does work better in a climate in which the six necessary and sufficient conditions are present.

63

THE PERSON-CENTRED THERAPIST'S JOB IS TO FOLLOW WHEREVER THE CLIENT LEADS, PUTTING ASIDE THEORETICAL UNDERSTANDING AND ANY OTHER 'EXPERT' KNOWLEDGE

Although it follows from the whole concept of the non-directive attitude, it is worth emphasising that, whatever experience and knowledge person-centred therapists bring to the practice, their job is to immerse themselves in the client's experience and to respond to that and only that. Theory and knowledge inform practice and they can be helpful in preparing therapists and sustaining them but they must not get in the way of paying high-quality attention to what the client is saying and experiencing. When as therapists we 'know' something about what our client is going through, has experienced and is likely to experience we can become distracted from what they are actually telling us and/or experiencing in our presence. This runs counter to what person-centred theory tells us is likely to be helpful. What is helpful is to track the client's experience as closely as possible and to trust that, if you do this, the clients will do what they need to do. Perhaps the best way to illustrate this is by a story.

When I was training as a therapist I had a client from West Africa. In our first session she told me a story of multiple loss. She had recently miscarried, a close relative had died and she was far from her family and culture. I was mentally rubbing my hands. This was about loss and grieving. I knew about the grief process – I had read the books and attended the lectures. All my client had to do was to tell me her story as a way of facilitating her progress through the stages of grief and she would be fine.

My client came to the second session and I expectantly waited for her to tell me about her losses. She didn't. After a few brief words, her head went down and nothing more was said. I knew about silence, silence is good. After half an hour I was less sure of this. Surely my client wasn't making use of her time with me? Shouldn't she be experiencing and processing her grief? I gently informed her that we were halfway through the session. She looked up and smiled sadly but said nothing. Her head went down once more. With five minutes to go, I spoke again. Still nothing but a sad smile. At the end of the session, we made another appointment. OK, I thought, surely next time we will get to the meat of what she needs to do.

The next and subsequent sessions passed in exactly the same way. I began to question my abilities as a therapist. I must be doing something wrong because this wasn't going at all the way the books said it would. This was confirmed for me in our tenth session at the end of which my client said that she wouldn't be coming any more. She had exams and she thought she should apply herself to them. I thought she was letting me down gently for clearly I hadn't helped her grieve.

About a month after our last session, my client came to find me bearing a gift. She told me how wonderful I had been and that she had passed her exams with flying colours. This was all due to me. I was a bit taken aback but I thought about our process together. Of course, I have no idea what actually happened for my client (and it doesn't really matter exactly what was helpful) but the way I have explained it to myself is that she was using the time we spent together to return to her homeland in her imagination and that I was somehow a companion on that journey. To her, there was something important about the time to reflect and the companionship.

Whatever the truth of the matter is, I learned a great deal about the power of paying attention, staying with the client's actual process and experience (rather than seeking to push in the direction of one that would be 'good' for the client) and the importance of letting go of my knowledge. The more I have practised, the more it has seemed to me that it is high-quality attention, really being with and tuning into how my client *is*, which matters as much as what I say. It seems to me that when my client knows I am really 'listening' with understanding and acceptance they benefit in some way. I guess I do this by watching and feeling as much as by hearing.

Of course theory is important as is an understanding of how clients might react to life events but it is more important to put the client before the knowledge.

5.4

THE NECESSARY AND SUFFICIENT CONDITIONS IN PRACTICE

64

THE NECESSARY AND SUFFICIENT CONDITIONS ARE ALL IT TAKES FOR SUCCESSFUL THERAPY

It is axiomatic that the necessary and sufficient conditions for constructive personality change are precisely that. Therefore, certainly from at least the classical client-centred position, all that is required of person-centred therapists is to ensure contact and, once it has been established, to hold the three therapist conditions in such a way as to allow their clients to perceive empathic understanding and unconditional positive regard. The primary way in which this is done is by 'checking perceptions'. The implicit question behind a majority of therapist responses is 'This is what I think you mean/how you feel/what you are experiencing ... have I got that right?' However, questions as such are not amongst the primary tools of person-centred therapists so they are more likely to check and communicate their understanding by conveying their sense of what has been said or their impression as to what the client is currently experiencing. 'You are sad' is probably a more effective response than 'I think you are telling me that you are sad. Am I right?' On the other hand, in person-centred terms, both are better than 'Are you sad?' and certainly than 'How do you feel about that?'. Crudely, this is the 'technique' of reflection. Often there is more concern with reflecting feelings than reflecting anything else but what the client is thinking is also of importance and deserves to receive a response. Certainly, even when the client is talking about past events, the primary focus of the therapist is on current experiencing – in the first instance that of the client but also (for a variety of reasons including monitoring congruence) their own. This does not mean that person-centred therapists ignore historical accounts of either the 'When I was a kid ...' or 'On my way here ...' kind and all things between but rather just as the client is telling the story from the perspective of the present, so the therapist responds to it in and from the present ideally picking up on just what the client is experiencing with respect to the story being told.

In reality, the process of person-centred therapy and the response of the person-centred therapist are a lot more sophisticated than simply 'reflecting' the client's experiencing. For a start, because person-centred therapy is always about the particular individuals and the particular relationship, how this is done varies from relationship to relationship and, as the client moves through the seven stages of process (Point 17), over time. Responses of different kinds may be required to accord with the therapist's different reactions to the client's material. Although many person-centred therapists would see empathic responses as the primary tool in person-centred therapy, there may be times when, perhaps in order to maintain or regain congruence, a response of a different kind is necessary. This section is about how the necessary and sufficient conditions are implemented and just how sophisticated this can be.

65

CONTACT IN PRACTICE

The first of the necessary and sufficient conditions is that the therapist and the client are in (psychological) contact. This is defined as each making at least a minimal impression on the experiential field of the other. For most of us, most of the time, this can be taken as a given. We almost always know when we are in the presence of another person and are taking at least some note of who, how and what they are, what they are doing and how all this impinges on us. We are also likely to have some awareness of how we are affecting the other person. However, this does not mean that, in person-centred practice, contact can be assumed and neglected – it is something to be deliberately cultivated and the acknowledgement of the client by the therapist is fundamental to successful therapy. Also, there are different degrees of contact and the depth of contact will influence or guide the manner in which the therapist responds to the client. As Sanders (2013: 15) says, 'the therapist has to *deliberately attend* [original emphasis] to making contact with the client'.

In the normal course of events, there is an immediate mutuality to contact. It involves recognition and acknowledgement by each of the other. Coming into contact is entering a relationship. It is through contacting others that we are able to perceive ourselves as meaningfully present, the acknowledgement of another confirms our actuality. This is one of the reasons why contact is fundamental to effective therapy.

In the normal course of events, contact between individuals occurs via a variety of channels. Everything we do or say is a communication and communication involves contact. The way we dress, how we sit or stand, our facial expressions and gestures, even our scent as well as what we say contribute to contact. Even in our words there are a number of things that influence contact. Tone of voice, accent, para-verbal expression ('ummm', 'ahhhh' and so on) and the pace of our speech all contribute to the seemingly simple but actually complex process of contact. At least to some extent, the practice of person-centred therapy involves the therapist in paying attention to each of these things – and probably others. However, to add to the complicated nature of contact, it is important that it is congruent. It is a mistake to (for example) speak in a soft, mild tone in the interests of 'contact' if this does not accord with the therapist's inner state or to 'dress down' (or dress up) in order to 'fit in' when this is too different from the therapist's normal way of being. So, the way each of us contacts others and is available to be contacted is personal. Contact is best assured by being true to one's nature. Also, how contact is ensured and conveyed will vary from relationship to relationship and with time in any particular relationship. Thus, there are no definitive rules about how to contact another other than that it involves acknowledging their presence and being opened to being contacted by them. In person-centred therapy, it involves the development of shared meaning and the co-creation of a working relationship. However, there can be obstacles to initiating and/or maintaining contact and the effectiveness of therapy may relate to its depth.

66

THE THERAPIST'S AVAILABILITY FOR CONTACT

It is a fact of human nature that most of us, at times, are limited in our availability for contact and our willingness to receive another. Sometimes this is because we have burdens of our own that responding to the needs of another would seem to increase so it is easier, even on the face of it necessary, to screen others out, for example, when we are tired or ill or immersed in our own psychological or emotional processes. Sometimes it is about being unaccepting of another's way of being, deciding that they are mad, bad or sad and that we want nothing to do with them. We may (for example) block contact or at least limit its depth when we are confronted by behaviour of which we disapprove, when the person before us provokes fear or connects us with our prejudices or when we are afraid that being seen will lead us to being rejected. All of these things limit availability for what Cameron (in Tolan 2003: 87–92) calls 'basic contact'.

While it is probably true that the client almost always makes at least a minimal impression on the experiential field of the therapist, it is also true that there are times when we are liable to bring such attitudes with us into the therapy room. This brings person-centred therapists a responsibility to monitor their availability for contact and, when it is or may become limited, to address whatever might block it. This is about attending to well-being through, for example, ensuring sufficient rest and recreation, continual attention to personal and professional growth and, perhaps above all, getting good supervision.

As well as things that may interfere with or limit basic contact, there are things that may interrupt the process. These (after Cameron, p. 92) include:

- distracting thoughts about things outside the session ('What shall I have for tea?');
- concern about being a good enough therapist ('Was that a good response?');
- or, conversely, self-congratulation ('Wow – I was really empathic just then!');
- feeling shocked ('You did what!');
- identification ('When that happened to me …');
- feeling attracted to the client ('I really fancy you – I wish we could …');
- interpreting/analysing the client ('Although you haven't said so, that sounds to me like you have been abused');
- irritation or annoyance ('You're whining again and I'm getting pissed off').

Such interruptions to the ongoing flow of contact are a normal part of relating to others. However, the role of person-centred therapist brings with it a responsibility to monitor and address such things. Mostly this is about catching the distracting thought or feeling and getting back on track there and then. This may involve a congruent response – that is an open owning of the distraction – 'When you told me that I was shocked' or 'I'm very sorry but I drifted off into my own thoughts then' because it is likely that the client noticed something was amiss. Alternatively, particularly if there is a pattern to the failure to maintain contact then noting what occurs, when it occurs and what happens as a result and addressing this in supervision or personal therapy is probably the way forward.

67

THE CLIENT'S AVAILABILITY FOR CONTACT

By definition, clients for person-centred therapy are incongruent, being vulnerable or anxious. This may very well limit their ability for sustained contact – certainly contact at depth (but note that the basic hypothesis does not require 'depth' of contact and there are differences of opinion about the quality of contact). In some cases, the potential client may be in a state or have a way of being that prevents meaningful contact. This is where pre-therapy and contact work come into their own. These are dealt with separately (Points 34 and 68). Clients who have the capacity for contact but for whom it is (temporarily) difficult can be facilitated in the direction of deeper and more sustained contact.

A client's availability for contact may be limited or impeded by the nature of their current experiencing. Anger, fear or a sense of being swamped by events can all result in a tendency to withdraw and act in a guarded fashion. Likewise, a client under the influence of alcohol or one or more other drugs (prescribed or otherwise) may be distant or remote, appearing to be cut off from experiencing their current environment, giving the therapist the impression that they are not quite in the world (or at least the same world as the therapist although Cameron (2012a: 122) takes the view that being 'under the influence' does not completely rule out sufficient contact). For some maintaining distance from others or limiting contact is a response to conditions of worth. Allowing other people close is dangerous, perceived as threatening. And just as therapists may be limited in their availability for contact by physical and emotional ailments, so it is with clients. Exhaustion – even everyday tiredness, virus infections, ill-health, worry about a third party and emotional disturbances of many kinds (for example, depression, anxiety, panic or the numbness brought about by bereavement or trauma) – may also inhibit contact. In each and any of these cases, it is up to the person-centred therapist to act in such a way as to enhance the contact.

Often, communicating the close attention the therapist is paying to the client will at least begin to deepen contact. Responding empathically in such a way as to recognise the lack of contact may be helpful – a response such as 'You seem distracted and caught up in your thoughts' may very well help the client come back into contact. Sometimes a process comment may be helpful: 'When we talk about … I lose my sense of you and what is going on for you' may help the client contact the reality of loneliness and isolation. However, it is really important to realise that a silent, withdrawn client is not necessarily a client out of contact. For example, in the course of my training, I had a client who, week after week, apart from a few words at the beginning of the session and 'goodbye' at the end spent the whole session in silence, scarcely even responding to my reminders of the passing of time ('We are halfway through our time now', 'We have five minutes'). She decided to halt her time with me because she had forthcoming exams. I thought she was letting me down gently. Clearly, I had been no use to her. After the exam period, my client came to find me – she told me that I had been wonderful, I was the reason she made it to and through her exams (she passed with flying colours) and that she couldn't thank me enough for my efforts. Whatever else was going on for my client, it is clear that she was aware of my presence (I made at least a minimal impression on her experiential field) and that it was important to her.

The story above indicates some of the difficulty of assessing the client's availability for and degree of contact. It is a judgement call, one that perhaps improves with experience but which even experienced therapists can get wrong. Ultimately, it is for the client to judge if there is a sufficient degree of contact. Nevertheless, when the therapist is in doubt about mutual contact, it is important to respond to that sense (empathically, congruently, with a process comment). It should not be ignored but responses should be tentative, gentle and encouraging, never compelling the client to contact of a kind they do not desire or need. If the client really is out of contact, it may be worthwhile making simple contact reflections (Points 34 and 65) but this should not be confused with 'doing pre-therapy'.

68

CONTACTING THE 'UNAVAILABLE' CLIENT – CONTACT IMPAIRMENT AND PRE-THERAPY OR CONTACT WORK

Although there are acute causes to the limitation of the ability for contact, these can be worked with in the 'normal' person-centred way (Point 64). However, there are clients for whom their unavailability for contact is a chronic condition. Such clients may include those with severe learning difficulties, serious mental disturbance or both. For such clients pre-therapy or 'contact work' may be suitable therapeutic strategies (Point 34). However, although pre-therapy can sound deceptively simple it is actually difficult to do well.

Apart from that it is more difficult to do than it seems, perhaps the first thing to realise about pre-therapy is that although its founder, Garry Prouty, referred to his way of working with clients as a series of 'techniques' this does not mean that they can be applied in a detached, mechanistic way. Pre-therapy is a person-centred way of working and, as such, its efficacy is predicated on the assumption that it is in the therapeutic relationship that constructive change occurs. Responsibilities of the pre-therapy practitioner additional to those incumbent on any person-centred therapist and in addition to using techniques are given by Sanders (2007c: 21–22).

The practitioner:

* assumes full responsibility for contacting the client;
* validates the client's experience (including, for example, psychotic experience);

- values the importance of the client's expressions;
- recognises that e.g. hallucinations and delusions are meaningful;
- acknowledges the client's self-autonomy process towards meaningful experience;
- contributes to the client's healing process.

In essence, the objective of pre-therapy is to encourage clients towards contact with self, the world and others. Therapists and contact workers do this by offering contact. This is a slow, reiterative process requiring discipline and patience. In contact work, everything the client does is important and so it is necessary to pay close attention to expressions of all kinds (for example, grimaces, tugging at clothing, kicking the furniture, smiling, staring), posture (for example, slouching, self-hugging, crossing and uncrossing legs), words (no matter how random and unconnected they appear to be) and para-language (for example, grunts, humming, screams, clicking noises) and so much more. The worker's task is to respond to what the client does by making contact reflections (see Point 34).

Sanders (2007d: 30) points out that pre-therapy work proper is very demanding of the practitioner for the (slightly adapted) following reasons:

- It is a special sort of communication for special circumstances.
- It can be embarrassing or awkward to use contact reflections at first.
- It requires time and patience, since it can sometimes take a long time to produce noticeable results.
- People already qualified as helping professionals will almost certainly have problems in scaling down their responses to the minimalist, concrete responses necessary for successful contact work.
- Some of the time spent doing contact work can be in silence, or at a slow tempo to match the lived experience of the client which may add to the awkwardness for people unused to silent or slow-paced attention-giving (although, paradoxically, sometimes the client's behaviour can be extremely rapid).

- When helpers get involved in the process with their client they can forget to keep it very simple and absolutely basic in the heat of the moment.

It is beyond the scope of this book to give a full account of doing pre-therapy. Sanders (2007f) and Van Werde and Prouty (2013: 327–342) provide introductions but, for anyone wishing to use pre-therapy in their work, there is no substitute for good training.

69

DEALING WITH CLIENT INCONGRUENCE

One of the most important things to remember when faced with an incongruent client is that is how they are *supposed* to be. To put it another way, it is a *sense* of their incongruence (manifesting as vulnerability and/or anxiety) that brings clients to therapy or, as Sanders (2006b: 43) puts it, 'the client needs help, and knows it'. This is in accord with the second of the necessary and sufficient conditions and recognising and accepting client incongruence is a fundamental task of person-centred therapy.

Incongruence results from a gulf between the perceived self and the actual experience of the total organism and, in fact, person-centred therapy is about increasing (or bringing about) harmony between self and experience, the inner world and the outer such that they are in accord and situations evaluated and choices made in line with a personal valuing system rather than an introjected one. Introjected value systems give rise to conditions of worth and these are seen as a principal cause of incongruence (Point 12).

Incongruence and conditions of worth can take many forms. They may impede or limit the client's ability to make psychological contact and likewise the ability to perceive communication from others in an undistorted way. Points 65 and 68 deal with the enhancement or repair of contact and these can be seen as ways of addressing client incongruence.

A way of viewing incongruence is to see it as arising from a lack of (or insufficient) unconditional positive regard. Conditions of worth result from conditional positive regard from a significant other. Because conditions of worth disturb a person's internal evaluating process it prevents movement towards the state of being 'fully functioning'. This, by definition, results in incongruence. Thus the 'corrective' for incongruence is the consistent perception of unconditional positive regard from a significant other. In the context of person-centred therapy, it is the role of the therapist to provide this unconditional positive regard. In a nutshell, the unconditional positive regard of the therapist facilitates the unconditional positive self-regard of the client who is thus no longer incongruent. So, unconditional positive regard is seen by at least some person-centred therapists as the curative factor in therapy (see, for example Bozarth 1998: 83 and Wilkins 2000: 33–34). When it is experienced from one person to another it overturns conditions of worth and promotes congruence.

To summarise, person-centred therapists deal with client incongruence not (usually) by confronting it or challenging it but by unconditionally accepting clients as they are in a climate of their own congruence and empathic understanding. This is what the next few Points are about.

70

BEING CONGRUENT OR INTEGRATED IN THE RELATIONSHIP AS A THERAPIST

The third of the necessary and sufficient conditions requires the person in the role of the therapist to be congruent or integrated *in the relationship*. The first thing to understand about this is it is not a requirement to be some sort of permanently perfect being. Person-centred therapists are not expected and certainly not obliged to be completely congruent in all their dealings, all the time. Rogers (1959: 215) was very clear about that, going so far as to say that if it were indeed so there would be no therapy (because it would demand an impossible level of perfection). There is a recognition that therapists are limited in their ability to be congruent. Indeed, it may even be that part of being congruent is the acknowledgement to one's self of all the imperfections and flaws that make us human and the acceptance of these. Whatever may be the case, the congruence required of person-centred therapists to be effective in their role is, strictly speaking, limited to that role.

The second important thing about being congruent is that it is precisely that – it is about *being* totally yourself and fully present without façade and not necessarily (and certainly not usually) *doing* something. In person-centred theory, congruence is defined in terms of the distinction between self and experience *not* in terms of therapist behaviour. Brodley (2001: 59) emphasises the relational nature of congruence, stating that it is about the relation between the contents of experience and the symbols representing the contents but it is not the contents per se. To restate and reframe that, being congruent in the relationship does not call for action but an openness to experience (internal and external) *is* required. This includes an open and honest acceptance of the things that conflict with being a 'good' therapist such as fear of the client, fear of failing the client, becoming absorbed in one's own thoughts, losing concentration and so on.

In terms of classical person-centred theory, the third important thing about congruence is that there is no requirement that it is communicated to or perceived by the client. However, the therapist's congruence probably 'works' because it results in the client's perception of the therapist as someone who is authentic and thus to be trusted. An authentic therapist is one whose unconditional positive regard and empathic understanding can be received and believed. Certainly, because it throws doubt on those same therapist attitudes, it is assumed that the perceived incongruence of the therapist, albeit as a vague, uncomfortable feeling rather than as a conscious thought, is counter-productive. This is because when, for example, the therapist is irritated with the client but unaware of it or suppressing it then this directly contradicts attempts to convey unconditional positive regard and empathic understanding. Such contradictory messages, however subtly received, confuse clients and tend to make them distrustful. Even so, momentary lapses in concentration or judgement that (almost inevitably) occur in practice, if accurately symbolised in awareness, can be recognised and owned by the therapist and, if necessary or advisable, admitted to the client and so are unlikely to be disruptive of the therapeutic process. Indeed in most cases such fleeting distractions, preoccupations or failures in unconditional positive regard are not perceived by others. They remain a part of the private inner processes of the therapist. As long as they are not distorted or denied it is probable that no great harm results. Such lapses are part of being a fallible human being; however, especially if there is a pattern to them, it is well worth reflecting on them and taking them to supervision or addressing them in personal therapy.

The congruence of the therapist offers the client the genuine reaction of another person who can be trusted and who honours the client's value system rather than imposing their own. This is extraordinarily powerful; at its fullest, it is the meeting of the deepest, most real, most vibrant and vital self of the therapist with the client – it is encounter (see Point 31) in the truest sense and it is of great potency in the client's quest for transformation.

71

DEVELOPING AND ENHANCING THERAPIST CONGRUENCE

In many ways, because it is about being rather than doing and therefore the 'skills' element to be learned and practised is minimal or non-existent, developing congruence appears to be difficult particularly to therapists in the early stages of their career. Indeed, becoming acquainted with the flow of internal experience and how that matches outward expression is a demanding task. However, because congruence is about the relation between experience and its symbolisation it is really a matter of self-awareness and self-acceptance. Developing congruence is about learning to acknowledge all your internal responses without distorting or denying them – in the context of the practice of person-centred therapy perhaps especially those you have in response to your client regardless of whether or not they fit your preconception as to what it means to be a good therapist. So, it is at least partly about learning to listen for and become aware of all the thoughts and feelings you have in relationship with a client. As Tolan (2003: 45) points out, the second thing is to learn when and how to communicate that awareness to your client.

For a person-centred therapist, being self-aware means that all thoughts, feelings, sensations and intuitions are available to consciousness. For most of us, developing self-awareness is a never-ending task. In this context, self-awareness means that therapists' feelings are available to their consciousness. However, being congruent is not about turning your gaze inward and concentrating on your own experience for that would defeat the very object of person-centred therapy. Rather, it is about trusting yourself and being enough at ease with yourself to allow the free-flowing of your experience *while* you concentrate on the lived experience of another. This is something which can be developed and enhanced.

Perhaps it is stating the obvious to point out that the degree to which we can be self-aware and therefore congruent is limited by our self-acceptance, our ability to offer unconditional positive self-regard. So, the first way to develop congruence is to pay attention to our own personal development. Personal development can be understood as attending to personal needs in such a way as to increase the ability to be with clients in a safe way and which incrementally improves effectiveness. It is about dealing with blind spots and resistance so that the therapist is better able to accompany the client on what may be a painful and challenging journey without blocking them because they seek to enter areas that are frightening or painful for the therapist. For person-centred therapists as for therapists of many other stripes a recognised way of doing this is to engage in personal therapy. This can be of the 'normal' one-to-one one hour a week kind but alternatives such as group therapy or occasional residential sessions may do just as well. It is a question of preference, availability and cost. As well as personal therapy, supervision, debate and discussion with colleagues, reflective writing or journal keeping, reading and some form of meditation or spiritual practice may severally or together serve to aid the enhancement of congruence.

Personal development is helpful in increasing the capacity to be congruent; however, even for those with an enhanced capacity to be congruent in the therapeutic relationship there are advantages to taking deliberate steps to lay aside petty distractions, clearing the mind of the issues of the day (what to have for dinner, personal relationships and so on). Leijssen (2001: 151–155) recommends 'clearing a space' and describes an exercise to achieve this. By 'clearing a space' she means paying attention to your own world in such a way as to allow your own concerns to fade into the background thus preparing yourself for contact with clients.

72

MAKING CONGRUENT RESPONSES

At least for some therapists who identify with the classical client-centred approach to therapy, for therapists to make responses from their own frames of reference should be rare if it happens at all. This is because anything but an empathic, 'checking perceptions' response may deflect clients from their own processes. That is, any response other than one that is in accord with the client's frame of reference and current experience is directive and therefore contrary to one of the principles of person-centred practice. However, there are other thoughts about this and it may be that, on occasions, therapists' willingness to express themselves *about their reaction to the client's experience* is helpful to their clients.

There are several ways in which this may be so. First, a response from the therapist's frame of reference (as long as it is about or enhancing of the relationship) can be experienced as 'humanising' the therapist and thus contributing to a sense of the therapeutic endeavour as a collaborative enterprise. A personal response can help dispel the mystique surrounding therapy and go some way towards the equalisation of power. Second, if the therapist has feelings towards the client other than unconditional positive regard, particularly if these are distracting and/or persistent, it *may* be helpful to openly own them. This is because feelings such as irritation or boredom may in any case have already been picked up by the client and masking them may be experienced as incongruent and unaccepting and because sometimes naming the therapist's feeling is what clears it. However, the notion of responding 'congruently' should not be taken as licence for self-disclosure other than of the most limited and relevant kind. When they are appropriate, congruent responses are genuinely felt reactions to the client's current experience and only that. Also, note that congruence per se is different from what Tolan (2003: 54) calls 'authentic communication' (that is, making congruent responses) and that this in turn is different from self-disclosure or a 'willingness to be known' on the part of the therapist. Congruence is about being integrated in the therapeutic relationship; authentic communication is about the facilitative expression of the therapist's response to the client's current lived experience while self-disclosure is about therapists communicating their own experience from their own frames of reference. The latter may have a function in the therapeutic relationship ('When that happened to me ...' may be helpful in terms of willingness to be known) but, because the therapist's self-disclosure is a deflection from the client's process, it should be approached with caution. However, if the initiative comes in the form of questions from the client ('How old are you?', 'Are you married?') then it is probably best to answer briefly and honestly. But this has nothing to do with being congruent.

In their discussion of congruence, Mearns and Thorne (2007: 130–133) describe three ways in which a therapist may 'resonate' with a client's experience. First, there is self-resonance which is the reverberation of the therapist's own thoughts and feelings triggered by the client's account but not related to it in any other way. Second, there is empathic resonance as 'concordant' – the depiction as accurately as possible of the client's expressed experience (also called 'accurate empathy') and as 'complementary' which is when, as a response to an empathic sensing, the therapist adds something to the client's expressed experience perhaps delving into 'edge of awareness' material (see Point 22). Third, there is personal resonance in which the therapist (p. 131) 'includes her own responses, as a reasonable person, to the client's experiencing'. When making a personally resonant response, therapists are communicating their side of the relationship. It is a sharing of the therapist's personal, feeling reaction to the client's material in a way that is relevant to the client's process and consistent with a non-directive attitude. Mearns and Thorne (p. 131) are of the opinion that such responses encourage the client to move into relational depth (Point 38).

73

BEING YOURSELF, PSYCHOLOGICALLY MATURE AND PRACTISING ACCORDING TO YOUR PERSONAL STYLE: THE MULTIFACETED NATURE OF THERAPIST CONGRUENCE

Wyatt (2001b: 79–95) argues that congruence is complex and describes the therapist's congruence as 'multi-faceted'. In her view (pp. 84–85) the therapist's congruence comprises three core elements, each having implications for practice. These elements are:

- *Being myself*: Each of us has a unique way of being in the world and a task of person-centred practice is to bring this uniqueness into the therapeutic relationship rather than to hide behind a professional façade.
- *Psychological maturity*: Being integrated in the therapeutic relationship depends upon self-awareness (knowing and owning strengths and weaknesses, recognising that there is almost certainly more to discover), an ability for autonomous action while remaining a relational being and an ability to appreciate the person in the client role as equally autonomous and unique. In terms of person-centred theory, congruence relies on a flexible enough self-structure to allow most experiencing to be accurately symbolised in awareness – that is, denial and distortion are at minimal levels. Or, more simply, your degree of psychological maturity accords with the extent of your openness to experience.

- *Personal style of the therapist*: Because each of us is unique with our own way of being in the world, we are different in what we do and how we do it. This means that even though they share core theoretical beliefs and a commitment to non-directive practice, each person-centred practitioner will be different in the ways that they offer the therapist conditions and in their responses to clients. So, there is no 'right' way to do person-centred therapy except, within the framework of person-centred theory, to allow the natural development of a personal style. The way you practise in a person-centred way will be different from the way the next person does it. What is important is that there is harmony between how you are in the therapeutic relationship (which is at least subtly different from what you do – it is how you do things that result from your personal style) and the person-centred approach.

Wyatt (2001b: 85–93) goes on to describe the 'facets' of the therapist's congruence. Briefly, these are:

- *Being open to moment to moment experiencing*: The congruent therapist has a fluid enough self-concept to accurately symbolise most experience into awareness including experiences arising from the therapist's way of being, the client's way of being and the relationship between them. There are other sources, for example, experiences also result from sensory impressions of the environment. Openness to experience allows the therapist to make judgements about its potential significance to the client and the therapeutic relationship. For example, some experiences may reveal unconditional positive regard for and/or empathic understanding of the client while some may result in uncomfortable feelings or a sense of vulnerability. The latter indicate that incongruence has been triggered and this will probably need to be addressed in the session, in supervision, in personal therapy or in some combination thereof.
- *How to be with our incongruities*: At times every therapist is incongruent with a client. Such incongruence may be

the result of a lack of awareness of feelings or the resistance to communicating feelings of which the therapist is aware even if they are relevant to the client and the relationship. Whatever its nature, the therapist's incongruence relates to unresolved personal issues. These can be dealt with in personal therapy. However, with respect to dealing with incongruity in the ongoing therapeutic relationship, Wyatt (p. 87) writes of the importance of 'communicating … incongruency congruently'. This is to be done openly and honestly but with sensitivity towards the client and the client's process.

- *Genuine empathic understanding and unconditional positive regard*: The therapist's congruence ensures that empathy and unconditional positive regard will be perceived of as genuine. They are received in this way only when clients know that the therapists are genuinely interested in them and their experiences.
- *The therapist's behaviour*: How the therapist behaves towards the client directly influences the client's perception (not least of the therapist-provided necessary and sufficient conditions). Practising in accordance with a developed personal style and in a non-defensive way is at the heart of the therapist's congruence.
- *Limits and concerns regarding the therapist's expression*: Wyatt (pp. 91–92) asks 'what is appropriate therapist self-expression?' and notes that although it is impossible to delineate or codify them, there are always limits. Some therapist behaviour is inappropriate. The therapist's self-expression is returned to in Point 74.

74

THE THERAPIST'S SELF-EXPRESSION AND SELF-DISCLOSURE IN PERSON-CENTRED THERAPY

The issue of the degree to which person-centred therapists may express and disclose themselves in the person-centred relationship is contentious. However, there is general agreement that self-expression, self-disclosure and a 'willingness to be known' are different from congruence. What is certain is that, even under the (misunderstood) label of 'being congruent', there is no licence to 'tell it how it is' and the excuse 'I felt it so I said it' runs directly contradictory to person-centred practice. There is nothing in the necessary and sufficient conditions to indicate the desirability of the therapist responding to the client from the therapist's frame of reference and in classical client-centred therapy this would be done only exceptionally if at all. Also, an investigation by Barrett-Lennard (1998: 265) of the effect on the therapist's willingness to be known on the progress and success of therapy indicated no correlation – but it did show the importance of empathic understanding. Nevertheless, the issue of the therapist's self-disclosure to the client is constantly revisited and many take the view that, at times and in limited ways, this may be a useful thing to do. Just what to do and when to do it is debatable and there are no commonly agreed guidelines. Even Rogers himself can be considered inconsistent with respect to his views in this matter. Perhaps when and how to make responses from one's own frame of reference is something that arises from our personal style and it is for each of us to make up our minds about this facet of practice. To help, there are some key points.

Self-disclosure and self-expression are most likely to be helpful to the client and the therapeutic relationship when:

- they are relevant to the client and the client's current experiencing;
- they are a response to the client's experience;
- a reaction to the client is persistent and particularly striking.

From a classical client-centred position, Brodley (1999: 13–22) gives reasons why (p. 13) 'client-centered therapists may speak to their clients from their own frame of reference'. In brief, these include:

- *In response to questions and requests from the client* – to answer openly and honestly helps dispel mystique; however, therapists are entitled to privacy and it is sometimes OK to say 'I'm sorry but I don't want to tell you that because …'
- *When it seems that the client wishes to ask a question but does not directly voice it.*
- *To make an empathic observation* – that is, to express a perception of an aspect of the client's communication or emotional expression. Brodley (p. 15) distinguishes such a response from empathic understanding because it is rooted in the therapist's experience of the client rather than the client's current experience.
- *To correct for loss of acceptance or empathy or incongruence.*
- *To offer insights and ideas* – but only very occasionally and when it is clear that the insight relates to an issue the client is currently exploring and trying to understand and when there is explicit permission from the client. It is also wise to ask the client if the timing of the offer is appropriate.
- *In an emotionally compelling circumstance* – this refers to the impulsive emission of a personal emotional reaction from the therapist's frame of reference to the client's expressed experience. This is hazardous because the therapist's reaction may not accord with that of the client.

So, although person-centred therapists do sometimes make responses from their own frames of reference, this is something best done rarely and only with the intention to aid the client's therapeutic process. Even then, the principles of person-centred theory must be borne in mind. In general, if you have any doubt that a response from your own frame of reference will be helpful, don't make it.

75

DEVELOPING YOUR UNCONDITIONAL POSITIVE SELF-REGARD

The extent to which any of us can offer another unconditional positive regard relies directly on our ability to accept ourselves. Even though most of us embark upon training in person-centred therapy thinking of ourselves as accepting people, because of this, unconditional positive regard is the hardest of the therapeutic attitudes to develop. It cannot be effectively faked and tolerance (the ability to patiently endure or allow something) is no substitute. What we need to be effective in the role of person-centred therapist is positive self-regard.

According to Bozarth (1998: 84), it is unconditional positive self-regard that reunifies the self with the actualising tendency. One consequence of this is that there is a weakening of and loosening of the defences of distortion and denial and an amelioration of conditions of worth. In the context of the therapeutic relationship, because the defensive reactions of the therapist to the client's material are counter-therapeutic, it is necessary for person-centred therapists (and therapists of other kinds) to have unconditional positive self-regard; that is to prize, respect and feel warmth towards themselves. Unconditional positive regard for another comes from an understanding that everyone has a reason for what they do and how they are and the recognition that each of us is prompted by our actualising tendency to make the best possible choice given the circumstances as we experience them. It follows that unconditional positive self-regard means holding this attitude towards ourselves. Paradoxically, this may include an acceptance that we will sometimes fail to do so.

Successful person-centred therapy depends upon approaching clients without prejudice, with respect for whom and what they are and with recognition that they are self-determining persons. However, we each have values and opinions and few of us are without pain and shame so this can be very difficult. Because the therapist's unconditional positive self-regard is fundamental to a successful therapeutic relationship, it is imperative that person-centred therapists take positive, constructive steps to develop and maintain such an attitude towards themselves. Perhaps the first thing each of us needs to accept is that our ability to offer unconditional positive regard to others is limited and variable. The second is to discover these limits and what it is that causes us to vary in our ability to extend the attitude towards others (tiredness, personal difficulties, mood are each amongst several possibilities). Having discovered your limitations, seek to expand them (while working within them in the interim); having recognised the reasons for any variations in your ability, address them – perhaps through increased self-care. How to do all this is a matter of choice and opportunity. Personal therapy is a well-known and time-honoured route; joining a personal growth/self-development group may be helpful (not least because it will expose you to not only the foibles of others but because you will also learn something of how others see yours) but it might be that meditation or some other contemplative practice serves as well. Perhaps it matters less what you do as long as you do something to increase your self-acceptance, self-prizing and self-warmth.

76

DEVELOPING UNCONDITIONAL POSITIVE REGARD

In the previous point, the deep connection between unconditional positive regard for others and unconditional positive self-regard was explored. In a way, to separate the development of one from the other is artificial; they are inextricably linked. However, given that work continues on the latter, there are some things that can be done to promote the former.

First, it may help to re-examine and re-evaluate attitudes to practice and to clients. Rigid adherence to the conventions of practice and to the 'categorisation' of clients is often unconducive to unconditional positive regard. Certainly, it is worth critically appraising existing conventions of practice and developing a credulous attitude towards clients and the ways in which we behave towards them. Boundaries of all kinds are there to facilitate effective, safe working and not to dictate the course and shape of therapy regardless of the needs of the client and the therapist.

It is also worth monitoring attitudes towards clients. For example, any notion of the client as attention-seeking or manipulative has little to do with unconditional positive regard. If someone is attention-seeking doesn't that bespeak a deep need to be attended to? It isn't that in person-centred practice the communication of unconditional positive regard demands a permissive, laissez-faire, 'anything goes' attitude towards clients (far from it) but it may be that the uncritical acceptance of and rigid adherence to the structures and conventions of therapy sometimes runs counter to it.

Second, it is important to find ways of seeing the world as the client experiences it. I once had the task of working with a client who, at least seemingly, had very different attitudes and beliefs from my own at that time. He had a deep admiration for the military way of being and a love of the trappings of war. He also expressed deeply misogynistic and racist views. This was a real challenge. However, I knew that to be effective as his therapist I had to genuinely accept him. It wouldn't do for this to be faked and any limitation of my attitude would limit the success of therapy. As I listened and responded to him, I began to think about what life-experiences could have led him to such extreme views. The tale he told was of being brutalised as a child and 'robbed' of his home and possessions as a consequence of a messy and bitter divorce. Also, between sessions, I read about how prejudice may arise. Almost without noticing, I slipped from being challenged and repulsed by my client's views to an appreciation of him as a person of worth in spite of them. As this happened there was a softening – in him, in us and in me – and we moved to a relationship characterised by companionship and humour.

We were both changed by the process. I found that I had moved to a position of deeply embodying the knowledge that unconditional positive regard meant the issue of my approval or disapproval was irrelevant and immaterial. Each of us is doing the best we can and what is necessary to our continued existence even if, because of our lived experience and the way we perceive the world to be, this conflicts with the values of others. I also had an even deeper realisation that when my ability to accept another just as he was is challenged, it is my job to move myself to a position in which I can genuinely hear, respect, prize and feel warm towards the other. Or, if I cannot do this, to withdraw from the therapeutic contract (see Point 32 on person-centred assessment).

To summarise, the ability to develop and convey an attitude of unconditional positive regard depends on a willingness to approach each person as an individual with unique needs. This is not without tensions and, sometimes, these can only be resolved on a case-by-case basis. For example, if your unconditional positive regard is limited by ignorance (as was mine with respect to the origins of prejudice), take steps to learn. If there is something about your client's experience that scares or disquiets you or arouses your own unresolved issues, take this to personal therapy or supervision.

77

UNCONDITIONAL POSITIVE REGARD IN PRACTICE: PAYING ATTENTION TO THE WHOLE CLIENT

Unconditional positive regard for another involves recognising and attending to the whole person, hearing everything
that is said – and even recognising what is not said. This must
be done without judgement even if that judgement would be
'positive' or in agreement with the client's own estimation
or expressed attitude. Unconditional positive regard does not
(usually) involve the therapist in taking any position whatsoever with respect to the client's experience, views, reactions,
etc. except one of impartiality. UPR does not of itself involve
therapists in liking clients but it does mean the former prizing,
respecting and experiencing warmth towards the latter. There
is no need for the therapist to share the values or beliefs of the
client. Indeed, any sense of recognition ('She's just like me!')
or disagreement ('That's just plain wrong!') may interfere
with or inhibit unconditional positive regard – both positive
and negative personal reactions to the client and the client's
attitudes and lived experience have nothing to do with unconditional positive regard which can only be truly experienced
when these are set aside. To some extent, as difficult as it can
be, this is obvious. What is far trickier is avoiding what might
be thought of as responding with unconditional positive regard
to only part of the client's experience.

Tolan (2003: 71) writes about the 'partial hearing' of the client's material. 'Partial' has three meanings, existing only in part
(a bit of), favouring one side in a dispute (being biased) and having a liking for. Each of these is relevant to unconditional positive regard because each interferes with it. For example, paying

more attention to one bit of the client's experience than another (or others) may result in the client feeling unaccepted for the whole of who and what they are while favouring one of the client's views over another does much the same thing. 'Liking' your client for some of the ways they are is equally detrimental.

Clients often express themselves in complex and self-contradictory ways (see Tolan 2003: 71–73 for a good example). Hearing and accepting everything that is said is complicated but necessary. When the therapist responds to only one of the things the client expresses, even if that seems to be constructive and positive when others don't, is a failure of UPR and is likely to block the client's progress. Tolan's example is about the consequence of the therapist responding to the abused client's wish to leave her partner while not picking up on the love the woman feels for her abuser or her fear of having to make a fresh start elsewhere. Although as a concerned person any one of us might want to see an abused woman out of the hands of her abuser, as a person-centred therapist it is an aim to facilitate the client to make her own choices. This is most likely to happen when the client feels accepted (and acceptable) in her totality. However, such choices are rarely simple and easily made (if they were why would the client bring them to therapy?). For example, continuing with Tolan's example, if the abused woman were to leave her partner, she might be risking her status and acceptance in her own social circle or family. In some cultures there may even be a strong cultural imperative to stay.

Whatever the case, for the therapist to respond strongly to only part of what a client has said (whether approvingly or with apparent neutrality) is likely to result in the client feeling unheard and thus only conditionally accepted. In Tolan's example the abused woman may feel that if she does what the therapist appears to sanction (leaving her partner) she will be acceptable but that her tender feelings for him and her fears about *being* alone are not. She will not perceive the therapist's positive regard as unconditional therefore one of the necessary and sufficient conditions will not be met and constructive personality change will not occur.

78

UNCONDITIONAL POSITIVE REGARD IN PRACTICE: THE AVOIDANCE OF POSITIVE REINFORCEMENT AND PARTIALITY

Sometimes, one of the difficult things about unconditional positive regard is the avoidance of positively reinforcing aspects and attitudes of the client that seem beneficial and growth-promoting. While it is important to value and respect the client, this is very different from praising the client or confirming the client's thought, feeling or action. The latter involves making a judgement, is far from impartial and it is directive (because it points the client in the direction of a particular way of being/doing). To put it another way, the confirmation comes from the therapist's frame of reference and may involve the client in succumbing to an external locus of evaluation. One of the healing processes of person-centred therapy is clients' establishment of internal loci of evaluation; that is, an increased ability to trust their experiences and perceptions and to form judgements accordingly rather than to take on board the values and opinions of others in a way that supersedes their own.

Relatedly, the conclusion from theory is that for the therapist to offer unconditional positive regard to the client will effect constructive personality change. However, for the therapist to have that as an expectation and certainly as a desire (however well intentioned) may be counter-therapeutic. Holding another in unconditional positive regard involves accepting their right *not* to change. While it is natural for person-centred therapists to want their clients to change, and perhaps even to form a view of to what change might lead, for at least some clients change only becomes possible when the therapist lets go of the desire for it.

The relatively straightforward conflict with basic person-centred theory is not the only problem when therapists are tempted into praising or reinforcing clients in particular views. By confirming and approving of some part of the client's experience, there is a strong likelihood that the therapist is in effect rejecting another. Also, it is a simplistic mistake to think that person-centred therapy is always supporting 'growth-promoting' aspects of the client. We are all complex creatures full of ambiguities and contrary views, some growth-promoting, some less so and we experience support for one of our experiences or values as rejection of another or others. Paradoxically, favouring (apparently) growth-promoting aspects of the client while ignoring or downplaying other aspects is likely to be counter-therapeutic because, in effect, the therapist ends up offering the client a conditional relationship. It is particularly difficult for therapists to avoid positive reinforcement when only part of a client's experience or way of being in the world has been revealed – which is most of the time. It is probably best always to assume that there is more to the client than meets the eye. Not only that, but the totality of the client's experience is a result of the prompting of the actualising tendency. Even apparently harmful aspects have their purpose and stand in need of empathic understanding and unconditional positive regard. For this reason alone it is unwise to praise or show approval of the client, the client's actions or intended actions.

It is also wise to avoid the sometimes facile attitude 'Although I disapprove of what you do, I accept you as a person of worth' (also occasionally put as 'Hate the sin but love the sinner'). It is extremely unlikely that any of us wholly separate what we do from who we are – clients are no exception. Not only that but the behaviour that seems reprehensible to the therapist may be equally so to the client who may feel a great deal of shame about it. For the therapist to express (in words or otherwise) disapproval of the behaviour (past or present) will be experienced as rejecting and it may very well compel the client to lock away feelings of shame. The disapproved-of behaviour becomes a no-go area. The therapist's disapproval may very well be even more harmful when the client *doesn't* see anything wrong with what has been done or said.

This doesn't mean that person-centred therapists have to approve of or accept (for example) criminal or immoral behaviour. Rather it is that in person-centred therapy approval and disapproval are equally irrelevant. In practice, unconditional positive regard is precisely that; there are no conditions, no limitations and, one way or another, the personal values of the therapist must be set aside.

79

UNCONDITIONAL POSITIVE REGARD IN PRACTICE: THE AVOIDANCE OF RESCUING THE 'HELPLESS'

It is common for person-centred therapists to hear their clients express attitudes about themselves that the therapist doesn't believe to be true. For example, a client may say that they are so worthless that they would be better off dead when it is apparent to the therapist that they have the potential for a bright and happy future. Or someone who has been assaulted may blame themselves for being in the wrong place at the wrong time, dressed the wrong way and having had too much to drink when the therapist knows we should all have the freedom to walk through our streets unafraid. Sometimes, there is a strong urge to contradict the client, pointing out the error in what they say. Because it is fundamentally unaccepting, it isn't helpful to say to a suicidal person something like 'But you are so young, with so much ahead of you.' This holds even if the therapist believes it to be true. Likewise, to say to someone who blames herself for being raped that she is not to blame probably isn't helpful. It may be that what she is doing is giving voice to her feelings of shame and that when these are heard and responded to with empathic understanding and unconditional positive regard she will be able to move on from them to her own recognition of her innocence and to express her justified anger.

Contradicting a client (for example by pointing out their strengths when they are identifying themselves as weak) or distracting them from their feelings (by, for example, assuring someone in tears that they are a strong, capable, coping person) can be seen as an attempt to rescue the client from pain and distress. Although this may arise from the desire to reassure, comfort and encourage the client it is about the therapist's need, not the client's. It may even be that the therapist is uncomfortable with or upset by the client's distress. When there is even the slightest suspicion of this it is a matter for supervision and personal therapy.

Whatever the reason for the attempt to rescue the client, it is a failure to offer unconditional positive regard. For clients, the experience is that their pain and distress have not been heard; or they have been brushed aside. This is likely to make them seem shameful and unacceptable (when our feelings are unaccepted we feel our person is unaccepted and unacceptable). Not to accept that someone feels they would be better off dead is to reject an important part of that person's experience. Not to accept that someone blames herself for getting raped is equally rejecting. What is intended as reassurance actually blocks the client's expression. Inadvertently and with the best of intentions, by not accepting clients as they see themselves, therapists run the risk of creating whole areas of the clients' experiences that cannot be brought to therapy.

80

ACCEPTING THE WHOLE OF THE CLIENT: UNCONDITIONAL POSITIVE REGARD AND CONFIGURATIONS OF SELF

The danger of positive reinforcement may be particularly evident when the client has obvious 'configurations of self' (Point 27). There is often a temptation to respond to one or more configurations at the expense of others especially if some seem more constructive while others are inhibiting or even destructive. It is important to respond to all aspects of the client and to respect and accept them equally – even those that Mearns and Thorne (2000: 115–116) call 'not for growth' configurations. The examples they give of not for growth configurations include those that want to retreat from the world and do nothing, those that want to return to some previous state and those that have angry and/or aggressive feelings towards the therapist. They acknowledge that to pay attention to not for growth configurations can be very challenging for the therapist but point out that (p. 115) 'the therapist must actively value this part of her client as well as understanding its nature and existence'. Person-centred therapists are tasked with the responsibility to respond congruently and with empathic understanding and unconditional positive regard to the totality of the client. As Mearns (1999: 127) points out, it is not only one or even a few of the configurations comprising a client's self-concept which is important but all the configurations comprising that client and the dynamics between them. He states that if any parts are missed or banned from therapy because they are too difficult for the therapist what results is a conditional and possibly counter-therapeutic relationship. It is important and helpful to remember that all configurations of self, however 'negative' they may seem to the therapist, came about because they were useful – indeed they may even have been about survival and/or protection. Seen in this light, it is usually easy to comprehend the necessity of extending unconditional positive regard to them all.

Whether or not the concept of configurations of self makes sense to you, and even if it does and there are no apparent configurations of self in the client with whom you are working, it still remains true that it is vital to accept the whole of your client regardless of how contradictory, self-condemning and self-deprecating they may be. To do otherwise is to deny the validity of your client's experience.

81

DEVELOPING YOUR EMPATHY

Empathy is the natural, innate ability of human beings to perceive the subjective experience of others – it is usually used to refer to the sensing of the feelings of another but, at least arguably, it applies to all other aspects of their current being including their thoughts and visceral sensations. That is to say that how the experience of another is sensed and what form that sensing takes varies both from time to time and with individuals. In person-centred practice, whatever shape empathy takes therapists are aware that what they are sensing relates to the experience of the other. It is an 'as if' experience. Therapists accurately perceive something of the inner frame of reference of the client *as if* they were the other person but all the time hanging on to the 'as if' awareness. It is not unusual for me to literally 'feel' empathy; that is to pick up on a physical sensation. For others it is different. For example, one of my supervisees would 'see' sometimes very elaborate images and when she described these to her clients their experience was of deep, accurate empathic understanding.

I (Wilkins 1997c: 8–9) and others (for example, Baughan and Merry 2001: 233–234) have made a case that empathy is a universal human trait that has evolutionary advantages. Knowing something about the experience of others facilitates social living and thus survival. However, for many of us, our experience of the world leads us to lose touch with our empathic sense. There are things we can do to reconnect with and enhance our ability to connect with the inner experience of another. This is a process of discovery (literally the uncovering of something) not of learning a technique. Indeed, to treat 'becoming empathic' as a matter of learning appropriate responses might very well result in becoming less empathic. Increasing the capacity for empathic understanding is about discovering your own way of connecting with the experience of others 'as if' it were your own. You may do this as perceiving thoughts, as feeling bodily sensations, as 'seeing' images, as having a sense of transpersonal connection, as any or all of these in combination or in some other way altogether. You may sometimes get the 'as if' experience one way, sometimes another. Discovering your ability for empathic understanding is about tuning into and trusting these 'as if' sensations however vague they may be. As with many things, it is practice that makes for effectiveness.

Empathy is often spoken of as an art. If it is, in the first place it is the art of paying close attention to another. Empathic sensing is most likely to arise when you stay with and in your client's frame of reference. Needless to say, this isn't as easy as it sounds. We are all distracted at times and there are things we just don't want to hear. Practice may help us deal with distraction; personal therapy may help us expand our capacity to hear. The second 'art' of empathic understanding is to communicate what you have sensed of the experience of another. This improves with time and practice. Initially, it is about responding to what you have heard by making what are sometimes called 'reflections of feeling'. With experience, it is possible and likely that you will 'hear' something which has not been said or communicated directly via some other form of expression (but beware of responding to things not offered by your client). This may be in some form other than words. Communicating this tentatively to your client so that it can be easily accepted, denied or amended is likely to be helpful. If what you are doing is a genuine attempt to understand the experience of your client (as opposed to interpret it, offer some conclusions about it, etc.) then even if you are wrong your response is likely to be well received.

82

COMMUNICATING YOUR EMPATHIC UNDERSTANDING

Empathic understanding involves connecting with and communicating awareness of the client's meaning and experience. It is much more than parroting of the client's words and even of 'reflection of feeling' (although that is sometimes a good place to start). Each of us has our own way of being empathic. Often this takes us beyond the client's words or outward expression. For example, I was meeting with a young woman client for the first time. She had a smile on her face and was talking in a bright and bouncy way. As she spoke, telling me how great her life was, I was aware that the flesh between my shoulder blades was creeping and squirming and that I felt physically very uncomfortable, even slightly nauseous. This physical discomfort seemed linked to emotional distress (although I could not tell of what kind). Although this appeared to have nothing to do with my client's overtly expressed experience, I was sure the feeling wasn't mine – that it was an 'as if' experience. So, rather than repeat to her what she had said, I told her about my physical sensations and she burst into tears telling me that was how she felt all the time. Because I had somehow sensed the level of her distress, she was able to connect with it in my presence and to tell me about what lay behind it.

An important thing about this story is that, although my empathy was what has been described as 'somatic empathy' or (Cooper 2001: 222–223) 'embodied empathy', to communicate it to my client I had to use words. Similarly, for those who 'receive' visual images the most usual way of communicating them is to describe in words the content of the image.

Even when we are responding directly to what a client has said, it is usually best to avoid 'parroting' the exact words spoken (because this can be perceived as involving only a superficial understanding of the communicated experience). There is always much more to communication than the words spoken. Tone, pacing, facial expressions, posture and your own inner experience all add something to the content and meaning of what is being expressed. All these enhance the empathic connection.

In responding empathically, using exactly the same words as the client can seem like a passive, automatic response so it is usually best to translate what the client said into your own words because this demonstrates a real effort to understand – and, more sophisticatedly, allows you to respond to what has been expressed non-verbally. To do this and to communicate empathic understanding as fully as possible it is really helpful to have an extensive vocabulary – perhaps especially of words for emotions and emotional states. This is because to communicate what you have thought, felt, 'seen' or otherwise sensed 'as if' it were your own experience as accurately as possible it is helpful to have as many words as possible at your disposal. It is also because English is a very rich language and has many words for feelings – these have nuanced differences (for example, consider words connected with fear – worried, scared, frightened, terrified, anxious, panic-stricken all have different meanings) – using the one closest to what your client has communicated (regardless of which was spoken) is likely to result in a greater sense of being understood. However, sometimes using the same word as the client is exactly the right thing to do. Sometimes, regardless of what you might think is an equivalent word or a better word for what your client is expressing, the client in effect rejects your word by re-stating their own. For example, the client says 'a bit scared', responding to the intensity of feeling you sense (sweating, shaking, quavering voice), you say 'terrified' but the client repeats 'a bit scared'. This probably means either your client doesn't understand you or, more likely, the word they are using has particular weight and meaning for them and it is important that you 'hear' it. In such cases repeating the client's words is the most helpful thing you can do (even if your client is terrified, not merely a bit scared).

83

FACILITATING THE CLIENT'S PERCEPTION OF THE THERAPIST'S UNCONDITIONAL POSITIVE REGARD AND EMPATHY

At first glance, there is not much difference between the therapist's attempt to communicate unconditional positive regard and empathic understanding and the client's perception of them. However, the 1959 version of the necessary and sufficient conditions is concerned with the client's *perception* and this is something about which person-centred practitioners and theoreticians have been thinking and writing (see, for example, Wyatt and Sanders 2002). And there are indeed subtle differences between 'communication' and 'perception'. What the therapist 'communicates' is not necessarily perceived. For example, there is a possibility that your empathic sensing will be 'right' but denied by the client. To illustrate, as a young man and client, I was 'told' by my therapist that I was angry. In my self-concept, anger was a sub-human emotion, beneath my dignity. I could not understand why my therapist was suggesting I might be angry. While it didn't irreparably damage our relationship I certainly went away with a different view of her skills. Of course, she was absolutely right and had accurately communicated her empathic understanding but I didn't realise that for years. She had gone beyond my 'edge of awareness' into some part of me that I could not/would not admit into awareness. I was unable to perceive my therapist's empathic understanding. So, in effect, in this case condition six was not met. 'However accurate it may be, will my client be able to receive it?' is something to bear in mind when offering empathic understanding. This is one reason why 'taking only what is given' (see Grant 2010: 225) is an important guideline.

The situation with respect to unconditional positive regard is similar – but different. As explained in Points 77–79, the communication of unconditional positive regard is less to do with what is said and more to do with the therapist's attitude to the *whole* of the client. The client's perception of unconditional positive regard relies upon the sincerity of this attitude. In a way, for most of us, perceiving the unconditional positive regard of another is the greatest challenge for it undermines the core of the 'self' that has arisen through our experience of the world (and the 'self' as distinct from the organism is an adapted and adaptive structure 'built' for protection and defence). With respect to facilitating the perception of unconditional positive regard perhaps what is necessary is patience, consistency and genuineness – of intent and of acceptance.

84

THE THERAPIST-PROVIDED CONDITIONS AS A WHOLE: PREPARING FOR AND FACILITATING 'PRESENCE' AND/OR 'RELATIONAL DEPTH'

Although there is general agreement that 'presence' (Point 25) cannot be brought about on demand and that it is something which 'just happens' when there is a peculiar and particular set of circumstances, paradoxically, some practitioners do think that there are things that may be done to enhance the possibility of this special state in which both parties are transformed. For example, Geller and Greenberg (2002: 77) indicate that it is possible to prepare for the possibility of 'presence' and increase its likelihood. They discuss strategies of two types; those that are implemented immediately prior to or at the beginning of the session and those which are about the way of being of the therapist – what they call 'in life' preparation.

The former involves actively 'clearing a space' by deliberately putting away personal concerns and issues. This allows the therapist to approach the client with an attitude of openness, interest, acceptance, and in a non-judgemental manner. The therapist approaches the client with naivety of a special kind, a not-knowing combined with an openness to knowing whatsoever there is to know (the task is to understand the client's subjective experience almost as if the therapist was 'inside' it).

In life preparation involves a philosophical commitment to presence in the daily life of the therapist. This includes a 'commitment to personal growth as well as practising presence in their own lives, with friends, partners, and in everyday encounters' (Geller and Greenberg 2002: 77). Daily meditation is also seen as a way of preparing for presence as is attending to the personal needs and concerns of the therapist outside the session.

Geller and Greenberg (2002: 77–80) go on to discuss what the therapist does when in presence in a session with a client. They say that this involves:

- *Receptivity* – that is (p. 78) 'fully taking into one's being in a palpable and bodily way, the experience of a session'. This receptivity is multi-sensational involving all channels of perception (kinaesthetic, sensual, physical, emotional and mental). It is a process of 'allowing', letting in experience and allowing it to flow freely through the therapist's self.
- *Inwardly attending* – this is about the therapist attending to their inner flow in response to the received experience. This inward attention allows therapists to use themselves as instruments trusting their spontaneous reactions and to respond to the client by conveying the inward experience which may be in the form of (p. 79) 'images, visions, intuitions, guiding voices, techniques, emotions or bodily sensations'.
- *Extending and contact* – this involves therapists extending themselves and their boundaries in such a way as to meet and contact their clients in an 'immediate' way. Extending (p. 79) 'is the act of emotionally, energetically and verbally reaching outwards to the client, and offering one's internal self, images, insights or personal experience'. Contact (p. 79) 'involves directly encountering and meeting the essence of the client, whether in shared silence or in verbal expression'.

Although they don't use quite the same language, in their discussion of 'facilitating a meeting at relational depth', Mearns and Cooper (2005: 113–135) suggest very similar strategies and attitudes. They write about the importance of:

- the therapist 'letting go' (of aims, lusts, anticipations and techniques) (pp. 114–118);
- high-quality attention to the whole of the client and the client's experience (pp. 118–124);
- an openness to being affected by the client (pp. 124–126).

Arguably, although these strategies are presented as those for the facilitation of presence and meeting at relational depth, they are simply those that will enhance any person-centred encounter.

Section 6

PERSON-CENTRED THEORY AND PRACTICE WHEN WORKING WITH REACTIONS TO LIFE EVENTS

85

PERSON-CENTRED THERAPY AND THE 'ONE SIZE FITS ALL' APPROACH

Amongst at least classical client-centred therapists there has been a traditional resistance to the idea of describing person-centred ways of working with different client groups. This is because, ideally, person-centred therapists should have exactly the same way of being in response to any client no matter what brings them to therapy. That is to say, no matter what the client's experience is or how they view themselves and the world, the person-centred therapist is charged with responding non-directively and in such a way as to offer the therapist-provided conditions of congruence, unconditional positive regard and empathic understanding. Person-centred therapists take their direction from their clients, work at their clients' pace and in accordance with their clients' ways of being. Nothing more is necessary and, indeed, it is argued that to introduce more may be counter-therapeutic. It is the quality of attention that is important not expert, theoretical knowledge of the client's situation, life experience or reactions to life events. As Bozarth (1998: 100) puts it, 'contamination occurs when therapists assume they know what is best for clients, what is wrong with clients or in what direction clients should go'. At the very least such knowledge brings the danger of distraction from the client's actual experienced process (see my story in Point 67) and the valuing of the model in the therapist's head over what the client is actually experiencing. Also, clients are whole people with a range of emotions, thoughts and reactions. Nobody is (for example) just a user of drugs or alcohol, nobody is just a survivor of abuse, no one experiences bereavement and only that. To put knowledge of such reactions to life events at the forefront of practice or to treat different clients differently because of what has happened to them (rather than because of whom they are and their way of being in the world) is a mistake.

However, just as a thorough grounding in person-centred theory is essential to good person-centred practice, so it can be helpful to have some knowledge of the ways in which person-centred therapy can be done with people who have certain life experiences. This is less to do with how to be with the clients (although such knowledge may be helpful in aiding therapists to pick up some of the more subtle signs and communications) and more to do with aiding therapists to deal with their own uncertainties.

However, if held lightly, theory and knowledge of particular life experiences can help therapists stay with their clients. Having some understanding of what may be happening for a client allows the therapist to remain congruent and thus more able to experience unconditional positive regard and express empathic understanding. It is imperative that knowledge is 'held lightly'. Theory is a general statement about people rather than statements about a particular individual and the same is true for knowledge of reactions to life events. Nobody exactly follows the textbook and some may have experiences very far from those described.

The next three Points explain and examine how person-centred therapy is practised with clients who are experiencing reactions to specific life events. This is meant to indicate and exemplify the applicability of person-centred therapy. To do this, I have summarised, adapted and added to the work of experienced practitioners with particular client groups as this appears in Tolan and Wilkins (2012). It is not an exhaustive list and it is most certainly not a set of prescriptions for person-centred ways of working. The client and the client's actual experience always come first.

86

THERE ARE PERSON-CENTRED APPROACHES TO CLIENT ISSUES ARISING FROM LIFE EVENTS

Things happen to people and they respond variously and peculiarly. This point is concerned with person-centred theory and practice when a client's presenting issue relates directly to some outside event such as loss and bereavement, a traumatic incident or having been sexually abused as a child.

Haugh (2012: 16–17) notes that there are many theories of loss and bereavement. She says that, although they may be useful, there is a danger that the idea of a grief process will be taken too literally and interpreted as being fixed phases through which a bereaved person must be helped to pass. This is an error. No two clients grieve in exactly the same way. To put the notion of a grief process before the client's experience can be counter-therapeutic because it may involve the loss of unconditional positive regard (the client is doing what should be done) and empathic understanding (the therapist does not 'hear' what does not fit the model). Similarly, the idea that grief is something to be surmounted does not sit easily with person-centred theory. It is more important to understand individual reactions to loss than to grasp some global process.

From a person-centred perspective, a healthy grieving process is the one the client is experiencing because (by definition) a person reacts in the healthiest way for them at the time. It is not possible to know what parts of their self-concept are being protected by their current way of being. What is called for is trust in their actualising tendency and commitment to the knowledge that clients know better than an outsider (for example, the therapist) what it is they need at any particular time. This is why it is a mistake to think in terms of directing a client towards addressing their issues of loss or to assume that there is a particular process they should follow.

Turner (2012: 32–33) notes that responses to trauma and critical incidents are various but they are susceptible to a person-centred explanation. For example, it is very common for people who have witnessed or been directly involved in a critical incident to have disrupted sleep and disturbed and disturbing dreams. In person-centred terms, difficulty in sleeping may be understood as due to excessive brain activity because the mind has not yet assembled a coherent symbolisation of the event. After a day or so the feeling of a 'racing mind' diminishes and then the dreams are likely to start. The mind is continuing the same process, that of making order out of chaos.

Sometimes the threat to the self-concept following a traumatic incident is so great that an intolerable incongruence is created and some people solve that difficulty by denial or distortion of awareness. The incongruence causes their mind to 'blow a fuse' every time they think about it so the solution they adopt is not to think about it and thus the normalisation process is frustrated or even stopped. This may result in what is sometimes called 'post-traumatic stress disorder' or PTSD. Turner (2012: 37–41) describes 'psychological processing' as an additional strategy for dealing with the effects of traumatisation. The most important task is for a traumatised person to symbolise the new, and often painful, knowledge which is the consequence of the event. Although psychological processing may at first seem directive, if it is done sensitively, this is not necessarily so. Even person-centred therapists who use psychological processing when working with clients who have been traumatised may choose to explain to the client that examining the traumatising event closely may be helpful.

Power (2012: 50–51) argues that this reversal of the therapist-provided conditions by an abuser causes the child to experience a huge psychological and physical threat to her/his organism. Indeed abuse is experienced cognitively, emotionally and somatically: the abused child is transformed accordingly. Abused children may habitually fear their organismic responses in case something should slip out.

As with other traumatic life events, abuse can lead to dissociation. The many different feelings and contradictory values may need to be 'shared out' more safely between different aspects of self or even different selves. Practical experience with clients who have experienced abuse and trauma as children has identified extreme incongruence and the development of plural selves as directly related to early childhood difficulties. Power (2012: 52–57) lists some of the ways in which an adult abused as a child may be incongruent.

There is no formula for working with abuse issues because each person's experience and reaction is different. A therapeutic encounter with an abused person will not necessarily have anything to do with the abuse – at least not in terms of content. Regardless of how 'important' the abuse may seem to the therapist it is not for them to set the agenda regardless of whether or not the client is addressing the issue of abuse. That said, when working with people who have been abused as children, it is helpful to have some awareness of how life can be for an abused child and how this can play out in adult life.

There are huge issues around power and control for abused people, so developing a collaborative process throughout the relationship and particularly during contracting may be the first opportunity for a client to exercise some personal power in a relationship. The process of bringing memories of abuse into awareness, and all the hidden feelings surrounding them, can be extremely difficult. Some clients bring their experiences of childhood abuse to therapy at the outset; others develop awareness during therapy. It is the congruent expression of unconditional positive regard and responding to the client's story, difficulties in telling the story, ambivalence about the abuse and so on that provide a climate in which the client can explore the abusive experience and its effects to the extent that is right for them at that time.

87

PERSON-CENTRED THERAPY AND EMOTIONAL REACTIONS TO LIFE EVENTS

We each have individual emotional responses to life events. What makes one of us anxious depresses another while someone else may feel fine. When it comes to helping clients who present with an emotional reaction as a presenting issue, person-centred therapists are not likely to be concerned with its cause except in as much as it matters to the client. There are, however, aspects of the person-centred understanding of, for example, depression or anxiety and panic which are likely to be helpful in the therapeutic endeavour.

While Rundle (2012a: 68–69) expresses disquiet about the 'medicalisation of misery', she points out the usefulness of person-centred therapy to people who characterise themselves as depressed or who are so characterised by others. For example (p. 69), she points out that because depression is often marked by a feeling of an inability to be in a relationship, the therapeutic encounter may be a significant chance to experience being connected with someone else again. She (pp. 70–79) goes on to consider a variety of ways in which clients may experience depression. Sometimes an accumulation of life events may lead to feelings of being overwhelmed and to helplessness, sometimes there may be no apparent explanation for feeling so dreadful, so lacking in energy, so miserable, so hopeless. Sometimes it may seem that things are so bad suicide may be the only solution seen. Rundle shows how it is the provision of the therapist-provided conditions that allows clients to explore their feelings, mobilise their actualising tendency and to address aspects of their self-structure which may no longer be useful. In the light of some current person-centred thought (see Points 91, 92), it is important to realise that depression may very well be a response to environmental or social factors and conditions. Someone in financial difficulty or who is poorly housed may very well be 'depressed'. Similarly social isolation can be depressing. However, not everyone responds to such stimuli in the same way. There are always personal, familial and social reasons why one individual responds to an event with an experience of depression and another does not.

Bryant-Jefferies (2012: 81–84) offers an understanding of anxiety and panic in terms of person-centred theory. Writing of his practice with clients experiencing anxiety and panic, he (pp. 85–94) demonstrates that person-centred therapy provides an opportunity for the person to risk acknowledging the existence of the discrepancy or contradiction between their self-concept and the new material entering awareness. When an anxious client is confused by the emerging awareness and perhaps even doubts who they are (a long-maintained self-concept may be under threat of extinction) what is required is not active intervention or reassurance but a steadfast maintenance of the therapist-provided conditions. This is true even when a client experiences high anxiety or even panic in the course of a session.

88

THERE ARE PERSON-CENTRED STRATEGIES FOR DEALING WITH BEHAVIOURAL REACTIONS TO LIFE EVENTS

Sometimes when people are disturbed or distressed by things that happen to them their recourse is to some aspect of behaviour. Cameron (2012a: 115) states that person-centred theory admits no drive towards atrophy or self-destruction but the effects of any one (or more) 'maladaptive' behaviours such as the use of an addictive substance (Cameron 2012a), eating problems (Douglas 2012) or self-injury (Cameron 2012b) can lead to the conclusion that the actualising tendency cannot be at work in someone so self-damaging. However, the opposite is true. Rogers (proposition XII, 1951: 507) discusses how some needs are denied symbolisation in awareness if incompatible with the self-concept. The next proposition (1951: 509) implies that sometimes we find ourselves doing something we think we shouldn't, or can't, and then saying, and believing, that 'it wasn't me', or 'something took me over'. The 'something' was the actualising tendency pressing to meet an organismic need. In other words an apparently damaging behaviour is likely to be experienced as a relief and release. The person is making the best choice they can in the circumstances as they understand them.

However, as Cameron (2012a: 117) points out, excessive substance use eases psychological tension in some ways but can also increase it. This is true of other problematic behavioural reactions. A self-perpetuating cycle may ensue, in which the person '(mis)behaves' to ease psychological tension, feels wonderful (or at least better) whilst experiencing the effect but even more distressed when the effect wears off and more inclined to seek relief through behaving in the same way.

In a way, there is a danger that being in therapy may be counter-productive when the presenting issue is a behavioural reaction. There is an ever-present danger that, as the client becomes more aware of underlying psychological tension, the internal pressure to drink, cut, over- or under-eat again will become overwhelming. It may therefore be that the client who stops or reduces (for example) drug or alcohol use, and takes time to adjust to this before exploring very sensitive issues, gives themselves the best chance of working through these without resuming their previous habit. Understanding and respecting the client's process of coming to terms with a behavioural problem is an essential foundation to offering a relationship that is neither directive nor collusive.

After Cameron (2012a) and applying her 'things of which to be aware when working with drug and alcohol issues' and broadening them to behavioural reactions to life events as a whole, it's possible to draw out some principles for practice. For example:

- (p. 124) As a result of hiding their behaviour, most users of mood-altering substances, self-injurers and problem eaters become expert in the art of deceit and can detect incongruence with paranormal speed and accuracy. It may be tempting to try to hide a reaction of disgust or disappointment so as not to shame the client further but it is probable that the client's skill in detecting incongruence will outweigh the therapist's skill in hiding it.
- (p. 127) Maintaining unconditional positive regard can be challenging when a client is behaving in a way that seems very self-destructive. This is not just because it is painful to stay emotionally connected to people who are hurting themselves but also because unconditional acceptance of the client however they behave means not minimising their behaviour. There may be a temptation to minimise the client's behaviour in order to ameliorate their shame.

However, this would impede the therapeutic need to symbolise the experience without distortion.

- (p. 128) With respect to empathic understanding, some knowledge about the general effects of a substance can be useful in understanding what using it, or not using it, may mean to the client. For example, a client using heroin is likely to have been in considerable emotional (or physical) pain prior to using it. Amphetamines on the other hand make the user feel wide awake and fully alive and a client who particularly likes their effect may have a low intensity fragile process that leaves them feeling deadened inside.

NEWER DEVELOPMENTS, ADVANCES AND UNDERSTANDINGS: EXPANDING PERSON-CENTRED THERAPY FOR THE TWENTY-FIRST CENTURY

89

IN COUNSELLING FOR DEPRESSION (CFD), PERSON-CENTRED THERAPY HAS AN APPROVED EVIDENCE-BASED INTERVENTION

In the UK, 'Counselling for Depression' (CfD) is an approach to therapy approved by the National Institute for Health and Care Excellence (NICE) and as such is available as a treatment within the framework of the Improving Access to Psychological Therapies (IAPT) programme (see Sanders 2013: 21). It is an integrative model drawing on classical client-centred and emotion-focused therapy (EFT) and developed specifically for working with people who experience depression. It is intended to be delivered in up to twenty sessions. While in the context of person-centred therapy as a whole limitations to the number of sessions offered is often seen as antithetical; arguments as to the practicality of 'brief person-centred therapy' have often been made (see, for example, Tudor 2008: 1–5, 13–28).

CfD was developed from the work of leading theorists and practitioners working in the fields of person-centred and experiential therapies and is supported by increasingly impressive research evidence. In the context of evidence-based practice and person-centred and experiential therapies as a whole, Hill and Elliott (2014: 14–20) present and summarise research on the effectiveness of person-centred and experiential therapies with depression.

Much of the work done in developing the theory behind CfD applies more widely to person-centred therapy as a whole. For example, as well as a consideration of the evolution of research evidence for and the competencies necessary for the practice of the model, Sanders and Hill (2014: 99–115) includes an important, careful and useful presentation of 'depression' in terms of person-centred and EFT theory and practice (pp. 132–181). Perhaps because of the traditional resistance of person-centred therapists to 'diagnosis', attempting to understand the experience people describe as 'being depressed' (by themselves or professionals they may encounter) in terms of person-centred theory does not seem to have been done before. Indeed, Sanders (personal communication 2014) is of the view that this is the first time any consistent and coherent attempt to frame and interpret any 'medical disorder' in terms of person-centred theory has been made.

Drawing on theories from person-centred and emotion-focused therapies, the authors (pp. 100–115) consider 'four cornerstones' to the understanding of the experience of depression. These are:

- the nature of self;
- self-discrepancy;
- self-configuration dialogue;
- the nature of emotions.

Sanders and Hill (2014: 100–115) also offer and develop a number of statements as part of their theory of depression.

Although (because of a resistance to 'diagnosis' and the perceived manualisation of practice) the development and implementation of CfD has not been without controversy in the person-centred world, many see it as constituting an important, well-implemented and well-intentioned effort to bring person-centred and experiential therapies once more to the fore as a recommended choice in primary care. Sanders and Hill (2014: 2) point out that this development allows counsellors to gain parity with the practitioners of cognitive behavioural therapy (CBT) who until recently were the therapists favoured by IAPT. As Sanders and Hill say, perhaps more importantly it offers service users a choice of therapies that now includes counselling.

Although, as Hill (2012: 223) points out, CfD 'is not pure person-centred counselling, it is a thoughtful integration of person-centred and emotion focused therapies, not claiming to be either', he is of the opinion that person-centred therapists are 'best placed to offer it'. This is because the CfD 'competencies' (broadly speaking the knowledge and abilities required to practise it) draw on person-centred theory and the exercising of the therapeutic skills person-centred practitioners already possess. Sanders and Hill (2014: 4) point out that the majority of CfD practice will be familiar to experienced person-centred practitioners who 'will be reassured to find a good portion of their everyday work here'.

90

THE PERSON-CENTRED APPROACH IS A POSITIVE PSYCHOLOGY: THE FULLY FUNCTIONING PERSON

Joseph and Murphy (2013a, 2013b) pointed out that person-centred theory and the objectives of the person-centred approach accord with the principles and aims of positive psychology. This follows on from Levitt (2008) which was concerned with 'bridging' the person-centred approach and positive psychology. Unlike many other approaches to understanding the human mind, positive psychology is concerned with what defines and contributes to well-being and optimum functioning. In doing this, positive psychologists move away from a disease model of the human mind. Seligman and Csikszentmihalyi (2000: 5) say 'the aim of positive psychology is to begin to catalyze a change in the focus of psychology from preoccupation only with repairing the worst things in life to also building positive qualities'. Joseph states his belief that person-centred personality theory offers the best psychological perspective of the human condition available and that it is a preferable alternative to the medical model for understanding human distress (see Joseph and Worsley 2005: i).

Person-centred therapists in general are resistant to a disease model as an adequate way to describe mental and emotional distress and person-centred theory offers more constructive ways of viewing the person placing emphasis on movement to increasing well-being as not so much an objective of therapy (although it is) but as an essential factor of human existence. So, in person-centred terms, mental health is more than the absence of disease; it is about flourishing as a human being, continually moving towards an ability to adapt and move with or absorb change and to achieve one's potential. This agrees with the precepts of positive psychology.

Writing in the mid-1950s, Shlien (2003: 17) pointed out that one of the few positive conceptualisations of mental health of which he was aware was Rogers' notion of the fully functioning person. The idea of the fully functioning person refers to a directional development, not a state of being; it is a process of 'becoming' (see Wilkins 2003: 52–53). Describing the 'process of functioning more fully', Rogers (1967: 191–192) wrote of the person who is 'psychologically free':

> He is more able to experience all of his feelings, and is less afraid of any of his feelings; he is his own sifter of evidence, and is more open to evidence from all sources; he is completely engaged in the process of becoming himself, and thus discovers that he is soundly and realistically social; he lives more completely in this moment, but learns that this is the soundest living for all time. He is becoming a more fully functioning organism, and because of the awareness of himself which flows freely in and through his experience, he is becoming a more fully functioning person.

In her discussion of what it means to be fully functioning, Freeth (2007: 37–38) put it thus:

> Essentially, the fully functioning person is completely congruent and integrated. Such a person, Rogers believes, is able to embrace 'existential living'. By this he means they are able to live fully in the here and now with personal inner freedom, with all its accompanying exciting, creative, but also challenging, aspects.

Implicit in these statements is that to be fully functioning is to be responsive to experience and to 'evidence'. Both these are susceptible to change and so what it means to be fully functioning is too.

Borrowing a phrase from Kierkegaard, Rogers (1967: 181) saw an objective of therapy, indeed of life itself, as to 'be that self which one truly is'. Rogers lists a number of characteristics a person in the process of becoming may have. Some which in particular pertain to positive psychology are:

- being increasingly a harmony of complex sensings and reactions, rather than being the clarity and simplicity of rigidity;
- being creatively realistic and realistically creative;
- feeling a growing pride in being a sensitive, open, realistic, inner-directed member of the human species, adapting with courage and imagination to the complexities of the changing situation.

Joseph and Worsley (2005) and Worsley and Joseph (2007) are two edited works emphasising person-centred approaches to a positive psychology of mental health while in Joseph and Murphy (2013a, 2013b) it is the interface of person-centred psychology and positive psychology that is explored and with the expressed intention of building bridges.

91

IN PERSON-CENTRED THERAPY IT IS ACKNOWLEDGED THAT THE ROOTS OF MENTAL AND EMOTIONAL DISTRESS MAY BE SOCIAL AND/OR ENVIRONMENTAL

Amongst person-centred thinkers, there is a widespread and increasing view that the causes of emotional and mental distress are not intrinsic, endogenous, solely interpersonal and a response to relationships with significant others but that their origin is social and/or environmental. Perhaps it would be more correct to say that distress is not entirely or primarily a response to internal processes and relationships but that these can be and are distorted by the social and environmental aspects of a person's life. There is also an assumption that 'madness' is socially defined and that social and political circumstances at least contribute to and exacerbate mental distress. For example, Proctor (2002: 3) shows that 'there is much evidence to associate the likelihood of suffering from psychological distress with the individual's position in society with respect to structural power'. Sanders (2006a: 33) states that there is growing evidence that psychological distress has social, not biological causes. Indeed, he goes as far as to say that there is no such thing as mental illness. As supportive evidence for his position, he (p. 34) notes that (for example):

> People who have suffered sexual abuse are three times more likely to receive a diagnosis of schizophrenia; people who are subject to poverty and ethnic discrimination are three times more likely to receive a diagnosis of psychosis other than schizophrenia;

childhood neglect and abuse are highly correlated with ... earlier age at first admission to psychiatric care and a higher number of admissions.

In Sanders (2007e: 184):

- he shows that in spite of the introduction of neuroleptic drugs, recovery rates from schizophrenia have not improved in fifty years;
- declares that (p. 186) psychological disorders are names for theories not names for things that exist in nature;
- and (p. 188) states that there is evidence that growing up in poverty has implications for psychological distress.

To summarise:

- distressed societies beget distressed people;
- distressed people act in distressing ways;
- people disconnected from a sense of the Universal We may act as individuals rather than persons;
- such behaviour results in yet further social distress and yet more emotional distress for individuals;
- there are financial implications to dealing with emotional and mental distress.

If emotional and mental distress has social origins then it makes sense to take social action.

92

PERSON-CENTRED THERAPY HAS A SOCIAL DIMENSION

Of late, person-centred theorists have returned to the centrality of relationship to the nature of human beings. This is at the heart of what has become known as a dialogical approach, a primary advocate of this way of being in a therapeutic relationship is Peter Schmid (see Point 31). Schmid (2003: 110) emphasises the 'fundamental We' as a basic characteristic of the person-centred approach. He states that each of us only exists as part of a 'We' and (p. 111) 'we are unavoidably part of the world' and that:

> This We includes our history and our culture. It is not an undifferentiated mass, nor is it an accumulation of 'Mes'; it includes commonality *and* difference, valuing both equally. Only a common esteem for diversity constitutes and accepts a We.

He (pp. 111–112) goes on to say that to ignore this We has dreadful implications including the growth and spread of totalitarianism and terrorism. So, in person-centred terms, the organism is relational and what it relates to is We where We is the whole of which it is part. To thwart or distort this relationship results in personal and social distress. For me (after Wilkins 2006: 12):

- The We implies a connectedness, an inter-relatedness that goes beyond the organism.
- It is possible to conceive of the We as a meta-organism to which we all belong.
- To harm the 'We' is to harm the me.
- We is more than an immediate community, more than humanity, more than all living things. It is our planet in its totality.

This has implications not only for therapy but for the conductance of life (being in the world).

This conceptualisation of the need to tackle social issues as well as personal experiences if mental and emotional distress (indeed the well-being of humanity as a whole and the environment on which we depend) is to be addressed has led to the beginning of articulation of 'person-centred sociotherapy' (see Schmid 2014; Wilkins 2012).

To summarise the case for sociotherapy (after Wilkins 2012: 243–244):

- We need others and are needed by them.
- Encounter and communication are at the heart of a satisfying existence.
- It is in our interest to be loving, caring, charitable and helpful because if we collectively are not then existence (of the person, the community, the human race, the planet) is threatened.
- Social human beings are more likely to survive than unsocial human beings.

Ignoring these principles causes distress not only to individuals but to groups, societies, nations. Because of this my contention (Wilkins 2012: 245) is that prevention is better than cure and that we should think in terms of a public health dimension to person-centred therapy. This Schmid (2014) sees as:

- a therapy for society
- a therapy of society.

And that it's:

- a (multidisciplinary), practical, social science and form of therapeutic social work that deals with theory, research and practice of the person and his/her environment and this environment.

93

PERSON-CENTRED PRACTICE IS APPROPRIATE FOR PEOPLE EXPERIENCING SEVERE AND ENDURING DISTRESS

As will be evident from many of the earlier points, in spite of the popular (but declining) view that person-centred therapy has no role in working with clients experiencing severe and enduring mental and emotional distress, increasingly, its theoreticians and practitioners are presenting their ideas about and ways of working with settings, clients and issues which have been regarded as 'beyond therapeutic reach' (see Pearce and Sommerbeck 2014: v–vi). Sanders (2013: 18) points out, even though the history of the approach indicates otherwise, 'for many years, person-centred therapy suffered from the ill-informed criticism of only being suitable for the problems of the "worried well"'. Sommerbeck (2014b: 159) attributes the belief that person-centred therapy is unsuitable for such people to 'four mistakes'. These are:

- the idea that empathic understanding of psychosis colludes with it or reinforces it;
- the confusion of 'non-directive' with 'unstructured' (see Points 13, 46, 50);
- the notion that person-centred therapy is too in-depth and exploratory;
- the confusion of the theory of therapy with the theory of personality.

She (pp. 160–168) goes on to examine each of these points in turn and demonstrates how and why they are erroneous. She

267

(p. 161) argues that 'expression of accurate empathic understanding', far from being collusive, gives clients no reason to defend their perception of reality. It is this which allows the client to consider alternative points of view whereas 'reality correction' constitutes a potentially harmful, threatening confrontation.

Of the notion that person-centred therapy can be too in depth for clients at the difficult edge, Sommerbeck (p. 163) agrees that to (however subtly and well intentioned) direct them to deeper levels of experiencing and thus to closer contact with emotionally stimulating material may easily turn out to be harmful. She says that for such clients (pp. 163–164) ' "ordinary" accurate empathic understanding of the client's inner frame of reference or psychological landscape' is to be preferred to additive empathy, empathy at the edge of awareness or working at relational depth (see Points 28, 38). Sommerbeck (p. 167) is of the opinion that 'One only has to be convinced of the potency of the core conditions and that offering [them] to a client is the best one can do, as a psychotherapist, to facilitate actualization of the client's most constructive potentials.' This is because the reasons behind the distress are 'of no real consequence to the actual practice of person-centred therapy'. However, it is not necessary to agree with this 'theory-free' approach to accept the truth of Sommerbeck's (pp. 169–170) statement that:

> It is, thus, a myth that person-centred therapy is not useful with clients diagnosed with severe psychopathology. It is the opposite of the truth. Person-centred therapy is eminently suited for these clients and with the extension of Pre-Therapy [ed.: see Point 34], person-centred therapy can reach clients in the most remote corners of the back wards of psychiatry.

Sommerbeck (2014c: 171–186) also discusses therapists' limits at the difficult edge. These include (pp. 171–180) limits to therapeutic competence, setting limits (pp. 180–183) and idiosyncratic limits (pp. 183–185).

94

PERSON-CENTRED PRACTICE AND SEVERE AND ENDURING DISTRESS

Person-centred therapy has many strengths when it comes to working with people experiencing severe and/or enduring mental and emotional distress. This is increasingly apparent from the published accounts of person-centred practitioners in the UK and elsewhere. Continually, there are accounts of the applications of person-centred theory and practice being applied to new client groups and in new settings. This leads to developments and extensions to theory which are in turn taken and used in innovative ways. This includes the re-conceptualisation of trauma as, in the context of person-centred therapy, 'the springboard for transformational changes in a person's life – referred to as posttraumatic growth' (see Murphy and Joseph 2014: 3). Murphy and Joseph (2014: 3–13) are, with reference to therapeutic interventions with a client 'Denise', expanding on Joseph's (2003, 2004, 2005) work explaining how post-traumatic stress can be understood from within person-centred theory. Of their approach, Murphy and Joseph (2014: 12) state that it constitutes 'a radical ontology for trauma'. This is because, as opposed to other current therapies recommended for working with clients experiencing post-traumatic stress, 'it is the client and not the therapist that determines the direction of the therapy'.

Sanders (2013: 21) has pointed out that Kirshen Rundle and Wendy Traynor are independently actively researching 'the difficulties of establishing person-centred psychological treatments in a largely biomedical psychiatric system'. Amongst other things, both Rundle and Traynor have an interest in working in a person-centred way with people who hear voices. Drawing on Rundle (2010), Sanders (2013: 20) summarises how, in terms of person-centred theory and practice, the experience of hearing voices may be understood, therapeutic strategies for working with voice hearers and the possible outcomes of therapy. Rundle (2012b) and Point 91 also relate to Rundle's work with people who experience 'reality' differently. Traynor *et al.* (2011) deals with the perspectives of person-centred therapists who work with clients experiencing psychotic processes and Traynor (2014) is an account of researching the effectiveness of person-centred therapy with adults experiencing 'psychotic' process. Of her research, Traynor (p. 202) reports 'the most dramatic and general finding ... is the role of PCT in enhancing client social and interpersonal skills'. She (pp. 202–203) goes on to comment that this change is essential in helping clients to improve their quality of life and shows that this is consistent with previous findings.

Rundle (2012b: 100–111) presents accounts of her practice with people who experience reality differently and contextualises these with respect to theory. She (p. 105) writes that empathising with and accepting the client's experience, however bizarre, does not amount to 'collusion'. However, she does note that 'we must be clear about what is different for us and acknowledge that to the client'. It is the truth and consistency of the therapist which 'enables a scared or vulnerable client to feel safe enough to risk exploring issues that may never have been addressed before'. Accepting and responding empathically to a client's experience must be grounded in what is actually said but (p. 106) 'it is important to listen for clues to discover idiosyncratic meaning'.

95

PERSON-CENTRED THERAPY AND THE 'DIFFICULT EDGE', LIFE STAGES AND 'DIFFERENT' WAYS OF BEING

Person-centred therapy is being effectively used with a range of clients who, and issues which, may be seen as outside the usual remit of psychotherapy. According to Pearce and Sommerbeck (2014: v), some of these have been thought of as 'beyond therapeutic reach'. Their examples include people who are contact-impaired due to learning disabilities or autism, severely withdrawn, demented or terminally ill. Their book demonstrates that person-centred therapists have much to offer people who are what they refer to as the 'difficult edge'. Person-centred therapists also work effectively with people who are not 'ill', probably not necessarily distressed but who have particular circumstances with respect to (for example) their age, the nature of their relationships or some kind of special need. What follows are some examples of person-centred practice with clients in these two categories.

There has been an expansion of person-centred therapy into working with people with dementia. Lipinska (2009, 2014) has written of her therapeutic relationships with people with dementia over a 30-year period and Dodds *et al.* (2014) have detailed their work in applying pre-therapy to working with the same client group valuing, amongst other things, the way contact work provides (p. 115) 'emotion-oriented work to help staff sustain a sense of continuing to see the person alongside the dementia'.

Person-centred practices with people who, rather than necessarily being distressed, think differently from those of us who

are (more or less) 'neurotypical' and who therefore sometimes have difficulties interacting with the 'normal' world
are also in the process of development and promulgation. For
example, Rutten (2014: 75–79) describes autistic process and
(pp. 80–84) counselling clients with autistic process and some
of the differences and similarities of this to counselling neurotypical people. Carrick and McKenzie (2011: 73–88) publish
their research examining the application of pre-therapy skills
(see Point 34) and the person-centred approach in the field
of autism. Similarly Hawkins (2005, 2014) has shown that
person-centred therapy is a valid and valued way of working
with people with learning difficulties.

Person-centred approaches are also being employed with
people at different life stages or who have special needs. For
example:

- Pörtner writes of the application of person-centred principles to everyday care of the elderly (2008) and people
  with special needs (2007). Washburn and Humboldt
  (2013: 304–308) write of person-centred therapy with older
  people.
- Person-centred work with children and young people is
  represented by Behr *et al.* (2013), Cornelius-White and
  Behr (2008) and Keys and Walshaw (2008).
- Writing about person-centred therapy with couples and
  families includes Gaylin (2001, 2008), O'Leary (1999, 2008,
  2012) and O'Leary and Johns (2013).

96

PERSON-CENTRED THEORY AND PRACTICE SHARE APPROACHES, STRATEGIES AND IDEALS WITH OTHER THERAPEUTIC INTERVENTIONS

Sanders (2013: 19–20) notes that many aspects of person-centred theory and how it is practised accord with newer approaches to working with people experiencing severe and enduring mental distress ('psychosis'). Sanders compares the person-centred approach to recently developed theory and practice and states that (more or less word for word):

- The actualising tendency and idea that humans have inherent organismic wisdom overlaps with the idea of encouraging clients to use self-coping strategies and the CBT technique of coping strategy enhancement (Tarrier *et al.* 1990). This accords with the process in person-centred therapy by which clients are freed of the constraints of their actualising tendencies to enable their natural abilities to manage their own recovery (see Point 9).
- The actively acceptant non-judgemental position of person-centred therapists (see Points 19, 80) chimes with the work of (e.g.) Romme and Escher (2000) on accepting voices, hallucinations and other unusual ideation. In person-centred therapy, all experiences, behaviour, affect and ideation have meaning (see, for example, Points 36, 91 and 96). Person-centred therapists strive to empathically understand their clients' experiences (see Points 20, 28 and

82). This in turn often reveals implicit meanings hitherto
out of the client's awareness.

- There is no categorisation of experience or behaviour in
person-centred therapy and thus no therapist-directed distinction between types or degrees of behaviour beyond
those clients apply to themselves (see Point 32). This echoes (for example) Bentall (2003) who demonstrated the
continuity between normal and abnormal experience. It
also demonstrates how person-centred therapy has been
a model of anti-stigmatising practice and has ceaselessly
drawn attention to the clinical, social and cultural iatro-
genic nature of diagnosis (see Point 37) for over seventy
years (see, for example, Sanders 2005, 2006a; Shlien 1989).
- Mosher (1999: 37) described the 'treatment' at the original
Soteria House as '24 hour a day application of interpersonal
phenomenologic interventions'. Since person-centred therapy is the premier phenomenological therapy method (see
Point 4), Mosher's description is more than a fair approxi-
mation to much contemporary person-centred practice.
- Rogers (1959) was explicit in his definition of empathy,
making a pointed distinction between the actual (client)
and the reflected (therapist) experience ('as if' it were the
client's, without losing the 'as if'). This is analogous to
recent ideas in attachment theory, for example, the work
of Fonagy (e.g. Allen *et al.* 2008) regarding 'marked mirroring'. The person-centred therapeutic relationship as an
integrated experience meets the criteria for the type of relationship deemed important for initiating and sustaining
mentalising in clinical practice.

The person-centred attitude to diagnosis present from the time
of its origins (see Point 32) is also reflected in changing and
developing attitudes to the labelling of people who experience
mental distress. Examples include the positive psychology
movement (see Point 94), the increasing recognition that mental and emotional distress has social and environmental causes
(see Points 37 and 95) and a whole raft of books including the
'A Straight Talking Introduction to …' series published by

PCCS Books (for example Coles *et al.* 2013; Johnstone 2014; Johnstone and Dallos 2013; and Read and Sanders 2010). Sanders (2013: 18) points out that there is a natural alliance between person-centred practitioners and psychiatric service-user movements and 'all efforts to destigmatise mental health problems by demedicalisation in both philosophy and vocabulary'. This too has been at the core of person-centred theory and practice since the outset.

'THE FACTS ARE FRIENDLY': RESEARCH EVIDENCE INDICATES THAT PERSON-CENTRED THERAPY IS EFFECTIVE

There is research evidence for the efficacy and efficiency of person-centred therapy. Although this has been there from the very start of the approach, the most relevant and persuasive of this evidence dates from the 1990s onwards. In his review of recently published outcome research studies Bozarth (1998: 172–173) found no evidence that specific treatments are effective for specific dysfunctions but that it is the quality of the relationship between therapist and client which is significant. Cooper *et al.* (2010b) provides a review of the research demonstrating that person-centred and experiential therapies 'work' including investigations of effectiveness, meta-analyses and the development of measures.

The contemporary research evidence for the efficacy of person-centred therapy includes:

- *Outcome studies*: meta-analyses (for example Elliott *et al.* 2004a) indicate that a significant proportion of people improve as a result of PCT when compared with being on a waiting list or not receiving therapy.
- *Studies of the effectiveness of person-centred therapy for different psychological problems*: Elliott *et al.* (2004a), once researcher allegiance is controlled for, indicate that person-centred therapy is as effective as cognitive behavioural therapy (CBT) and process-experiential therapy for a range of mental and emotional difficulties including anxiety disorders, depression and schizophrenia.

- *The key ingredients of an effective therapeutic relationship and the necessary and sufficient conditions*: the largest review of empirical studies of the elements of the therapeutic relationship and how these affect outcome (see Norcross 2002) demonstrates that empathy is an effective element of therapeutic relationships and indicates that positive regard and congruence are probably effective.

Elliott and Freire (2008) completed a major project to integrate sixty years of research on the effectiveness of person-centred and related therapies. Their sample of more than 180 scientific outcome studies provides multiple lines of evidence demonstrating that these therapies are highly effective. Their main findings as to effectiveness were:

- *Person-centred and experiential therapies (PCE) are associated with large pre-post client change.* On average, these therapies make a big difference for clients. Furthermore, this is particularly true for symptom measures like the CORE-OM, as indicated by the two large UK-based studies by Stiles *et al.* (2006, 2008).
- *Clients' large post-therapy gains are maintained over early and late follow-ups.* Clients retain the benefits of PCE therapy over time. If anything, clients in PCE therapies show slight further gains during the first year after therapy. This stability of post-therapy benefit is consistent with the PCE philosophy of enhancing client self-determination and empowerment, indicating that clients continue to develop on their own after they have left therapy.
- *Clients in PC therapies show large gains relative to clients who receive no therapy.* In order to show that there is a causal relationship between PCE therapy and client change, it is necessary to compare clients who get therapy to those who don't.

Elliott and Freire (2010) also offered a review of meta-analyses demonstrating the effectiveness of person-centred therapies and Elliott (2013) presented an updated version of the research evidence for the effectiveness of person-centred therapies with data in the following categories (after Sanders 2013: 22–23):

Pre-post studies

- 'Open clinical trials' and effectiveness studies;
- 191 studies; 203 research samples; 14,235 clients;
- Conclusion: person-centred and experiential therapies *do* cause positive client change.

Controlled studies

- Versus waiting list or non-treatment conditions;
- 63 research samples; 60 studies, including 31 randomised controlled trials (RCTs); 2,144 clients; 1,958 controls;
- Conclusion: person-centred and experiential therapies *are* better than waiting list or no treatment, with large effect sizes.

98

PERSON-CENTRED THERAPIES ARE AT LEAST AS EFFECTIVE AS OTHER MODALITIES

As well as seeking to demonstrate that person-centred therapies are effective, research effort has gone into establishing that they are at least as effective as other approaches to psychotherapy. In this regard special attention has been given to how PCTs compare with CBT but this isn't the exclusive focus of comparative studies. One important finding from comparative studies of person-centred therapy and other approaches is that, when 'researcher allegiance' is accounted for, Elliott *et al.* (2004a) show that an apparent difference between the efficacy of person-centred therapy and other approaches disappears. In terms of outcome, they are equally effective. This is true of studies across the psychotherapy research literature. One of the most recent of these is the study by Stiles *et al.* (2006) using CORE-OM (Clinical Outcomes in Routine Evaluation – Outcome Measure) and data from 1,309 'patients' in which outcome data for cognitive behavioural therapy, person-centred therapy and psychodynamic therapy was compared. This showed that clients receiving each therapy markedly improved and that there was no real difference between the approaches.

Similarly, in his summary of Elliott and Freire (2008), Elliott (personal communication 2010) showed that:

- *PC therapies in general are clinically and statistically equivalent to other therapies.* That is, PCE therapies were neither more nor less effective than other therapies.
- *PC therapies in general might be trivially worse than CBT.* It is commonly assumed by CBT therapists, government

officials and the general public that CBT has better out-comes than other therapies such as PCE therapies. At first, PCE therapies appeared to be slightly but trivially less effective than CBT. However, this effect disappeared when researcher allegiance is statistically controlled for.

• *So-called 'non-directive/supportive' therapies have worse outcomes than CBT but other kinds of PC therapy are as effective or more effective than CBT.* It seems that in some studies what are referred to as 'non-directive/supportive' therapies are watered-down, typically non bona fide versions of PCE therapies, commonly used by CBT researchers, especially in the USA. Once the non-directive/supportive therapies are removed from analyses, it is clear that bona fide PCE therapies are statistically equivalent in effectiveness to CBT.

Sanders (2013: 23) presents a very brief summary of what is known from comparative studies of PCT with other modalities (non-PCE therapies). He says that evidence from 135 compari-sons; 105 research samples; 100 studies; 91 RCTs; 6,097 clients leads to the conclusion that PCE therapies are as effective as other therapies (main comparisons with CBT) with trivial effect sizes for differences (Overall −0.01, weighted, RCTs only).

What isn't known from quantitative, evidence-based research is how, when, where and with whom is person-centred therapy the preferred choice. It is a matter of faith for some person-centred practitioners that their practice offers something unique (and uniquely useful) and this is implicit in research of other kinds including case study research and qualitative studies. Cooper *et al.* (2010b: 240) stress the 'urgent need' not only to con-duct high-quality randomised control studies but also 'qualita-tive investigations of effectiveness using consumer groups and clients' perceptions and understandings'. They (p. 248) suggest that case studies of various kinds may offer a 'particularly valu-able' research method having 'the capacity to provide rigorous evidence to support, and develop, [person-centred] therapies, while also being based on idiographic, qualitative data'.

99

PERSON-CENTRED THERAPY IS ALIVE, WELL AND INCREASINGLY RELEVANT TO MEETING THE NEEDS OF HUMANITY IN THE TWENTY-FIRST CENTURY: EXPERIENCE AND BEYOND

Person-centred therapy has been evolved by reflecting on experience, research and a pragmatic approach to problem-solving. It is this that led (and leads) to the development of theory, practice and service provision. This started with Rogers (who in their account of his ground-breaking contributions to psychotherapy research, Elliott and Farber (2010) refer to as an idealistic pragmatist and a pioneer of psychotherapy research) and continues to the present time. Person-centred therapy is an advancing and dynamic approach responsive to the needs of people (individuals, groups and perhaps even nations) in the twenty-first century. What follows is a summary of some of the ongoing developments in person-centred therapy and the person-centred approach as a whole.

Many of the theoretical expansions to classical person-centred therapy as described in the seminal works of Rogers (e.g. 1951, 1957, 1959) are referred to in or are the subject of previously stated 'points' in this book (see especially Section 3, Points 23–38 but also how newer ideas have been incorporated into considerations of the principles and philosophy underpinning the approach and classical person-centred therapy per se). As

implied in the opening paragraph to this point, this expansion
to theory is an ongoing process. For example:

- Two editions of *Person-Centered and Experiential
  Psychotherapies* (2012, Volume 11, Issues 3 and 4) were
  devoted to papers on non-directivity.
- The necessary and sufficient conditions continue to be reap-
  praised and reconsidered. See, for example, Grant (2010) on
  empathy, Murphy *et al.* (2012) consider the mutuality of contact and perception and *Person-Centered and Experiential
  Psychotherapies* (2013, Volume 12, Issue 3) which concerns
  experiencing congruence and incongruence.
- The role of the client in the effectiveness and efficacy of
  person-centred therapy is explored. See, for example,
  Bohart and Tallman (2010) and Hoener *et al.* (2012).
- The concept of relational depth (Point 38) continues to be
  actively researched (see, for example, Knox and Cooper
  2011; Knox *et al.* 2013; and Wiggins *et al* 2012).

Understanding the how, why and wherefore of person-centred
practice with specific client issues and/or client groups is also
the subject of contemporary research and (re-)conceptualisa-
tion. Some of this is apparent in Points 86–92, 93, 96 and 97 but
there is also, for example:

- Case study research including into social anxiety (MacLeod
  and Elliott 2014), client and therapist mutuality (Tickle
  and Murphy 2014) and *Person-Centered and Experiential
  Psychotherapies* (2014, Volume 13, Issue 2) which is a special edition on case studies.
- The ongoing, extensive research conducted into counselling in schools (see Cooper 2006, 2008, 2013b and Pattison
  et al. 2007). This has been followed by a drive to establish a
  sound evidence base through conducting randomised controlled trials (see, for example, Cooper *et al.* 2010a).

Following on from Proctor *et al.* (2006) outlining the ways
in which the person-centred approach presents an agenda for

social change and Point 95, the social/political dimension to the person-centred approach remains a focus of attention and the politics of difference and diversity is also a hot issue. For example:

- Schmid (2012) argues that a political understanding is essentially inherent in the person-centred approach and (2013) explores the anthropological, epistemological and ethical foundations of the person-centred approach as a practice of social ethics.
- Proctor (2011) presents an argument against 'embracing the diversity rhetoric' because it obscures inequalities and therefore perpetuates existing power structures. She (p. 231) expresses the hope that the person-centred approach can focus on power and inequalities.
- Lago (2011b: 235) points out the need for person-centred therapists who work with people who are deemed 'different' or 'diverse' to be sensitive to 'multiplicity of factors that are socially constructed and determined'.
- Pete Sanders (personal communication 2015) has an expressed interest in and commitment to the politics of counselling and psychotherapy and links this to the demedicalisation of distress (see Point 98) and continues to address these via workshops, conference presentations, etc. He sees the person-centred approach as having a natural ally in the 'user movement' (that is, people who make use of psychological and psychiatric services because of their own needs).

THERE ARE STILL ASPECTS OF PERSON-CENTRED THERAPY AND ITS EFFECTIVENESS OPEN FOR RESEARCH

While throughout this book there are many references to how, when and where person-centred therapy has been researched and Point 99 directly addresses the evidence for its effectiveness, as Elliott (2013: 476) notes, 'there are many questions open for PCE therapy research'. His list of these (pp. 476–478) to which he adds expansions comprises:

1. How effective are PCE therapies with specific client populations?
2. How effective are PCE therapies with particular clients?
3. What are the effects of the facilitative conditions on the outcome of PCE therapies?
4. What are the immediate in-session effects of therapist facilitative responses on the depth of client-processing?
5. What do clients experience as most helpful in PCE therapy?
6. What are the characteristics of transformative moments in therapy?
7. What do PCE therapists know about how to help facilitate different kinds of productive client work in therapy?
8. What are the effects of change processes in PCE therapy/counselling training?

He (pp. 478–479) goes on to point out that there are many ways for person-centred therapists to reclaim their scientific heritage 'building ... humanizing research that is completely consistent with the values and practices of PCE therapies'.

Cooper *et al.* (2010b: 243–249) also outline seven key priorities for researching PCE therapies in the short to medium term. These are:

- conduct randomised controlled trials of a type that might impact upon policy makers;
- continue preparation and publication of rigorous, high-quality meta-analyses;
- highlight the ingredients of effective therapy by conducting process-outcome research;
- develop and validate PCE-friendly measures – instruments that measure outcomes in ways that are congruent with PCE theories;
- use research to develop new practice and theory;
- continue to develop person-centred research methods – these will be needed to complete the challenge to the hegemony of randomised controlled trials;
- continue to be at the forefront of the development of case study research.

Already, how the principles and ethics of the person-centred approach can be the basis of research has been explored through, for example, the development of measures (Freire and Grafanaki 2010; Freire *et al.* 2014) and directly incorporating person-centred attributes into the research process per se (Haselberger and Hutterer 2013; Wilkins 2010). However, there remains much to be done, as Elliott (2013: 479) states, 'Not only is research a political necessity, it is also one of the purest expressions of the actualizing tendency.'

REFERENCES

Allen, J. G., Fonagy, P. & Bateman, A. W. (2008) *Mentalizing in Clinical Practice*. Arlington, VA: American Psychiatric Publishing.

Barrett-Lennard, G. T. (1997) The recovery of empathy – toward others and self. In A. C. Bohart & L. S. Greenberg (eds) *Empathy Reconsidered: New Directions in Psychotherapy*. Washington DC: APA Books.

Barrett-Lennard, G. T. (1998) *Carl Rogers' Helping System: Journey & Substance*. London: Sage.

Barrett-Lennard, G. T. (2005) *Relationship at the Centre: Healing in a Troubled World*. London: Whurr.

Barrett-Lennard, G. T. (2007) The relational foundations of person-centred practice. In M. Cooper, M. O'Hara, P. F. Schmid & G. Wyatt (eds) *The Handbook of Person-Centred Psychotherapy and Counselling*. Basingstoke: Palgrave Macmillan.

Baughan, R. & Merry, T. (2001) Empathy: an evolutionary/biological perspective. In S. Haugh & T. Merry (eds) *Empathy. Rogers' Therapeutic Conditions: Evolution, Theory and Practice*. Vol. 2. Ross-on-Wye: PCCS Books.

Behr, M., Nuding, D. & McGinnis, S. (2013) Person-centred therapy and counselling with children and young people. In M. Cooper, M. O'Hara, P. F. Schmid & A. C. Bohart (eds) *The Handbook of Person-Centred Therapy & Counselling* (2nd edn). Basingstoke: Palgrave Macmillan.

Bentall, R. P. (2003) *Madness Explained: Psychosis and Human Nature*. London: Allen Lane/Penguin.

Biermann-Ratjen, E.-M. (1996) On the way to a client-centered psychopathology. In R. Hutterer, G. Pawlowsky, P. F. Schmid & R. Stipsits (eds) *Client-Centered and Experiential Psychotherapy: A Paradigm in Motion*. Frankfurt-am-Main: Peter Lang.

Biermann-Ratjen, E.-M. (1998) Incongruence and psychopathology. In B. Thorne & E. Lambers (eds) *Person-Centred Therapy: A European Perspective*. London: Sage.

Bohart, A. C. (2004) How do clients make empathy work? *Person-Centered and Experiential Psychotherapies* 3 (2) 102–116.

Bohart, A. C. (2013) The actualizing person. In M. Cooper, M. O'Hara, P. F. Schmid & Bohart, A. C. (eds) *The Handbook of Person-Centred Psychotherapy and Counselling* (2nd edn). Basingstoke: Palgrave Macmillan.

Bohart, A. C. & Greenberg, L. S. (eds) (1997) *Empathy Reconsidered: New Directions in Psychotherapy*. Washington DC: American Psychological Association.

Bohart, A. C. & Tallman, K. (1999) *How Clients Make Therapy Work: The Process of Active Self-Healing*. Washington DC: American Psychological Association.

Bohart, A. C. & Tallman, K. (2010) Clients as active self-healers: implications for the person-centred approach. In M. Cooper, J. C. Watson & D. Hölldampf (eds) *Person-Centered and Experiential Therapies Work: A Review of the Research on Counseling, Psychotherapy and Related Practice*. Ross-on-Wye: PCCS Books.

Bozarth, J. D. (1996) Client-centered therapy and techniques. In R. Hutterer, G. Pawlowsky, P. F. Schmid & R. Stipsits (eds) *Client-Centered and Experiential Psychotherapy: A Paradigm in Motion*. Frankfurt-am-Main: Peter Lang.

Bozarth, J. D. (1997) Empathy from the framework of client-centered theory and the Rogerian hypothesis. In A. C. Bohart & L. S. Greenberg (eds) *Empathy Reconsidered: New Directions in Psychotherapy*. Washington DC: American Psychological Association.

Bozarth, J. D. (1998) *Person-Centered Therapy: A Revolutionary Paradigm*. Ross-on-Wye: PCCS Books.

Bozarth, J. D. (2007) Unconditional positive regard. In M. Cooper, M. O'Hara, P. F. Schmid & G. Wyatt (eds) *The Handbook of Person-Centred Psychotherapy and Counselling*. Basingstoke: Palgrave Macmillan.

Bozarth, J. D. (2012) 'Nondirectivity' in the theory of Carl R. Rogers: an unprecedented premise. *Person-Centred and Experiential Psychotherapies* 11 (4) 262–276.

Bozarth, J. D. (2013) Unconditional positive regard. In M. Cooper, M. O'Hara, P. F. Schmid & A. C. Bohart (eds) *The Handbook of Person-Centred Psychotherapy and Counselling* (2nd edn). Basingstoke: Palgrave Macmillan.

Bozarth, J. D. & Wilkins, P. (eds) (2001) *Unconditional Positive Regard. Rogers' Therapeutic Conditions: Evolution, Theory and Practice. Vol. 3*. Ross-on-Wye: PCCS Books.

Brodley, B. T. (1999) Reasons for responses expressing the therapist's frame of reference in client-centered therapy. *The Person-Centered Journal* 6 (1) 4–27.

Brodley, B. T. (2001) Congruence and its relation to communication in client-centered therapy. In G. Wyatt (ed.) *Congruence. Rogers' Therapeutic Conditions: Evolution, Theory and Practice*. Vol. 1. Ross-on-Wye: PCCS Books.

Brodley, B. T. (2005) About the non-directive attitude. In B. E. Levitt (ed.) *Embracing Non-Directivity: Reassessing Person-Centered Theory and Practice in the 21st Century*. Ross-on-Wye: PCCS Books.

Brodley, B. T. (2006) Non-directivity in person-centred therapy. *Person-Centered and Experiential Psychotherapies* 5 (1) 36–52.

Brodley, B. T. & Brody, A. (1996) Can one use techniques and still be client-centered. In R. Hutterer, G. Pawlowsky, P. F. Schmid & R. Stipsits (eds) *Client-Centered and Experiential Psychotherapy: A Paradigm in Motion*. Frankfurt-am-Main: Peter Lang.

Bryant-Jefferies, R. (2012) Anxiety and panic: person-centred interpretations and responses. In J. Tolan & P. Wilkins (eds) *Client Issues in Counselling and Psychotherapy*. London: Sage.

Cain, D. J. (2002) The paradox of nondirectiveness in the person-centered approach. In D. J. Cain (ed.) *Classics in the Client-Centered Approach*. Ross-on-Wye: PCCS Books.

Cameron, R. (2003a) Psychological contact – basic and cognitive contact. In J. Tolan (ed.) *Skills in Person-Centred Counselling and Psychotherapy*. London: Sage.

Cameron, R. (2003b) Psychological contact – emotional and subtle contact. In J. Tolan (ed.) *Skills in Person-Centred Counselling and Psychotherapy*. London: Sage.

Cameron, R. (2012a) Working with drug and alcohol issues. In J. Tolan & P. Wilkins (eds) *Client Issues in Counselling and Psychotherapy*. London: Sage.

Cameron, R. (2012b) A person-centred perspective on self-injury. In J. Tolan & P. Wilkins (eds) *Client Issues in Counselling and Psychotherapy*. London: Sage.

Carrick, L. & McKenzie, S. (2011) A heuristic examination of the application of pre-therapy skills and the person-centred approach in the field of autism. *Person-Centered and Experiential Therapies* 10 (2) 73–88.

Coles, S., Keenan, S. & Diamond, B. (eds) (2013) *Madness Contested: Power and Practice*. Ross-on-Wye: PCCS Books.

Cooper, M. (1999) If you can't be Jekyll be Hyde: an existential phenomenological exploration on lived-plurality. In J. Rowan &

M. Cooper (eds) *The Plural Self: Multiplicity in Everyday Life*. London: Sage.

Cooper, M. (2001) Embodied empathy. In S. Haugh & T. Merry (eds) *Empathy. Rogers' Therapeutic Conditions: Evolution, Theory and Practice*. Vol. 2. Ross-on-Wye: PCCS Books.

Cooper, M. (2006) *Counselling in Schools Project, Glasgow, Phase II: Evaluation Report*. Glasgow: University of Strathclyde.

Cooper, M. (2007) Developmental and personality theory. In M. Cooper, M. O'Hara, P. F. Schmid & G. Wyatt (eds) *The Handbook of Person-Centred Psychotherapy and Counselling*. Basingstoke: Palgrave Macmillan.

Cooper, M. (2008) The effectiveness of humanistic counselling in secondary schools. In M. Behr & J. H. D. Cornelius-White (eds) *Facilitating Young People's Development: International Perspectives on Person-Centred Theory and Practice*. Ross-on-Wye: PCCS Books.

Cooper, M. (2013a) Development and personality theory. In M. Cooper, M. O'Hara, P. F. Schmid & A. C. Bohart (eds) *The Handbook of Person-Centred Psychotherapy and Counselling* (2nd edn). Basingstoke: Palgrave Macmillan.

Cooper, M. (2013b) *School-based Counselling in UK Secondary Schools: A Review and Critical Evaluation*. Glasgow: University of Strathclyde.

Cooper, M. & Bohart, A. C. (2013) Experiential and phenomenological foundations. In M. Cooper, M. O'Hara, P. F. Schmid & A. C. Bohart (eds) *The Handbook of Person-Centred Psychotherapy and Counselling* (2nd edn). Basingstoke: Palgrave Macmillan.

Cooper, M., Rowland, N., McArthur, K., Pattison, S., Cromarty, K. & Richards, K. (2010a) Randomised controlled trial of school-based humanistic counselling for emotional distress in young people: feasibility study and preliminary indications of efficacy. *Child and Adolescent Psychiatry and Mental Health* 4 (1) 1–12.

Cooper, M., Watson, J. C. & Hölldampf, D. (eds) (2010b) *Person-Centered and Experiential Therapies Work: A Review of the Research on Counseling, Psychotherapy and Related Practice*. Ross-on-Wye: PCCS Books.

Cornelius-White, J. (2007) Congruence. In M. Cooper, M. O'Hara, P. F. Schmid & G. Wyatt (eds) *The Handbook of Person-Centred Psychotherapy and Counselling*. Basingstoke: Palgrave Macmillan.

Cornelius-White, J. (2013) Congruence. In M. Cooper, M. O'Hara, P. F. Schmid & Bohart, A. C. (eds) *The Handbook of Person-Centred*

Psychotherapy and Counselling (2nd edn). Basingstoke: Palgrave Macmillan.

Cornelius-White, J. H. D. & Behr, M. (eds) (2008) *Facilitating Young People's Development: International Perspectives on Person-Centred Theory and Practice*. Ross-on-Wye: PCCS Books.

Coulson, A. (1995) The person-centred approach and the re-instatement of the unconscious. *Person-Centred Practice* 3 (2) 7–16.

Dekeyser, M., Prouty, G. & Elliott, R. (2014) Pre-therapy process and outcome: a review of research instruments and findings. In P. Pearce & L. Sommerbeck (eds) *Person-Centred Therapy at the Difficult Edge*. Ross-on-Wye: PCCS Books.

Dodds, P., Bruce-Hay, P. & Stapleton, S. (2014) Pre-therapy and dementia – the opportunity to put person-centred theory into everyday practice. In P. Pearce & L. Sommerbeck (eds) *Person-Centred Therapy at the Difficult Edge*. Ross-on-Wye: PCCS Books.

Douglas, B. (2012) Working with clients who have eating problems. In J. Tolan & P. Wilkins (eds) *Client Issues in Counselling and Psychotherapy*. London: Sage.

Dryden, W. (1990) *Rational Emotive Counselling in Action*. London: Sage.

Ellingham, I. (1997) On the quest for a person-centred paradigm. *Counselling* 8 (1) 52–55.

Elliott, R. (2013) Research. In M. Cooper, M. O'Hara, P. F. Schmid & A. C. Bohart (eds) *The Handbook of Person-Centred Psychotherapy and Counselling* (2nd edn). Basingstoke: Palgrave Macmillan.

Elliott, R. & Farber, B. (2010) Carl Rogers: idealistic pragmatist and psychotherapy research pioneer. In L. G. Castonguay, J. C. Muran, L. Angus, J. A. Hayes, N. Ladany & T. Anderson (eds) *Bringing Psychotherapy Research to Life: Understanding Change Through the Work of Leading Clinical Researchers*. Washington DC: American Psychological Association.

Elliott, R. & Freire, E. (2008) Person-centred & experiential therapies are highly effective: summary of the 2008 meta-analysis. *Person-Centred Quarterly*. November.

Elliott, R. & Freire, E. (2010) The effectiveness of person-centered and experiential therapies: a review of meta-analyses. In M. Cooper, J. C. Watson & D. Hölldampf (eds) *Person-Centered and Experiential Therapies Work: A Review of the Research on Counseling, Psychotherapy and Related Practices*. Ross-on-Wye: PCCS Books.

Elliott, R., Greenberg, L. S. & Lietaer, G. (2004a) Research on experiential therapies. In M. J. Lambert (ed.) *Bergin and Garfield's*

Handbook of Psychotherapy and Behaviour Change. Chicago, IL: Wiley.

Elliott, R., Watson, J., Goldman, R. & Greenberg, L. S. (2004b) *Learning Emotional- Focused Therapy: The Process-Experiential Approach to Change.* Washington DC: American Psychological Association.

Evans, R. (1975) *Carl Rogers: The Man and His Ideas.* New York: Dutton.

Fairhurst, I. (1993) Rigid or pure? *Person-Centred Practice* 1 (1) 25–30.

Freeth, R. (2007) *Humanising Psychiatry and Mental Health Care: The Challenge of the Person-Centred Approach.* Oxford: Radcliffe Publishing.

Freire, E. (2001) Unconditional positive regard: the distinctive feature of client-centred therapy. In J. D. Bozarth & P. Wilkins (eds) *Unconditional Positive Regard. Rogers' Therapeutic Conditions: Evolution, Theory and Practice. Vol. 3.* Ross-on-Wye: PCCS Books.

Freire, E. (2007) Empathy. In M. Cooper, M. O'Hara, P. F. Schmid & G. Wyatt (eds) *The Handbook of Person-Centred Psychotherapy and Counselling.* Basingstoke: Palgrave Macmillan.

Freire, E. (2012) Introduction to special issue on nondirectivity. *Person-Centered and Experiential Psychotherapies* 11 (3) 171–172.

Freire, E. (2013) Empathy. In M. Cooper, M. O'Hara, P. F. Schmid & Bohart, A. C. (eds) *The Handbook of Person-Centred Psychotherapy and Counselling* (2nd edn). Basingstoke: Palgrave Macmillan.

Freire, E., Elliott, R. & Westwell, G. (2014) Person-centred and experiential psychotherapy scale (PCEPS): development and reliability of an adherence measure for person-centred and experiential psychotherapies. *Counselling and Psychotherapy Research* 14 (3) 220–226.

Freire, E. and Grafanaki, S. (2010) Measuring the relationship conditions in person-centered and experiential psychotherapies: past, present and future. In M. Cooper, J. C. Watson & D. Hölldampf (eds) *Person-Centered and Experiential Therapies Work: A Review of the Research on Counseling, Psychotherapy and Related Practice.* Ross-on-Wye: PCCS Books.

Gaylin, N. L. (2001) *Family, Self and Psychotherapy: A Person-Centred Perspective.* Ross-on-Wye: PCCS Books.

Gaylin, N. L. (2008) Person-centered family therapy: old wine in new bottles. *Person-Centered and Experiential Therapies* 7 (4) 235–244.

Geller, S. (2013) Therapeutic presence. In M. Cooper, M. O'Hara, P. F. Schmid & A. C. Bohart (eds) *The Handbook of Person-Centred Psychotherapy and Counselling* (2nd edn). Basingstoke: Palgrave Macmillan.

Geller, S. M. & Greenberg, L. S. (2002) Therapeutic presence: therapists' experience of presence in the psychotherapy encounter.
Person-Centered and Experiential Psychotherapies 1 (1 & 2) 71–86.

Gendlin, E. T. (1978) *Focusing.* New York: Everest House (New British
Edition, London: Rider, 2003).

Gendlin, E. T. (1996) *Focusing Oriented Psychotherapy.*
New York: Guilford Press.

Gillon, E. (2013) Assessment and formulation. In M. Cooper, M.
O'Hara, P. F. Schmid & A. C. Bohart (eds) *The Handbook of
Person-Centred Psychotherapy and Counselling* (2nd edn).
Basingstoke: Palgrave Macmillan.

Grant, B. (2002) Principled and instrumental nondirectiveness in
person-centered and client-centered therapy. In D. J. Cain (ed.) *Classics
in the Client-Centered Approach.* Ross-on-Wye: PCCS Books.

Grant, B. (ed.) (2005) *Embracing Non-directivity: Reassessing
Person-Centered Theory and Practice in the 21st Century.*
Ross-on-Wye: PCCS Books.

Grant, B. (2010) Getting the point: empathic understanding in nondirective Client-Centered Therapy. *Person-Centred and Experiential
Psychotherapies* 9 (3) 220–235.

Haselberger, D. & Hutterer, R. (2013) The person-centered approach
to research. In J. H. D. Cornelius, R. Motschnig-Pitrik & M.
Lux (eds) *Interdisciplinary Handbook of the Person-Centered
Approach: Research and Theory.* New York: Springer.

Haugh, S. (1998) Congruence: a confusion of language. *Person-Centred
Practice* 6 (1) 44–50.

Haugh, S. (2001) A historical review of the development of the concept of congruence in person-centred theory. In G. Wyatt (ed.)
*Congruence. Rogers' Therapeutic Conditions: Evolution, Theory
and Practice. Vol. 1.* Ross-on-Wye: PCCS Books.

Haugh, S. (2012) A person-centred approach to loss and bereavement.
In J. Tolan & P. Wilkins (eds) *Client Issues in Counselling and
Psychotherapy.* London: Sage.

Haugh, S. & Merry, T. (eds) (2001) *Empathy. Rogers' Therapeutic
Conditions: Evolution, Theory and Practice. Vol. 2.*
Ross-on-Wye: PCCS Books.

Hawkins, J. (2005) Living with pain: mental health and the legacy of
childhood abuse. In S. Joseph & R. Worsley (eds) *Person-Centred
Psychopathology: A Positive Psychology of Mental Health.*
Ross-on-Wye: PCCS Books.

Hawkins, J. (2014) Person-centred therapy with people with learning disabilities: happy people wear hats. In P. Pearce & L.

Sommerbeck (eds) *Person-Centred Therapy at the Difficult Edge*. Ross-on-Wye: PCCS Books.

Hendricks, M. H. (2001) An experiential version of unconditional positive regard. In J. D. Bozarth & P. Wilkins (eds) *Unconditional Positive Regard. Rogers' Therapeutic Conditions: Evolution, Theory and Practice. Vol. 3*. Ross-on-Wye: PCCS Books.

Hill, A. (2012) Counselling for Depression. In P. Sanders (ed.) *The Tribes of the Person-Centred Nation: An Introduction to the Schools of Therapy Related to the Person-Centred Approach*. Ross-on-Wye: PCCS Books.

Hill, A. & Elliott, R. (2014) Evidence-based practice and person-centred and experiential therapies. In P. Sanders & A. Hill, *Counselling for Depression: A Person-Centred and Experiential Approach to Practice*. London: Sage.

Hill, M. (2004) Woman-centred practice. In G. Proctor & M. B. Napier (eds) *Encountering Feminism: Intersections between Feminism and the Person-Centred Approach*. Ross-on-Wye: PCCS Books.

Hobbs, T. (1989) The Rogers' interview. *Counselling Psychology Review* 4 (4) 19–27.

Hoener, C., Stiles, W. B., Luka, B. J. & Gordon, R. A. (2012) Client experiences of agency in therapy. *Person-Centered and Experiential Psychotherapies* 11 (1) 64–82.

Holdstock, L. (1993) Can we afford not to revision the person-centred concept of self? In D. Brazier (ed.) *Beyond Carl Rogers*. London: Constable.

Hölldampf, D., Behr, M. & Crawford, I. (2010) Effectiveness of person-centered and experiential psychotherapies with children and young people: a review of outcome studies. In M. Cooper, J. C. Watson & D. Hölldampf (eds) (2010) *Person-Centered and Experiential Therapies Work: A Review of the Research on Counseling, Psychotherapy and Related Practices*. Ross-on-Wye: PCCS Books.

Howe, D. (1993) *On Being a Client: Understanding the Process of Counselling and Psychotherapy*. London: Sage.

Iberg, J. R. (2001) Unconditional positive regard: constituent activities. In J. D. Bozarth & P. Wilkins (eds) *Unconditional Positive Regard. Rogers' Therapeutic Conditions: Evolution, Theory and Practice. Vol. 3*. Ross-on-Wye: PCCS Books.

Johnstone, L. (2014) *A Straight-Talking Introduction to Psychiatric Diagnosis*. Ross-on-Wye: PCCS Books.

Johnstone, L. & Dallos, R. (2013) *Formulations in Psychology and Psychotherapy: Making Sense of People's Problems* (2nd edn). Hove: Routledge.

Joseph, S. (2003) Person-centred approach to understanding post-traumatic stress. *Person-Centred Practice* 11 70–75.

Joseph, S. (2004) Person-centred therapy, post-traumatic stress disorder and post-traumatic growth: theoretical perspectives and practical implications. *Psychology and Psychotherapy: Theory, Research, and Practice* 77 101–120.

Joseph, S. (2005) Understanding posttraumatic stress from the person-centred perspective. In S. Joseph & R. Worsley (eds) *Person-Centred Psychopathology*. Ross-on-Wye: PCCS Books.

Joseph, S. & Murphy, D. (2013a) Person-centered theory encountering mainstream psychology: building bridges and looking to the future. In J. H. D. Cornelius, R. Motschnig-Pitrik & M. Lux (eds) *Interdisciplinary Handbook of the Person-Centered Approach: Research and Theory*. New York: Springer.

Joseph, S. & Murphy, D. (2013b) The person-centered approach, positive psychology and related helping: building bridges. *Journal of Humanistic Psychology* 53 (1) 26–51.

Joseph, S. & Worsley, R. (eds) (2005) *Person-Centred Psychopathology: A Positive Psychology of Mental Health*. Ross-on-Wye: PCCS Books.

Keil, S. (1996) The self as a systematic process of interactions of 'inner persons'. In R. Hutterer, G. Pawlowsky, P. F. Schmid & R. Stipsits (eds) *Client-Centered and Experiential Psychotherapy: A Paradigm in Motion*. Frankfurt-am-Main: Peter Lang.

Keys, S. & Walshaw, T. (2008) *Person-Centred Work with Children and Young People*. Ross-on-Wye: PCCS Books.

Kirschenbaum, K. (2007) *The Life and Work of Carl Rogers*. Ross-on-Wye: PCCS Books.

Kirschenbaum, H. & Henderson, V. L. (eds) (1990a) *The Carl Rogers Reader*. London: Constable.

Kirschenbaum, H. & Henderson, V. L. (eds) (1990b) *The Carl Rogers Dialogues*. London: Constable.

Knox, R. & Cooper, M. (2011) A state of readiness: an exploration of the client's role in meeting at relational depth. *Journal of Humanistic Psychology* 51 (1) 61–81.

Knox, R., Murphy, D., Wiggins, S. & Cooper, M. (eds) (2013) *Relational Depth: New Perspectives and Developments*. Basingstoke: Palgrave Macmillan.

Kovel, J. (1976) *A Complete Guide to Therapy: From Psychotherapy to Behaviour Modification*. New York: Pantheon Books.

Krietemeyer, B. & Prouty, G. (2003) The art of psychological contact: the psychotherapy of a mentally retarded psychotic client. *Person-Centered and Experiential Psychotherapies* 2 (3) 151–161.

Krupnick, J. L., Sotsky, S. M., Elkin, I., Simmens, S., Moyer, J., Watkins, J. & Pilkonis, P. A. (1996) The role of the therapeutic alliance in psychotherapy and pharmacotherapy outcome: health treatment of depression collaborative research programme. *Journal of Consulting & Clinical Psychology* 64 532–539.

Lago, C. (2007) Counselling across difference and diversity. In M. Cooper, M. O'Hara, P. F. Schmid & G. Wyatt (eds) *The Handbook of Person-Centred Psychotherapy and Counselling*. Basingstoke: Palgrave Macmillan.

Lago, C. (2010) On developing our empathic capabilities to work inter-culturally and inter-ethnically: attempting a map for personal and professional development. *Psychotherapy and Politics International* 8 73–85.

Lago, C. (ed.) (2011a) *The Handbook of Transcultural Counselling and Psychotherapy*. Maidenhead: Open University Press/McGraw-Hill.

Lago, C. (2011b) Diversity, oppression, and society: implications for person-centered therapists. *Person-Centered and Experiential Psychotherapies* 10 (4) 235–247.

Lambers, E. (1994) Person-centred psychopathology. In D. Mearns (ed.) *Developing Person-Centred Counselling*. London: Sage.

Leijssen, M. (2001) Authenticity training: an exercise for therapists. In G. Wyatt (ed.) *Congruence. Rogers' Therapeutic Conditions: Evolution, Theory and Practice*. Vol. 1. Ross-on-Wye: PCCS Books.

Levitt, B. E. (2005) Non-directivity: the foundational attitude. In B. E. Levitt (ed.) *Embracing Non-Directivity: Reassessing Person-Centered Theory and Practice in the 21st Century*. Ross-on-Wye: PCCS Books.

Levitt, B. E. (ed.) (2008) *Reflections on Human Potential: Bridging the Person-Centred Approach and Positive Psychology*. Ross-on-Wye: PCCS Books.

Lietaer, G. (1984) Unconditional positive regard: a controversial basic attitude in client-centered therapy. In R. H. Levant & J. M. Shlien (eds) *Client-Centered Therapy and the Person-Centered Approach*. New York: Praeger.

Lietaer, G. (1993) Authenticity, congruence and transparency. In D. Brazier (ed.) *Beyond Carl Rogers*. London: Constable.

Lietaer, G. (2001a) Being genuine as a therapist. In G. Wyatt (ed.) *Congruence. Rogers' Therapeutic Conditions: Evolution, Theory and Practice. Vol. 1*. Ross-on-Wye: PCCS Books.

Lietaer, G. (2001b) Unconditional acceptance and positive regard. In J. D. Bozarth & P. Wilkins (eds) *Unconditional Positive Regard. Rogers' Therapeutic Conditions: Evolution, Theory and Practice. Vol. 3*. Ross-on-Wye: PCCS Books.

Lipinska, D. (2009) *Person-Centred Counselling for People with Dementia*. London: Jessica Kingsley Publishing.

Lipinska, D. (2014) Person-centred therapy for people with dementia. In P. Pearce & L. Sommerbeck (eds) *Person-Centred Therapy at the Difficult Edge*. Ross-on-Wye: PCCS Books.

MacLeod, R. & Elliott, R. (2014) Nondirective person-centered therapy for social anxiety: a hermeneutic single-case efficacy design study of a good outcome case. *Person-Centered and Experiential Psychotherapies* 13 (4) 294–311.

Marshall, J. (1984) *Women Managers: Travellers in a Male World*. Chichester: Wiley.

Masson, J. (1992) *Against Therapy*. London: Fontana.

McLeod, J. (2002) Research policy and practice in person-centered and experiential therapy: restoring confidence. *Person-Centered and Experiential Psychotherapies* 1 (1 & 2) 87–101.

Mearns, D. (1994) *Developing Person-centred Counselling*. London: Sage.

Mearns, D. (1996) Working at relational depth with clients in person-centred therapy. *Counselling* 7 (4) 306–311.

Mearns, D. (1999) Person-centred therapy with configurations of self. *Counselling* 10 (2) 125–130.

Mearns, D. (2002) Theoretical propositions in regard to self-theory within person-centered therapy. *Person-Centered and Experiential Psychotherapies* 1 (1 & 2) 14–27.

Mearns, D. (2004) Problem-centered is not person-centered. *Person-Centered and Experiential Psychotherapies* 3 (2) 88–101.

Mearns, D. & Cooper, M. (2005) *Working at Relational Depth in Counselling and Psychotherapy*. London: Sage.

Mearns, D. & Thorne, B. (2000) *Person-Centred Therapy Today: New Frontiers in Theory and Practice*. London: Sage.

Mearns, D. & Thorne, B. (2007) *Person-Centred Counselling in Action* (3rd edn). London: Sage.

Merry, T. (1998) Client-centred therapy: origins and influences. *Person-Centred Practice* 6 (2) 96–103.

Merry, T. (2000) Person-centred counselling and therapy. In C. Feltham & I. Horton (eds) *Handbook of Counselling and Psychotherapy*. London: Sage.

Merry, T. (2002) *Learning and Being in Person-Centred Counselling* (2nd edn). Ross-on-Wye: PCCS Books.

Moerman, M. (2012) Working with suicidal clients: the person-centred counsellor's experience and understanding of risk assessment. *Counselling and Psychotherapy Research* 12 (3) 214–233.

Moodley, R., Lago, C. & Talahite, A. (eds) (2004) *Carl Rogers Counsels a Black Client: Race and Culture in Person-Centred Counselling*. Ross-on-Wye: PCCS Books.

Moon, K. & Rice, B. (2012) The nondirective attitude in client-centered practice: a few questions. *Person-Centered and Experiential Psychotherapies* 11 (4) 289–303.

Mosher, L. R. (1999) Soteria and other alternatives to acute psychiatric hospitalization: a personal and professional view. *Changes* 17 (1) 35–51.

Murphy, D. & Joseph, S. (2014) Understanding posttraumatic stress and facilitating posttraumatic growth. In P. Pearce & L. Sommerbeck (eds) *Person-Centred Practice at the Difficult Edge*. Ross-on-Wye: PCCS Books.

Murphy, D., Cramer, D. & Joseph, S. (2012) Mutuality in person-centred therapy: a new agenda for research and practice. *Person-Centered and Experiential Psychotherapies* 11 (2) 109–123.

Natiello, P. (1987) The person-centered approach: from theory to practice. *Person-Centered Review* 2 203–216.

Natiello, P. (1990) The person-centered approach, collaborative power, and cultural transformation. *Person-Centered Review* 5 (3) 268–286.

Natiello, P. (1999) The person-centred approach: a solution to gender splitting. In I. Fairhurst (ed.) *Women Writing in the Person-Centred Approach*. Ross-on-Wye: PCCS Books.

Natiello, P. (2001) *The Person-Centred Approach: A Passionate Presence*. Ross-on-Wye: PCCS Books.

Neville, B. (1996) Five kinds of empathy. In R. Hutterer, G. Pawlowsky, P. F. Schmid & R. Stipsits (eds) *Client-Centered and Experiential Psychotherapy: A Paradigm in Motion*. Frankfurt-am-Main: Peter Lang.

Norcross, J. C. (2002) *Psychotherapy Relationships That Work: Therapist Contributions and Responses to Patients.* New York: Oxford University Press.

O'Leary, C. J. (1999) *Counselling Couples and Families.* London: Sage.

O'Leary, C. J. (2008) Response to couples and families in distress: Rogers' six conditions lived with respect for the unique medium of relationship therapy. *Person-Centered and Experiential Therapies* 7 (4) 294–307.

O'Leary, C. J. (2012) *The Practice of Person-Centred Couple and Family Therapy.* London: Palgrave.

O'Leary, C. J. & Johns, B. J. (2013) Couples and families. In M. Cooper, M. O'Hara, P. F. Schmid & A. C. Bohart (eds) *The Handbook of Person-Centred Therapy & Counselling* (2nd edn). Basingstoke: Palgrave Macmillan.

Pattison, S., Rowland, N., Cromarty, K., Richards, K., Jenkins, P. I., Cooper, M., Polat, F. & Couchman, A. (2007) *Counselling in Schools: A Research Study into Services for Children and Young People in Wales.* Lutterworth: BACP.

Pearce, P. & Sommerbeck, L. (2014) *Person-Centred Practice at the Difficult Edge.* Ross-on-Wye: PCCS Books.

Pörtner, M. (2007) *Trust and Understanding: The Person-Centred Approach to Everyday Care for People with Special Needs.* Ross-on-Wye: PCCS Books.

Pörtner, M. (2008) *Being Old is Different: Person-Centred Care for Older People.* Ross-on-Wye: PCCS Books.

Power, J. (2012) Person-centred therapy with adults abused as children. In J. Tolan & P. Wilkins (eds) *Client Issues in Counselling and Psychotherapy.* London: Sage.

Proctor, G. (2002) *The Dynamics of Power in Counselling and Psychotherapy: Ethics, Politics and Practice.* Ross-on-Wye: PCCS Books.

Proctor, G. (2006) Therapy: opium of the masses or help for those who least need it? In G. Proctor, M. Cooper, P. Sanders and B. Malcolm (eds) *Politicizing the Person-centred Approach: An Agenda for Social Change.* Ross-on-Wye: PCCS Books.

Proctor, G. (2011) Diversity: the depoliticization of inequalities. *Person-Centered and Experiential Psychotherapies* 10 (4) 231–234.

Proctor, G. & M. B. Napier (eds) (2004) *Encountering Feminism: Intersections between Feminism and the Person-Centred Approach.* Ross-on-Wye: PCCS Books.

Proctor, G., Cooper, M., Sanders, P. & Malcolm, B. (eds) (2006) *Politicizing the Person-Centred Approach: An Agenda for Social Change*. Ross-on-Wye: PCCS Books.

Prouty, G. (2001) Humanistic therapy for people with schizophrenia. In D. J. Cain (ed.) *Humanistic Therapies: Handbook of Research and Practice*. Washington DC: American Psychological Association.

Prouty, G. (2002a) Pre-therapy as a theoretical system. In G. Wyatt & P. Sanders (eds) *Contact and Perception. Rogers' Therapeutic Conditions: Evolution, Theory and Practice. Vol. 4*. Ross-on-Wye: PCCS Books.

Prouty, G. (2002b) The practice of pre-therapy. In G. Wyatt & P. Sanders (eds) *Contact and Perception. Rogers' Therapeutic Conditions: Evolution, Theory and Practice. Vol. 4*. Ross-on-Wye: PCCS Books.

Purton, C. (2004) *Person-Centred Therapy: The Focusing-Oriented Approach*. Basingstoke: Palgrave Macmillan.

Read, J. & Dillon, J. (2013) *Models of Madness: Psychological, Social and Biological Approaches to Psychoses* (2nd edn.). Hove: Routledge.

Read, J. & Sanders, P. (2010) *A Straight-Talking Introduction to the Causes of Mental Health Problems*. Ross-on-Wye: PCCS Books.

Read, J., Mosher, L. R. & Bentall, R. P. (eds) (2004) *Models of Madness*. London: Brunner-Routledge.

Rennie, D. L. (1998) *Person-Centred Counselling: An Experiential Approach*. London: Sage.

Rice, L. N. (1974) The evocative function of the therapist. In D. A. Wexler & L. N. Rice (eds) *Innovations in Client-Centered Therapy*. New York: Wiley.

Rogers, C. R. (1939) *The Clinical Treatment of the Problem Child*. Boston, MA: Houghton-Mifflin.

Rogers, C. R. (1942) *Counseling and Psychotherapy*. Boston, MA: Houghton-Mifflin.

Rogers, C. R. (1951) *Client-Centered Therapy: Its Current Practice, Implications and Theory*. Boston, MA: Houghton-Mifflin.

Rogers, C. R. (1957) The necessary and sufficient conditions of therapeutic personality change. *Journal of Consulting Psychology* 21 95–103.

Rogers, C. R. (1959) A theory of therapy, personality, and inter-personal relationships, as developed in the client-centered framework. In S. Koch (ed.) *Psychology: A Study of a Science. Formulations of the Person and the Social Context. Vol. 3*. New York: McGraw-Hill.

Rogers, C. R. (1961) The process equation of psychotherapy. *American Journal of Psychotherapy* 15 27–45.

Rogers, C. R. (1963) The actualizing tendency in relation to 'motives' and to consciousness. In M. R. Jones (ed.) *Nebraska Symposium on Motivation*. Lincoln, NE: University of Nebraska Press.

Rogers, C. R. (1966) Client-centered therapy. In S. Areti (ed.) *American Handbook of Psychiatry*. New York: Basic Books.

Rogers, C. R. (1967) *On Becoming a Person: A Therapist's View of Psychotherapy*. London: Constable.

Rogers, C. R. (1975) Empathic: an unappreciated way of being. *The Counseling Psychologist* 5 (2) 2–11.

Rogers, C. R. (1977) *Carl Rogers on Personal Power: Inner Strength and Its Revolutionary Impact*. New York: Delacorte Press.

Rogers, C. R. (1980) *A Way of Being*. Boston, MA: Houghton-Mifflin.

Rogers, C. R. (1986) A client-centered/person-centered approach to therapy. In I. L. Kutash & A. Wolf (eds) *Psychotherapist's Case-book*. San Francisco, CA: Jossey-Bass.

Rogers, C. R. (2008) The actualizing tendency in relation to 'motives' and to consciousness. In B. E. Levitt (ed.) *Reflections on Human Potential: Bridging the Person-Centered Approach and Positive Psychology*. Ross-on-Wye: PCCS Books.

Rogers, N. (2007) Person-centred expressive arts therapy. In M. Cooper, M. O'Hara, P. F. Schmid & G. Wyatt (eds) *The Handbook of Person-Centred Psychotherapy and Counselling*. Basingstoke: Palgrave Macmillan.

Rogers, N. (2013) Person-centred expressive arts therapy: connecting body, mind and spirit. In M. Cooper, M. O'Hara, P. F. Schmid & A. C. Bohart (eds) *The Handbook of Person-Centred Psychotherapy and Counselling*. Basingstoke: Palgrave Macmillan.

Romme, M. & Escher, S. (2000) *Making Sense of Voices: A Guide for Mental Health Professionals Working with Voice-hearers*. London: Mind.

Rundle, K. (2010) Person-centred therapy and hearing voices. Presentation at the World Hearing Voices Congress, Nottingham, 4 November.

Rundle, K. (2012a) Person-centred therapy with people experiencing depression. In J. Tolan & P. Wilkins (eds) *Client Issues in Counselling and Psychotherapy*. London: Sage.

Rundle, K. (2012b) Person-centred approaches to different realities. In J. Tolan & P. Wilkins (eds) *Client Issues in Counselling and Psychotherapy*. London: Sage.

Rutten, A. (2014) A person-centred approach to counselling clients with autistic process. In P. Pearce and L. Sommerbeck (eds) *Person-Centred Therapy at the Difficult Edge*. Ross-on-Wye: PCCS Books.

Sanders, P. (2004) Mapping person-centred approaches to counselling and psychotherapy. In P. Sanders (ed.) *The Tribes of the Person-Centred Nation: An Introduction to the Schools of Therapy Related to the Person-Centred Approach*. Ross-on-Wye: PCCS Books.

Sanders, P. (2005) Principled and strategic opposition to the medicalisation of distress and all of its apparatus. In S. Joseph & R. Worsley (eds) *Person-Centred Psychopathology: A Positive Psychology of Mental Health*. Ross-on-Wye: PCCS Books.

Sanders, P. (2006a) Why person-centred therapists must reject the medicalisation of distress. *Self & Society* 34 (3) 32–39.

Sanders, P. (2006b) *The Person-Centred Counselling Primer*. Ross-on-Wye: PCCS Books.

Sanders, P. (2007a) The 'family' of person-centred and experiential therapies. In M. Cooper, M. O'Hara, P. F. Schmid & G. Wyatt (eds) *The Handbook of Person-Centred Psychotherapy and Counselling*. Basingstoke: Palgrave Macmillan.

Sanders, P. (2007b) Schizophrenia is not an illness – a response to van Blarikom. *Person-Centered and Experiential Psychotherapies* 6 (2) 112–128.

Sanders, P. (2007c) Introducing pre-therapy. In P. Sanders (ed.) *The Contact Work Primer*. Ross-on-Wye: PCCS Books.

Sanders, P. (2007d) Understanding and doing pre-therapy and contact work. In P. Sanders (ed.) *The Contact Work Primer*. Ross-on-Wye: PCCS Books.

Sanders, P. (2007e) In place of the medical model: person-centred alternatives to the medicalisation of distress. In R. Worsley & S. Joseph (eds) *Person-Centred Practice: Case Studies in Positive Psychology*. Ross-on-Wye: PCCS Books.

Sanders, P. (ed.) (2007f) *The Contact Work Primer*. Ross-on-Wye: PCCS Books.

Sanders, P. (ed.) (2012) *The Tribes of the Person-Centred Nation: An Introduction to the Schools of Therapy Related to the Person-Centred Approach* (2nd edn). Ross-on-Wye: PCCS Books.

Sanders, P. (ed.) (2013) *Person-Centred Therapy Theory and Practice in the 21st Century*. Ross-on-Wye: PCCS Books.

Sanders, P. & Hill, A. (2014) *Counselling for Depression: A Person-Centred and Experiential Guide to Practice*. London: Sage.

Sanders, P. & Tudor, K. (2001) This is therapy: a person-centred critique of the contemporary psychiatric system. In C. Newnes, G. Holmes and C. Dunn (eds) *This is Madness Too: Critical Perspectives in Mental Health Services*. Ross-on-Wye: PCCS Books.

Schmid, P. F. (1998a) 'Face to face' – the art of encounter. In B. Thorne & E. Lambers (eds) *Person-Centred Therapy: A European Perspective*. London: Sage.

Schmid, P. F. (1998b) 'On becoming a person-centred approach': a person-centred understanding of the person. In B. Thorne & E. Lambers (eds) *Person-Centred Therapy: A European Perspective*. London: Sage.

Schmid, P. F. (2002) Presence: immediate co-experiencing and co-responding. Phenomenological, dialogical and ethical perspectives on contact and perception in person-centred therapy and beyond. In G. Wyatt & P. Sanders (eds) *Contact and Perception. Rogers' Therapeutic Conditions: Evolution, Theory and Practice. Vol. 4*. Ross-on-Wye: PCCS Books.

Schmid, P. F. (2003) The characteristics of a person-centered approach to therapy and counselling: criteria for identity and coherence. *Person-Centered and Experiential Psychotherapies* 2 (2) 104–120.

Schmid, P. F. (2007) The anthropological and ethical foundations of person-centred therapy. In M. Cooper, M. O'Hara, P. F. Schmid & G. Wyatt (eds) *The Handbook of Person-Centred Psychotherapy and Counselling*. Basingstoke: Palgrave Macmillan.

Schmid, P. F. (2012) Psychotherapy is political or it is not psychotherapy: the person-centered approach as an essentially political venture. *Psychotherapy and Politics International* 12 (1) 4–17.

Schmid, P. F. (2013) A practice of social ethics: anthropological, epistemological and ethical foundations of the person-centered approach. In J. H. D. Cornelius, R. Motschnig-Pitrik & M. Lux (eds) *Interdisciplinary Handbook of the Person-Centered Approach: Research and Theory*. New York: Springer.

Schmid, P. F. (2014) *Person and Society. Towards a Person-Centred Sociotherapy*. pfs-online.at/papers/pp-keynote-buenosaires2014english.pdf. Accessed 29/12/2014.

Seligman, M. E. P. & Csikszentmihalyi, M. (2000) Positive psychology: an introduction. *American Psychologist* 55 (1) 5–14.

Shlien, J. M. (1984) A countertheory of transference. In R. H. Levant & J. M. Shlien (eds) *Client-Centered Therapy and the Person-Centered Approach*. New York: Praeger.

Shlien, J. M. (1989) Response to Boy's symposium on psychodiagnosis. *Person-Centered Review* 4 (7) 157–162.

Shlien, J. M. (1997) Empathy in psychotherapy: a vital mechanism? Yes. Therapist's conceit? All too often. By itself enough? No. In A. C. Bohart & L. S. Greenberg (eds) *Empathy Reconsidered: New Directions in Psychotherapy*. Washington DC: American Psychological Association.

Shlien, J. M. (2003) *To Lead an Honourable Life: Invitations to Think about Client-Centered Therapy and the Person-Centered Approach. A Collection of the Work of John M. Shlien* (ed. P. Sanders). Ross-on-Wye: PCCS Books.

Shlien, J. M. & Levant, R. F. (1984) Introduction. In R. F. Levant & J. M. Shlien (eds) *Client-Centered Therapy and the Person-Centered Approach: New Directions in Theory, Research, and Practice*. New York: Praeger.

Silverstone, L. (1994) Person-centred art therapy: bringing the person-centred approach to the therapeutic use of art. *Person-Centred Practice* 2 (1) 18–23.

Sommerbeck, L. (2011) An introduction to pre-therapy. *Psychosis: Psychological, Social and Integrative Approaches* 3 (3) 235–241.

Sommerbeck, L. (2012) Being directive in nondirective settings. *Person-Centered and Experiential Psychotherapies* 11 (3) 173–189.

Sommerbeck, L. (2014a) Combining person-centred therapy and pre-therapy with clients at the difficult edge. In P. Pearce & L. Sommerbeck (eds) *Person-Centred Practice at the Difficult Edge*. Ross-on-Wye: PCCS Books.

Sommerbeck, L. (2014b) Refutations of myths of inappropriateness of person-centred therapy at the difficult edge. In P. Pearce & L. Sommerbeck (eds) *Person-Centred Practice at the Difficult Edge*. Ross-on-Wye: PCCS Books.

Sommerbeck, L. (2014c) Therapist limits at the difficult edge. In P. Pearce & L. Sommerbeck (eds) *Person-Centred Practice at the Difficult Edge*. Ross-on-Wye: PCCS Books.

Speierer, G.-W. (1996) Client-centered therapy according to the Differential Incongruence Model (DIM). In R. Hutterer, G. Pawlowsky, P. F. Schmid & R. Stipsits (eds) *Client-Centered and Experiential Psychotherapy: A Paradigm in Motion*. Frankfurt-am-Main: Peter Lang.

Speierer, G.-W. (1998) Psychopathology according to the differential incongruence model. In L. S. Greenberg, J. C. Watson
and G. Lietaer (eds) *Handbook of Experiential Psychotherapy*.
New York: Guilford Press.

Spinelli, E. (1994) *Demystifying Therapy*. London: Constable.

Stiles, W. B., Barkham, M., Twigg, E., Mellor-Clark, J. & Cooper, M.
(2006) Effectiveness of cognitive-behavioural, person-centred
and psychodynamic therapies as practised in UK National Health
Service settings. *Psychological Medicine* 36 555–566.

Stiles, W. B., Barkham, M., Mellor-Clark, J. & Connell, J. (2008)
Effectiveness of cognitive-behavioural, person-centred, and
psycho-dynamic therapies as practiced in UK primary care routine
practice: replication in a larger sample. *Psychological Medicine* 38
677–688.

Tarrier, N., Harwood, S., Yusopoff, L., Beckett, R. & Baker, A. (1990)
Coping strategy enhancement (CSE): a method of treating
residual schizophrenic symptoms. *Behavioural Psychotherapy* 18
(4) 283–293.

Tengland, P.-A. (2001) A conceptual exploration of incongru-
ence and mental health. In G. Wyatt (ed.) *Congruence. Rogers'
Therapeutic Conditions: Evolution, Theory and Practice Vol. 1*.
Ross-on-Wye: PCCS Books.

Thorne, B. (1991) The quality of tenderness. In B. Thorne,
*Person-centred Counselling: Therapeutic and Spiritual
Dimensions*. London: Whurr.

Thorne, B. with Sanders, P. (2013) *Carl Rogers* (3rd edn). London: Sage.

Tickle, E. & Murphy, D. (2014) A journey to client and therapist mutuality in person-centred psychotherapy: a case
study. *Person-Centered and Experiential Psychotherapies* 13
(4) 237–351.

Tolan, J. (2003) *Skills in Person-Centred Counselling and
Psychotherapy*. London: Sage.

Tolan, J. & Wilkins, P. (eds) (2012) *Client Issues in Counseling and
Psychotherapy*. London: Sage.

Traynor, W. (2014) An investigation of the effectiveness of
person-centred therapy for 'psychotic' processes in adult clients.
In P. Pearce & L. Sommerbeck (eds) *Person-Centred Practice at the
Difficult Edge*. Ross-on-Wye: PCCS Books.

Traynor, W., Elliott, R. & Cooper, M. (2011) Helpful factors and outcomes in person-centred therapy with clients who experience
psychotic processes: therapists' perspectives. *Person-Centered and
Experiential Psychotherapies* 11 (2) 89–104.

Tudor, K. (2000) The case of the lost conditions. *Counselling* 11 (1) 33–37.

Tudor, K (ed.) (2008) *Brief Person-Centred Therapies.* London: Sage.

Tudor, K. & Merry, T. (2002) *Dictionary of Person-Centred Psychology.* London: Whurr.

Tudor, K. & Worrall, M. (1994) Congruence reconsidered. *British Journal of Guidance and Counselling* 22 (2) 197–205.

Turner, A. (2012) Person-centred approaches to trauma, critical incidents and post-traumatic stress disorder. In J. Tolan & P. Wilkins (eds) *Client Issues in Counselling and Psychotherapy.* London: Sage.

Van Werde, D. (1994) Dealing with the possibility of psychotic content in a seemingly congruent communication. In D. Mearns (ed.) *Developing Person-Centred Counselling.* London: Sage.

Van Werde, D. (2014) Pre-therapy at its edges: from palliative care to exercising newly recovered contact functioning. In P. Pearce & L. Sommerbeck (eds) *Person-Centred Therapy at the Difficult Edge.* Ross-on-Wye: PCCS Books.

Van Werde, D. & Prouty, G. (2007) Pre-therapy. In M. Cooper, M. O'Hara, P. F. Schmid & G. Wyatt (eds) *The Handbook of Person-Centred Psychotherapy and Counselling.* Basingstoke: Palgrave Macmillan.

Van Werde, D. & Prouty, G. (2013) Clients with contact-impaired functioning: pre-therapy. In M. Cooper, M. O'Hara, P. F. Schmid & A. C. Bohart (eds) *The Handbook of Person-Centred Psychotherapy and Counselling* (2nd edn). Basingstoke: Palgrave Macmillan.

Warner, M. S. (1996) How does empathy cure? A theoretical consideration of empathy, processing and personal narrative. In R. Hutterer, G. Pawlowsky, P. F. Schmid & R. Stipsits (eds) *Client-Centered and Experiential Psychotherapy: A Paradigm in Motion.* Frankfurt-am-Main: Peter Lang.

Warner, M. S. (2000) Person-centred therapy at the difficult edge: a developmentally based model of fragile and dissociated process. In D. Mearns & B. Thorne (eds) *Person-Centred Therapy Today: New Frontiers in Theory and Practice.* London: Sage.

Warner, M. S. (2001) Empathy, relational depth and difficult client process. In S. Haugh & T. Merry (eds) *Empathy. Rogers' Therapeutic Conditions: Evolution, Theory and Practice. Vol. 2.* Ross-on-Wye: PCCS Books.

Warner, M. S. (2002) Psychological contact, meaningful process and human nature: a reformulation of person-centered theory. In G. Wyatt & P. Sanders (eds) *Contact and Perception. Rogers'*

Therapeutic Conditions: Evolution, Theory and Practice. Vol. 4. Ross-on-Wye: PCCS Books.

Warner, M. S. (2005) A person-centered view of human nature, wellness and psycho-pathology. In S. Joseph & R. Worsley (eds) *Person-Centred Psychopathology: A Positive Psychology of Mental Health.* Ross-on-Wye: PCCS Books.

Warner, M. S. (2007a) Client incongruence and psychopathology. In M. Cooper, M. O'Hara, P. F. Schmid & G. Wyatt (eds) *The Handbook of Person-Centred Psychotherapy and Counselling.* Basingstoke: Palgrave Macmillan.

Warner, M. S. (2007b) Luke's process: a positive view of schizophrenic thought disorder. In S. Joseph & R. Worsley (eds) *Person-Centred Practice: Case Studies in Positive Psychology.* Ross-on-Wye: PCCS Books.

Warner, M. S. (2014) Client processes at the difficult edge. In P. Pearce & L. Sommerbeck (eds) *Person-Centred Practice at the Difficult Edge.* Ross-on-Wye: PCCS Books.

Washburn, A. & Von Humboldt, S. (2013) Older adults. In M. Cooper, M. O'Hara, P. F. Schmid & A. C. Bohart (eds) *The Handbook of Person-Centred Therapy and Counselling* (2nd edn). Basingstoke: Palgrave Macmillan.

Watson, J. C. & Sheckley, P. (2001) Potentiating growth: an examination of the research on unconditional positive regard. In J. D. Bozarth & P. Wilkins (eds) *Unconditional Positive Regard. Rogers' Therapeutic Conditions: Evolution, Theory and Practice. Vol. 3.* Ross-on-Wye: PCCS Books.

Wiggins, S., Elliott, R. & Cooper, M. (2012) The prevalence and characteristics of relational depth events in psychotherapy. *Psychotherapy Research* 22 (2) 139–150.

Wilkins, P. (1994) Can psychodrama be person-centred? *Person-Centred Practice* 2 (2) 14–18.

Wilkins, P. (1997a) Congruence and countertransference: similarities and differences. *Counselling* 8 (1) 36–41.

Wilkins, P. (1997b) *Personal and Professional Development for Counsellors.* London: Sage.

Wilkins, P. (1997c) Empathy: a desirable quality for effective inter-personal communication? *Applied Community Studies* 3 (2) 3–13.

Wilkins, P. (1999) The relationship in person-centred counselling. In C. Feltham (ed.) *Understanding the Counselling Relationship.* London: Sage.

Wilkins, P. (2000) Unconditional positive regard reconsidered. *British Journal of Guidance and Counselling* 28 (1) 23–36.

Wilkins, P. (2003) *Person-Centred Therapy in Focus*. London: Sage.

Wilkins, P. (2005a) Assessment and 'diagnosis' in person-centred therapy. In S. Joseph & R. Worsley (eds) *Person-Centred Psychopathology: A Positive Psychology of Mental Health*. Ross-on-Wye: PCCS Books.

Wilkins, P. (2005b) Person-centred theory and 'mental illness'. In S. Joseph & R. Worsley (eds) *Person-Centred Psychopathology: A Positive Psychology of Mental Health*. Ross-on-Wye: PCCS Books.

Wilkins, P. (2006) Being person-centred. *Self & Society* 34 (3) 6–14.

Wilkins, P. (2010) Researching in a person-centered way. In M. Cooper, J. C. Watson & D. Hölldampf (eds) *Person-Centered and Experiential Therapies Work: A Review of the Research on Counseling, Psychotherapy and Related Practice*. Ross-on-Wye: PCCS Books.

Wilkins, P. (2012) Person-centred sociotherapy: applying person-centred attitudes, principles and practices to social situations, groups and society as a whole. *Hellenistic Journal of Psychology* 9 240–254 (also at www.pseve.org/journal/UPLOAD/Wilkins9c.pdf).

Wilkins, P. & Bozarth, J. D. (2001) Unconditional positive regard in context. In J. D. Bozarth & P. Wilkins (eds) *Unconditional Positive Regard. Rogers' Therapeutic Conditions: Evolution, Theory and Practice. Vol. 3*. Ross-on-Wye: PCCS Books.

Wilkins, P. & Gill, M. (2003) Assessment in person-centered therapy. *Person-Centered and Experiential Psychotherapies* 2 172–187.

Wolter-Gustafson, C. (1999) The power of the premise: reconstructing gender and human development with Rogers' theory. In I. Fairhurst (ed.) *Women Writing in the Person-Centred Approach*. Ross-on-Wye: PCCS Books.

Wood, J. K. (1996) The person-centered approach: towards an understanding of its implications. In R. Hutterer, G. Pawlowsky, P. F. Schmid & R. Stipsits (eds) *Client-Centered and Experiential Psychotherapy: A Paradigm in Motion*. Frankfurt-am-Main: Peter Lang.

Worsley, R. (2002) *Process Work in Person-Centred Therapy: Phenomenological and Existential Therapy*. Basingstoke: Palgrave Macmillan.

Worsley, R. & Joseph, S. (eds) (2007) *Person-Centred Practice: Case Studies in Positive Psychology*. Ross-on-Wye: PCCS Books.

Wyatt, G. (ed.) (2001a) *Congruence. Rogers' Therapeutic Conditions: Evolution, Theory and Practice. Vol. 1.* Ross-on-Wye: PCCS Books.

Wyatt, G. (2001b) The multifaceted nature of congruence within the therapeutic relationship. In G. Wyatt (ed.) *Congruence. Rogers' Therapeutic Conditions: Evolution, Theory and Practice. Vol. 1.* Ross-on-Wye: PCCS Books.

Wyatt, G. (2007) Psychological contact. In M. Cooper, M. O'Hara, P. F. Schmid & G. Wyatt (eds) *The Handbook of Person-Centred Psychotherapy and Counselling.* Basingstoke: Palgrave Macmillan.

Wyatt, G. (2013) Psychological contact. In M. Cooper, M. O'Hara, P. F. Schmid & A. C. Bohart (eds) *The Handbook of Person-Centred Psychotherapy and Counselling* (2nd edn). Basingstoke: Palgrave Macmillan.

Wyatt, G. & Sanders, P. (2002) The history of conditions 1 and 6. In G. Wyatt & P. Sanders (eds) *Contact and Perception. Rogers' Therapeutic Conditions: Evolution, Theory and Practice. Vol. 4.* Ross-on-Wye: PCCS Books.

'This is an extraordinarily important book. Paul Wilkins did a great job in combining scholarly profound descriptions of the person-centred essentials with a clear and easy-to-read language.' – *Peter F. Schmid*, Sigmund Freud University, Vienna

Person-centred therapy, rooted in the experience and ideas of the eminent psychotherapist Carl Rogers, is widely practised in the UK and throughout the world. It has applications in health and social care, the voluntary sector and is relevant to work with people who are severely mentally and emotionally distressed. As well as being a valuable sourcebook and offering a comprehensive overview, this edition includes updated references and a new section on recent developments and advances.

The book begins with a consideration of the principles and philosophy underpinning person-centred therapy before moving to a comprehensive discussion of the classical theory upon which practice is based. Further areas of discussion include:

• The model of the person, including the origins of mental and emotional distress;
• The process of constructive change;
• A review of revisions of and additions to person-centred theory;
• Child development, styles of processing and configurations of self;
• The quality of presence and working at relational depth.

Criticisms of the approach are addressed and rebutted and the application of theory to practice is discussed. The new final section is concerned with advances and developments in theory and practice including.

• Counselling for Depression;
• The social dimension to person-centred therapy;
• Person-centred practice with people experiencing severe and enduring distress and at the 'difficult edge';
• A review of research.

Throughout the book, attention is drawn to the wider person-centred literature to which it is a valuable key. *Person-Centred Therapy* will be of particular use to students, scholars and practitioners of person-centred therapy as well as to anyone who wants to know more about one of the major psychotherapeutic modalities.

Paul Wilkins is a person-centred academic, practitioner and supervisor. After managing local authority mental health resources, he worked as a senior lecturer at Manchester Metropolitan University until 2009.

100 KEY POINTS & TECHNIQUES
Series Editor: Windy Dryden

PSYCHOTHERAPY AND COUNSELLING

Routledge
Taylor & Francis Group

ISBN 978-0-415-74371-6

9 780415 743716

an **informa** business

www.routledgementalhealth.com